On 23 August 1990, the world was outraged when five-year-old Stuart Lockwood was seen on television shying away fr uninvited attentions of Saddam Hussein, wi the hearts of viewers on every cont watching events in Kuwait and Iraq deepened.

Stuart's brave rejection of the Iraq instant hero around the globe and re Bush and Margaret Thatcher to libera Westerners being detained in Baghda policy. Stuart, his parents Derek and G elder brother Craig were among them.

Glenda Lockwood's diary, which she kept throughout the family's ordeal, and on which this book is based, evokes the terrifying circumstances of their long incarceration, during which Derek was twice separated from his wife and sons, when every night they went to sleep wondering if the next day would be their last, and when they were forced to participate in Saddam Hussein's inhuman schemes.

For the first time, in *Diary of a Human Shield* Glenda Lockwood is openly critical of the British Embassy in Kuwait which, she believes, by taking swifter action and giving better advice, could have prevented many of the hostages' being taken prisoner in the first place. At the same time she paints a moving picture of the way the women helped one another through the dark days when their husbands had been taken away to be held elsewhere, of the astounding stoicism and courage of all their children and, when the women and children were eventually allowed to go home, of the searing pain of being parted once more from the men who were left behind. Glenda and her sons were not to see Derek again for over three months.

The Lockwoods, happily reunited at last, are coming to terms with what happened to them, although Stuart is still scared of being shut in anywhere, Derek has problems sleeping and Craig loathes the unrelenting glare of publicity that has surrounded them since their return to Britain. They have, as Glenda gladly recognizes, been drawn much closer together as a family, but their experiences in captivity will remain with them, as with all who read this book, as an unforgettable nightmare.

Glenda Lockwood was born and brought up in Worcester. She worked as a secretary until her marriage at the age of twenty-one, and then travelled the world with her engineer husband, Derek. While living in Kuwait she became the manager of a children's playgroup, and now that she and her family have settled again in the Worcester area, one of her ambitions is to set up a similar venture in the UK. During the Gulf War, she was an active member of a Gulf support group in Worcestershire.

DIARY OF A HUMAN SHIELD

GLENDA LOCKWOOD

Glenda Lockwood

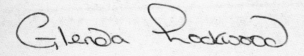

BLOOMSBURY

First published in Great Britain 1991
Bloomsbury Publishing Limited, 2 Soho Square, London W1V 5DE

The author gratefully acknowledges
the assistance of Christopher Mowbray

PICTURE SOURCES

Courtesy of Saddam Hussein: page 1 *top & bottom*
Daily Star: page 8 *top & bottom*
Times Newspapers: page 7
Worcester Evening News: page 6 *top & bottom*

All other photographs from the author's collection

A CIP catalogue record for this book
is available from the British Library

ISBN 0-7475-1090-3

10 9 8 7 6 5 4 3 2 1

Typeset by Hewer Text Composition Services, Edinburgh
Printed in Great Britain by Clays Ltd, St. Ives plc

CONTENTS

Foreword	vii
Before	1
Captivity	7
Freedom	145
After	225

FOREWORD

On 23 August 1990, millions of television viewers all over the world watched their screens in disbelief as a then unknown little British boy snubbed the Iraqi President, Saddam Hussein, and ruined the dictator's attempt to turn a group of Western hostages he was holding into a propaganda sideshow. The boy was five-year-old Stuart Lockwood who, with his parents and older brother, had been imprisoned as part of the 'human shield' policy designed to prevent a United Nations task force from liberating the neighbouring oil kingdom of Kuwait, which had been invaded by Iraq a month earlier. Stuart's television appearance lasted little more than three minutes, but it turned him into an international celebrity.

Stuart, his mother and his brother were freed along with other women and children ten days later, but his father, Derek Lockwood, was held in captivity for a further four harrowing months before being allowed to rejoin them in England. Throughout the period from the invasion of Kuwait to the family's reunion, Stuart's mother, Glenda Lockwood, kept a diary, on which this book is based. It tells a poignant story of how Saddam Hussein's most famous hostages survived the horrific dangers of detention by one of the bloodiest autocrats of the twentieth century and the intense pressure of the media attention upon their return home.

BEFORE

Life was very good to us throughout the four years we lived in the Middle East and we enjoyed a lifestyle and elegance most people never experience. Kuwait had become very rich because of its oil reserves, but the country needed our Western expertise and paid for it handsomely.

My husband, Derek, an engineer, had taken me and our two sons, Craig and Stuart, with him when he started a job working for the Kuwaiti Government as a technical adviser. Craig was only ten and Stuart was barely a toddler when we first arrived in Kuwait, so an important part of their early years was spent in exotic and unusual surroundings. At the time, the Iran-Iraq war was still raging just thirty miles away across the tip of the Gulf and a couple of emergencies brought the closeness of that trouble home to us: there was a missile attack on one of the islands just off the coast, and a saboteur blew up an oil storage tank at the refinery in Fahaheel. The housing estate next to it, where many Britons lived, had to be evacuated, but fortunately there was no explosive chain reaction, and the estate and the refinery were saved. Then the ten-year war between the two neighbouring Arab countries suddenly ended, and the whole of Kuwaiti society heaved a sigh of relief and got down to the serious business of working and enjoying itself.

We had really made ourselves at home by this time. I had obtained a job as the manager of an English playgroup owned by a Kuwaiti at Salwa, and we moved from an apartment down to a home on the housing estate next to the oil refinery at Fahaheel. The estate had originally been built to house the construction workers during the building of the refinery, but now it had become a privileged British society, closed to the outside world by locked gates and protected by its own guards. It even had its own private beach and this meant that all of us – men, women and children – could wander about in shorts and bathing costumes in the fierce desert heat. (This is generally forbidden in Kuwait, because the strict laws of Islam mean that women have to be covered at all times.)

Meanwhile, the world's top architects were putting the finishing touches to a fine, modern city nearby – Kuwait City – with its grand banking houses and official buildings, and its palm-lined coast road along which sprawled exclusive beach clubs with the best of restaurants and sporting facilities. There was plenty to do and we had plenty of time in which to do it – Derek worked from 7.00 a.m. to 1.00 p.m. and I worked from 8.00 a.m. to 1.00 p.m., so we had every afternoon and evening to ourselves. Craig, who received the benefit of a private education, went windsurfing, sailing and scuba diving regularly, and he was taught to play tennis by a world-class professional coach. The children swam every day in the private swimming pool on our estate, and we enjoyed good health with the help of a private medical scheme. Everyone had air-conditioned houses, offices and vehicles, and Mercedes and Rolls-Royces were a common sight on the roads. Even our boys had their own transport; Craig drove a motorbike, while Stuart pottered round the estate in a tiny electric-powered jeep.

Every day, we would get home from work and swim in the pool, organize a barbecue or go down town to gaze at the shops. We used to wander round the *souks* or markets, each one specializing in luxury consumer goods such as gold, Persian carpets and designer clothes. We would sometimes draw £1,000 in cash out of the cash-point at the bank and spend it almost without thinking if something took our fancy. We ate lavishly also, because the supermarkets were bulging with every kind of food imaginable from all over the world. We took it all for granted.

Nor were material possessions and long leisure hours the only things that made life so sweet. The glorious weather and blue skies, the days spent outdoors and the abundance of new-found friends all helped to make us think we had found the nearest earthly equivalent to paradise. Unlike some expatriates, we had a number of Kuwaiti friends whom I met through my work, so we also acquired a taste for the local culture. Kuwait was a place you either loved or hated, and we loved it. Derek's contract was originally for just over two years, but we had already obtained two extensions and were toying with the idea of settling out there for good.

There were a few disadvantages, however. My long telephone calls to my sister in England cost £2 a minute, though local calls inside Kuwait were free. Television programmes were generally poor by Western standards, and the British newspapers always arrived two days late, so we led a very insular existence. I have heard it said that if you are in Australia, you do not know what is happening elsewhere in the world, and the same was true of life in Kuwait. It was probably because of this that we did not notice the gathering Iraqi storm clouds until they were almost upon us.

Yes, life had been very good to us in Kuwait, but all that was about to change in the most dramatic fashion as we became caught up in events that shook the world, brought us four months of terror and made us reluctant media celebrities.

CAPTIVITY

Thursday 2 August 1990

The longest day of my life began with a roar at 5.30 a.m. when Derek and I were both jerked from our sleep into terrified consciousness by the sound of jets screaming low over the rooftops. Derek leapt out of bed, ran to the window and was just in time to see a fighter bank away sharply directly above our heads. The plane was so low that he almost felt he could reach out and touch it.

The day before, daily routine had been almost completely normal as the unsuspecting Middle East basked in the last day of peace. Naturally, there had been a lot of speculation as talks between Iraq and Kuwait broke down and there was a build-up of 100,000 troops on the border, but nobody had been prepared for the horrific months that lay ahead. I had gone to work as usual at 7.30 a.m. and returned shortly after lunch, but nobody I had spoken to, not even the Kuwaitis themselves, had seemed unduly concerned about the deteriorating political situation. We began to think that we were being alarmist. I did not then know it, but I would never again see my beloved playgroup where I had been so happy.

The only sign of panic had occurred at 6.00 p.m. when we had gone to get some money from the cash-point and found large crowds milling round the banks. We met some friends who told us that the money exchanges had closed because there had been a run on cash, and we all agreed it would be sensible to fill our vehicles with fuel and pack an emergency bag in case we had to make a run for it. Yet normality returned later the same evening when Derek had to go to the airport to pick up some friends returning from a two-week holiday in Cyprus. They told him they had telephoned the British Embassy in Kuwait to ask if they should stay where they were, but had been assured that it was safe to return.

Now, less than twelve hours later, Iraqi tanks, aircraft and ground troops were storming across the border and mercilessly crushing the light Kuwaiti defences in their path. Bazooka and machine-gun fire echoed through the streets of Kuwait City as the invading hordes gleefully set about the task of bludgeoning the little oil kingdom into submission in only twenty-four hours. Our fears had been well-founded. Saddam Hussein, the bloody dictator of Iraq, had not been bluffing.

Derek rushed into the lounge to get the World Service on our small short-wave radio. Fifteen minutes later, a friend knocked at our door and told us that he should go to a meeting in the clubhouse at 6.00 a.m. to receive instructions. While Derek was away, I slung some clothing and other bits and pieces into a bag and jerked our bewildered sons out of bed so that we could move at a moment's notice; but Derek returned at 6.15 a.m. to say we had been advised to sit tight. The invasion was announced on the 7.00 a.m. news. It appeared that a member of the Kuwaiti royal family had died defending the Dasman Palace, although the Emir, Sheikh Jaber al-Ahmed, had escaped to Saudi Arabia.

Iraq had already seized control of the radio and television stations, although one station was still managing to broadcast desperate appeals for help. The announcer, his shrill voice raw with terror, was screaming, 'We shall die but Kuwait will live. We will make the aggressors taste the chalice of death.'

Almost immediately, we received a telephone call from a friend in England to see if we were all right. He kindly took the telephone numbers of all the members of our family and promised to let them know we were safe.

As we apprehensively lay low in our house, we could hear the sound of shelling and gunfire in the distance, and it gradually got closer. We lived right by the sea, and the noise from explosions and the other sounds of war boomed at us across the open water. It seemed to get nearer all the time until it made our window panes literally rattle. We had never heard anything like it before, and it sent shivers of fear down our spines as our minds raced with the possibilities of what might happen to us.

Our next-door neighbours, George and Maggie, had gone

on holiday to Thailand only two days previously, and George's brother telephoned us to make sure that they had got away safely. He asked how we were and finished his call by saying, 'We're all thinking of you.' I burst into tears as the enormity of what he meant sunk home. They were the first of many tears I was to weep during the next five months.

Throughout the day, we desperately tried to keep busy and started packing our belongings into wooden boxes. We built an air-raid shelter under the table and put mattresses into it. We did our best to keep the children calm and make them think nothing was wrong, but we need not have worried about Stuart, who, at the age of five, thought the whole thing was one big, exciting game. As the battles raged in the countryside outside the town, we passed the time by playing games. Our menfolk had to go for further briefings at various times, but always the announcement from the British Embassy was the same: 'Sit tight.' If we had ignored this advice, we could have driven over the border to safety in Saudi Arabia within one and a half hours and spared ourselves the months of anguish and danger that lay ahead.

Our international telephone link with the outside world was by now virtually out of action, but a minor miracle occurred at 6.20 p.m. when my sister, Judy, managed to ring us from England, having tried all day to get through.

When darkness fell, we were, if possible, even more on edge because we were convinced that we would not see the following morning. We put the boys to bed on the mattresses in our home-made shelter, and Derek and I lay down on either side of them. If the invading soldiers came bursting in through the door, we wanted them to find us all together. I do not think we slept a wink that night as we waited for them to come and get us, lying restlessly with our ears straining to hear the slightest sound. We were frightened that the huge oil refinery situated behind our house might be bombed because, if that had all gone up, we would all have gone with it. We had heard tanks firing fairly close all day, but after midnight everything seemed to quieten down.

At 1.00 a.m. the telephone rang again, setting our nerves jangling. It was my niece, Hayley, who had managed to get through after trying all evening. She had been out to visit us for a holiday in April, and so she could visualize what was happening as I described it to her. She asked numerous questions and became very upset, and in the end we were both weeping down the phone as we talked. After she had rung off, a cell door seemed to slam on us because that was the last call we received from outside Kuwait. Our final link with the safe, sane world of England was broken.

Friday 3 August

The dawning of the new day was like the calm after the storm. There were no troops, and everything appeared to have returned to normal with people going about their daily business. Our neighbours were even pottering in their garden and we had a chat with them over the fence. We discussed the invasion with them and with other people in the area, and it appeared that the women were generally very nervous while the men were trying to stay calm, detached and logical. There was one point, though, on which everybody agreed: we should all have been on the road out of Kuwait to Saudi Arabia as soon as possible after the invasion began. We were only a short drive from the border, and our area had remained relatively quiet for the first thirty hours of the hostilities. But now it was too late. We little knew how bitterly we would come to resent and regret the advice of the Embassy to sit tight.

We saw Iraqi soldiers for the first time just after midday when a squad of about thirty of the élite Republican Guard came marching into our housing complex. Half went to the left, half to the right and they fanned out and did a thorough survey of the whole area. The operation looked very professional and they seemed to know exactly what they were doing. There was a missile station at the far end of the campus and we knew it would be of great interest to them. They found it and had a good look around, but everything seemed to be promising from our point of view because they were very civil to us and conducted themselves extremely well. They left after forty-five minutes without bothering us, and everybody started to relax because we thought, 'They know we are here and they just do not seem interested.'

Everyone's mood lightened to such an extent that two of the men even suggested opening up the clubhouse for a short time, and we all agreed that, after having been penned up in our houses for more than twenty-four hours, it would do us good to get together. The bar opened and we were just beginning to relax properly when two of the teenage boys, who had been for a walk, came rushing back with the news that they had met some more Iraqi soldiers. Two of the men went to see what was happening and were confronted by an Iraqi officer who wanted to inspect the missile station, but he left, apparently satisfied, after a few minutes.

We left the club at about 4.15 p.m. and returned home to do some more packing and prepare our evening meal. We had just sat down to eat it at 6.15 p.m. when there was an urgent knocking at the door and, when Derek went to answer it, he was confronted by an armed Iraqi soldier standing on the doorstep. The man asked Derek in Arabic if he was from the military, and when Derek replied, 'No, English,' the soldier seemed satisfied. We sat down to resume our meal, but within minutes we heard the fire alarm sounding. We knew that was normally the signal for everybody to congregate at the gates of the complex, but Derek told me and the boys to stay in the house while he went to see what was happening.

It was the last time we saw him for more than two weeks. The Iraqis gathered all our men together, loaded them on to a bus and took them away to the nearby town of Ahmadi for interrogation.

As news of what had happened spread through the complex like wildfire, panic broke out among the families the men had been forced to leave behind. Thirty-five wives, with only a handful of their teenage sons to protect them, were now at the mercy of goodness knows how many Iraqi soldiers. Our minds raced with fears of rape and other ugly kinds of abuse that women can suffer when they are innocently caught up in somebody else's war.

Yet within minutes, we were putting into operation an instant emergency plan which was to be our salvation during the days that lay ahead. The wives decided to stay in contact with one another by telephone, and it was agreed that groups of us should gather together in different houses where we could barricade ourselves in for mutual protection. The houses should be as close to one another as possible and should all have telephones so that we could keep in touch. Everything we managed to achieve subsequently became possible only because we had the telephone as our life-line. My next-door neighbour on the other side, Jean, and her children – Helen, and Craig's friend Stephen – came to stay with us, and we were soon joined by the girl from the house opposite. The seven of us took root in our front room.

We were all out of our minds with worry over our men because we did not have a clue what was happening to them. We managed to stay in touch by telephone with friends living in other parts of Kuwait, but this proved to be a mixed blessing. We kept receiving widely differing stories about what was going on and this made us even more frightened because we did not know what to expect next.

Three frantic hours later, we saw the children were becoming very tired, so we settled them down on the mattresses in the shelter Derek and I had erected the day before. When they had fallen asleep, we three adults sat and talked about our plan of campaign. We decided to barricade the doors with the large, heavy packing cases in which I had stowed our worldly goods ready for a 'quick' getaway, and then we went round the house making sure all the windows were locked and the curtains drawn. It was scant protection against some of the most efficient and professional troops in the Middle East, but it made us feel better. After we had finished our makeshift fortifications, Cassie, who had fled from the house opposite, peeped through the side of the curtains and saw that her home had already been occupied by Iraqi soldiers; she had only just got out in time. She was very concerned about what she was going to do in the future because she had with her just the clothes she was wearing, owing to her hurried departure. Her handbag, money, passport and other essential documents were now in enemy hands. It was obvious that it would have been useless and suicidal for her to try to return just then, and we decided that she should try the next day if it appeared the men had left.

We drew up a rota and took it in turns to keep watch, listen for any sounds of people trying to break in and man the telephone that kept us in touch with the girls in the other houses. The sound of guns firing had started again earlier, and, with the troops now in Fahaheel, the battle zone was very near. Yet, amazingly, the children slept on through all the noise, and this at least brought us some comfort because we knew that we must try to keep them calm. On reflection I do not think that Stuart and the other little ones realized what a dramatic and dangerous situation we had been placed in, and it must have seemed like an adventure to them – if only we could have been as carefree. We did not know where our men had gone, when or even if they would be back, or how long we would have to last out by ourselves. On top of this, we had to take account of what food stocks we possessed and try to work out a rationing system in case we were in for a long siege. I do not think any of the three of us slept at all throughout that long, lonely night.

The final irony was that it had already been dark when Derek and the other men were taken from us and so we had already drawn our curtains. We were never to open them again from that moment on because they were to be the only things that kept us hidden from the prowling Iraqi troops.

Saturday 4 August

This was the day when my elder son, Craig, had to face more danger and responsibility at the age of fourteen than many people have to face in a complete lifetime. After our safe return to England a month later, the media circus, which at times practically camped on our doorstep, was interested only in Stuart, because of his appearance on television with Saddam Hussein. Some of the reporters did not even seem to know that I had another son. Of course, Stuart was very brave and I shall always be proud of the way he behaved when the eyes of nearly the whole world were upon him, but in some ways Craig was even braver because, being nine years older, from the start he was under no illusions about the danger confronting us. Nor were my two sons unique: throughout the ordeal the children of all the hostages showed a bravery nobody had any right to expect from people of such tender years.

The burden of adulthood was thrust upon Craig's shoulders at 7.00 a.m. when we peeped around the curtains to see if it was safe for Cassie to try and return home to collect her important possessions. The house opposite appeared to be quiet and deserted, and Craig volunteered to run over the road with her. We moved the heavy boxes from the door and watched them as they dashed across – a terrified woman with only an unarmed teenage boy to protect her against the cream of the Iraqi army. They got as far as Cassie's back door, but heard the voices of men moving about inside and fortunately managed to escape back to our house without being seen. They flung themselves breathlessly inside and we slammed the door shut and shoved the barricades back in place. We abandoned all hope of returning to Cassie's house and settled down for the long day ahead of us.

The first news of our missing husbands came two hours later when one of the girls in another house telephoned to tell us that they had been taken by the Iraqis to Baghdad. We were completely devastated and began speculating about how the situation would resolve itself. We suddenly felt even more alone and vulnerable. Other scraps of information filtered through during the next twelve hours and were circulated among the families via our jungle telephone system. It appeared that the men were okay and were being held in a five-star hotel, the Mansour Melia, in the Iraqi capital, but this did not lessen our concern for their safety.

We also kept receiving news about the deteriorating situation in Kuwait, as we tuned into the BBC World Service every hour and were still able to receive telephone calls from friends elsewhere in the country who were worried about us. One friend told me she had just been out to one of the larger supermarkets on the sea front at Salmiya. She said all the coastline had been secured by the Iraqis, who had stationed hundreds of tanks and soldiers along the whole length of the coast road. There was absolute pandemonium in the shops as panic-stricken people queued to buy the fast-dwindling stocks of food, prices had become extortionate and, almost overnight, rampant inflation had decimated the Kuwaiti economy. Only three days previously the Kuwaiti dinar had been worth £2 and the Iraqi dinar 20p; but now both were worth the same.

Throughout the day, we kept watch from the edges of our closed curtains and saw a lot of Iraqi troop movements in and around our housing complex. In the main, the soldiers now appearing were just young lads, yet we found them more menacing than the hardened professionals we had seen earlier. The newcomers were all armed and they started larking about as immature, unsupervised men do, no matter what their race, creed or nationality. They managed to start up some of the cars and began hot-rodding them round the estate. Cassie's car was one of the first to go, and some of the others, which had been unlocked when the emergency started, were also soon being used as toys. We could only sit and listen as the madcap drivers spent hours screaming round the corners at horrendous speeds, bumping the vehicles into dustbins and other obstacles. The appalling driving convinced me that many of the soldiers had never been behind the wheel of a car before. Whenever a car ran out of fuel, its driver would simply abandon it on the nearby beach and then go in search of another.

The raucous shouting and erratic behaviour of some of the men suggested that they were drunk. This renewed our fears for our personal safety and we were haunted by the prospect of these loud-mouthed youngsters, fired up by drink, coming to seek us out. In a desperate attempt to minimize the risk of this happening, we scoured our houses for bottles of alcohol and poured every last drop down the drains. If only we could have done the same in the houses we had been forced to evacuate. If only it had not been brewed in the first place.

We were absolutely petrified as we heard them going on the rampage and driving our cars round the roads, and the fact that we could not see them properly only made it worse. All we dared do was pull back the outside edges of the curtains a bare half-inch and snatch a brief glimpse of what was happening outside. In a strange way, we would have felt better if we could have flung the curtains wide and glared at them, because at least we would have known for certain what they were up to, but such an action would have been reckless and stupid. We sat helpless in our half-darkened rooms and our imaginations built up terrible pictures based on what we could hear and the little we could see. It is impossible to describe the emotion that swamped us, but it was probably akin to what a man must feel as he sits condemned in a cell an hour from his execution.

Our telephone link really came into its own during these seemingly endless hours when we nervously strained our ears to pick up every sound, hoping against hope that each voice and each footfall we heard was not the signal for the start of what we most dreaded. Every movement of the soldiers was carefully monitored by all the girls watching with heart-hammering tension in their darkened houses from behind the closed curtains, and every scrap of information was shared out amongst us. We developed our own early-warning system, so that whenever a group of men tried the doors and windows at one house to see if they were locked, the families still in residence at the next house along the road were warned to be on their guard. We agreed to keep in touch with one another regularly until midnight and not to telephone one another after that time except in a dire emergency. There were many occasions when our doors and windows were rattled by unseen would-be intruders, and the sight of a man's shadow falling across a door or window made our hearts pound and our tongues stick to our palates as our mouths went dry with fear. No doubt most of these men were only trying to find empty houses in which they could set up home, but at the time it did not seem like it.

Another problem we had to wrestle with during the day was that of ensuring our larders could withstand the extra demands being made on them by the presence of the evacuees who had come to live with us. We were helped by a man named Mahmood, a native of the Yemen who had lived on the complex for several years and who was very upset when our husbands were taken away. He managed to get permission from an Iraqi officer to go into town and buy food supplies for whoever needed them. By means of the telephone again, a communal shopping list was prepared, and both it and the necessary money were collected by Mahmood from one of the houses. It was agreed that on his return he would take the provisions to the same house, where the purchases would be made into different food parcels which he would then deliver to the rest of our occupied homes.

Darkness had just fallen and I was on the telephone to one of the other houses when there was a knock at our door. That in itself was bad enough, because nobody had knocked at the door since Derek had answered it to the Iraqi officer the day before, and the fact that someone was knocking at it again now, when we knew every Briton on the estate was confined to a house, could mean only one thing. At the same time we heard the screams of children crying and we all stared at each other in open-mouthed horror. I nearly dropped the receiver and Craig almost completely flipped and started shouting something like, 'Get off the phone, for God's sake, there's children crying out there – they've got them.'

The knocking continued as we stood frozen to the spot, and, when we eventually dared to peep round the side of the curtain, we saw Mahmood standing there with our groceries in his arms. The sound of crying came not from desolate English children with bayonets held at their throats, but from our messenger's own youngsters who were having a petty squabble among themselves. Once again, we had imagined the worst because we could not see out of the house. The poor man had spent all day queuing for us at the supermarket and must have wondered why on earth we did not answer the door to take the groceries out of his aching arms, yet his only reaction was to apologize in his halting English for taking so long.

Later that evening, we noticed that other vacated houses now had lights on, and we realized that more Iraqi troops were moving on to the estate. The noise of cars being raced along the roads continued, but we managed to settle the younger children down to sleep and then played card games with the older ones to stop them brooding. We all went to bed by 1.00 a.m., leaving one person on watch by the telephone, but we had a far from restful night. On two occasions an unseen hand turned our door handle and once there was the sound of someone trying to force a window.

Throughout the whole month from the invasion of Kuwait to our liberation, this week that we spent in our own houses was the period when we felt most in danger and were most convinced we were going to die. It is nothing short of a disgrace that the British Embassy allowed it to continue.

Sunday 5 August

Two of the girls were subjected to the kind of ordeal we had all feared would eventually present itself. Five Iraqi soldiers broke into their house, threatened them with a knife and forced them to submit to a vicious sexual assault in front of two terrified children and two teenagers. The attack took place at the house from which our food parcels had been distributed, and this extra activity in and around the building may have drawn attention to them and led to their being singled out for special treatment. Fortunately, the women were saved from further humiliation or serious injury when a senior soldier arrived on the scene purely by chance and saw what was happening. He seemed very annoyed and marched the young men away, and we never saw them on the complex again. The girls happened to have been talking on the telephone to an Embassy official when the soldiers broke in, and the man on the other end heard everything that was happening. This incident, unpleasant though it was, gave us another idea for trying to protect ourselves. We all agreed that if we were attacked while speaking to someone in one of the other houses, we would leave the receiver off the hook so that they would know we were in trouble and hopefully could raise the alarm.

News of the attack filtered through to the rest of us on our telephone link-line and spread panic among the groups of women and children in their darkened homes. Our fears had been confirmed and we now knew that none of us could be safe while we remained on the estate where we had once lived so happily together. It was less than forty-eight hours since our husbands had been rounded up, yet it seemed like a lifetime. Someone contacted officials at the British Embassy, who immediately promised to ask the Iraqis if a member of their staff could take up residence on the estate until they could get us out permanently.

This time they took prompt action, and an Embassy man from Kuwait City arrived later in the afternoon and went straight to the house where the attack had taken place. The two women were understandably still in a dreadful state after what had happened to them, so our new guardian decided to stay in their house. The Iraqis agreed to his proposals quite readily and also accepted his suggestions for trying to ensure our safety. During the hours of daylight, he was to walk round to all our houses and keep us informed of any new developments communicated to him by the British Embassy.

We had already noticed that the young Iraqi men were quieter and better behaved when a senior officer was present to keep a watch on them, but whenever they were left to their own devices they seemed to go berserk. Upon his arrival, the Embassy man complained to the local Iraqi leaders about the assault, the joy-riding and the attempts to break into our occupied houses, and almost immediately there was a great improvement. The whole complex seemed to be much quieter throughout the afternoon and evening, and, apart from the occasional car being driven around the roads, some sort of peaceful normality returned. We hoped against hope that this would continue.

Earlier in the day, Cassie had been heartbroken as she looked through a chink in the curtain and saw her home being ransacked. We all peeped out when we heard a small truck being driven up the road and we saw it stop outside the house opposite. Cassie broke down and wept as she saw all her personal belongings – even the clothes from her wardrobe – being brought out by a small group of soldiers and loaded on to the vehicle. It numbed her to see everything she and her husband had worked for being pillaged and defiled by people who had no right even to touch it, but we were totally powerless to stop them. The truck drove away and we hoped that this was a sign the troops were moving out, but after a short while it returned empty and parked outside another vacated house. The whole process was then repeated, and we even saw one soldier walk off with a black leather briefcase. Shortly afterwards, the telephone rang and one of the other women told us she had seen things being taken from a third house. In this case, three soldiers had emerged with towels and diving equipment, and had walked along the road gleefully brandishing a knife. Clearly, the men intended to work their way through the estate looking for empty houses and stealing whatever took their fancy.

Despite everything that was happening to us, we had to try and keep the children quiet, calm and entertained. Fortunately, we had a number of children's videos in our house, and we played endless games of cards, Monopoly and Trivial Pursuit, and the air conditioning in our homes protected us from the searing heat of the Kuwaiti summer. There were times when the adults became fractious and there were one or two instances when, inevitably, we snapped at the youngsters. Fortunately, Cassie, Jean and I were all fairly level-headed women, and if ever one of us was down or moody, the other two would combine forces to keep her buoyed up. We agreed on the phrase, 'The dust is rising,' and whenever we used it, the person to whom it was addressed knew that she was getting a bit ratty and unreasonable, and would go off in a corner by herself until she felt better able to cope. We shall always remember it and it remains a friendly standing joke whenever we have our hostages' reunions.

Considering the circumstances, all the children were magnificent, and it was not until the late afternoon that they started showing signs of fatigue. Throughout the time we were trapped in our house, Stuart hardly ever asked to go outside to play, and yet formerly he had enjoyed the run of the complex and was always out and about. Young as he was, and even though he could not really understand what was going on, I am convinced he sensed that there was danger waiting for him if he left the house and wanted to keep away from it.

Night fell once more, and we settled the children in bed, and then sat and talked frankly about the awful situation we were in. We were almost out of our minds with the worry of what was happening to our husbands, and we feared for our children's safety should they fall into the hands of the Iraqis. However, we came to the conclusion that there was no chance of escape in the immediate future, and the only thing we could do was to keep our chins up and just plod on.

Somebody rattled the door handle once during the night, and the telephone rang twice with routine check calls from the other families, but apart from that we passed our quietest night since the invasion had started. We needed it after what we had been through.

Monday 6 August

Everyone was a bit cranky when they woke up, and the children, after being cooped up indoors for four days, started niggling each other from first thing. As usual, we tuned into the World Service and discovered that the situation in Kuwait was steadily deteriorating. We could not stop listening to the radio; hearing about our difficult situation had become like a drug we could not give up. The temporary 'ceasefire' on our housing estate seemed to be over because we could hear lots of movement again outside and the joy-riders were back behind the wheels of our cars.

Our Man from the Embassy called round to see us on one of his routine visits to make sure we were all right, but he had very little proper news to tell us apart from that efforts were being made to try and get us off the housing estate. They were attempting to obtain accommodation for us at either the Messila Beach Hotel or the International Hotel in Kuwait City, and failing that they might try to take us straight to Baghdad in Iraq. No decision had actually been made; there were only these vague possibilities floating round us. As usual, the official advice was 'Sit tight.' How we grew to hate that phrase.

Telephone calls were still coming in from friends in other areas of Kuwait, and all the reports we received seemed to confirm that the Iraqis were pretty well dug in right along the coastline and were definitely intent on staying. Food supplies in supermarkets were becoming scarcer by the hour and the prices had risen even further. People all over the country, particularly the expatriate community, were moving into communal houses and pooling all their food supplies just as we had done on our complex. The Iraqis appeared to be in total control, although the Kuwaitis were still putting up some resistance and had given the invaders a really good fight. There were even rumours that, as the days went on and the war progressed, the Kuwaitis were actually getting stronger.

During the morning, we received a telephone call from one of the houses on the right-hand side of the housing estate. The families living there were becoming very nervous because they were the only Britons still remaining in that particular area, and they asked if the house adjoining ours had been broken into. We had not heard anyone moving about in there, but we could not be certain and we did not dare to go round and find out. We promised them that we would ask Our Man from the Embassy to have a look when he made his routine visit a short time later, and he discovered that, amazingly, it had not been touched. We telephoned our friends to let them know and, when the street was deserted, they quickly and carefully moved into the vacant building. As soon as they arrived, we knocked a hole through the adjoining wall so we could all be together. The children were delighted because this meant there were now more of them to join in the games, and they quickly sorted out the sleeping arrangements to everyone's satisfaction. We adults were equally pleased, because we had so much to talk about and we all felt that little bit more secure. After all, they do say there is safety in numbers. We compared notes about what had happened to us and then made an inventory of the various supplies of food and other essentials we could muster between us.

We were rather worried, however, about Nikki, one of the newcomers, who was pregnant and had not been very well recently, and in an effort to keep her calm we tried to conceal bad news from her whenever it came through on the radio or the telephone. When I look back now at some of the tricks we employed and the confusion it caused, it is impossible not to laugh. We would all be gathered in the kitchen listening to the radio, for example, when Nikki would stroll in to join us. Straight away, off would go the radio and we would all rush about pretending to do something else and leave her standing there by herself. We all became very close to one another, and we developed friendships that will never be broken for as long as we live.

As the fifth day of our siege unfolded, some of the people

in the other occupied houses began to feel ill, particularly one or two of the children. The little commune in our double house included two nurses, who, as soon as they heard of this new problem, got to work on the telephone and asked everybody to let us have whatever medicines they possessed. Our Man from the Embassy was recruited to go round to collect them and bring them to us, and the nurses then made up a little medical pack for each house to ensure that everybody had at least the basics in case of an emergency.

During the afternoon, no less a person than the British Ambassador himself visited the estate, and Our Man from the Embassy took one or two of us from each house to meet him. I suppose there were about twenty of us altogether. The Ambassador had obviously come from Kuwait City to try and help us, but he was given a somewhat hostile reception. He still could not give us any positive hope of being moved out, and the seething bitterness and frustration of many of the women just boiled over. When one of the wives asked why we had not been moved out on the day of the invasion while there was still time to escape, he replied, 'We thought they would just come over the border. We didn't think they would come right into Kuwait.'

The discussion became quite heated, because the general feeling was that we had been advised just to sit and wait for the Iraqis to come and get us. I personally thought that all this arguing about what might have been was now irrelevant, and the most important thing was to work out some definite plan for us to be removed to a safer place.

After we had returned home and put the children to bed, the adults sat down for a game of cards, but this was interrupted at about 8.30 p.m. by the telephone. It was Our Man from the Embassy advising us to turn up our air conditioning to drown the sound of gunfire. Apparently, the Iraqis had broken into the police station at Salwa, taken the reservist list and gone to the various addresses on it to drag the Kuwaiti men from their homes and enlist them. The victims' angry wives had followed them into the streets and the soldiers had tried to disperse the women by firing volleys over their heads. We could hear the sound of gunfire almost into the small hours, and it was interspersed with the rattling of our doors and windows again by the Iraqis and the roar of cars screaming round our estate. It was one of the worst nights we spent together, and it was very late before any of us dropped off to sleep.

Tuesday 7 August

This was the most depressing and drawn-out day of our captivity so far, yet it started with a few minutes of sheer terror. We awoke early, merely relieved to have got safely through another night, and I walked through the hole in the wall to see if our friends next door were awake. Three of them were already up and about, and I had just started talking to them when the shadow of a man darkened the window as an Iraqi soldier began trying to break in. One of the other girls raced to the window and shouted 'Go away' at the top of her voice, but immediately a second shadow appeared at the kitchen door. We ran to it together and shouted again, and fortunately the men left. When we thought about it later, we burst out laughing. We realized we had made so much noise that the men were probably nearly as scared of us as we were of them. It is probable that they were just looking for another empty house to loot, and this house adjoining our home had been vacant until the day before. Nevertheless, it was an unpleasant experience because the men would have actually broken in if they had come a little earlier while everybody was still asleep.

By now, most of the empty houses on the complex had been stripped of everything that was movable. There were still a few cars that the Iraqis had not taken, but it was not for want of trying. Derek and I owned a four-wheel-drive jeep and the intruders had not managed to get into it because it had such a secure locking system, but I think even this might have been broken into eventually.

It was the older children's turn to have a bad day, and it was amazing that this had not occurred earlier. The boredom of being forced to sit inside four walls for days on end, coupled with the tension of having to shoulder the cares and responsibilities of adults, finally got to these ordinary, healthy teenagers. In the end, I let Craig and Stephen draw graffiti all over the walls of Craig's bedroom just so they could get rid of their frustration.

We women were not much better, either, because there was still no news of our men, we were no nearer to gaining our freedom and the general mood of depression seemed prevalent everywhere. Tempers were getting more than a little frayed, and we all had one or two occasions when we had to bite our tongues.

The one good thing was that our food supplies were lasting quite well, though drinks were becoming a problem. Fresh milk was running out and the hardest thing was to stop the children having the soft drinks they enjoyed so much. With the weather being so hot, before the invasion they had been used to drinking freely to keep their body fluid levels stable, but we had been forced to ration them from the start of the emergency.

During the afternoon, Mahmood came round to see us, but his visit did nothing to lift our spirits because he was being forced to leave the campus. The Iraqis had told him that if he wanted to escape with his family, he had to leave the next day. He had six children from about eight years old to a tiny baby, and he had no choice but to get out while he could. He was very upset about deserting us in our hour of need and he was actually crying as he told us about it. We all felt really low after he had left. He was so kind and considerate to us, and I often wonder what became of him and his brood.

As darkness approached, we heard what sounded like a lot of tank transporters moving very close to our campus. It appeared that the Iraqis were bringing tanks and heavy vehicles into the area to surround completely that potentially explosive oil refinery behind our homes. Yet something else to worry about! A couple of telephone calls came in from some of the girls in the other houses, but even those did not bring us any comfort or feeling of safety. They were as depressed as we were.

Wednesday 8 August

The news for which we had waited so long and so anxiously came at 10.20 a.m. We were told through a telephone call to be ready to leave for Kuwait City in twenty minutes and to take only one bag per family with us. Everything went mad. Within minutes, another call came through from the Embassy asking whether we still had our own transport available. We had our jeep and a Mazda, and next door also had two vehicles, so we hoped that between us we would find something that still had four wheels and worked. One bag of luggage between a woman and two boys really takes some organizing, but I managed it in double-quick time. I took two changes of clothes for Stuart and Craig and a change of underwear and a T-shirt for myself, then I crammed a few important official documents on top. The house was buzzing with everyone trying to get themselves into some sort of order and, in the middle of it all, Our Man from the Embassy suddenly appeared to check on the transport situation. Our jeep was fine and full of petrol, but we had to abandon the Mazda because it had been drained of fuel by the Iraqis. Both the cars belonging to next door had been damaged by joy-riders and only about twenty-five per cent of all the cars on the complex were usable, so we just had to pray that we had enough between us to get out of the hell-hole that had been our home.

Our last duty before leaving was our saddest. We had a pet parrot, which had previously belonged to the owner of the playgroup where I worked and which he had given to me twelve months earlier. We had named him Peter and he was not merely a great talker, he was bilingual and had a sense of humour. He used to say 'Daddy's coming' in Arabic, had picked up English phrases and even the odd swearword, and would imitate the ringing of the telephone so well that we would get up from our armchairs to answer it. One day when a new maid started working for us, he kept calling out 'Hello' until she was nervously walking through the house looking for an intruder. Stuart was particularly fond of him and spent hours feeding him and talking to him.

I was damned if I was going to leave such a fine pet, which had brought my son such happiness, in the hands of these people who had clearly demonstrated that they had no regard for the sanctity of even human life; so we carried Peter's cage into the garden and left it there with the top off so he could have the chance to fly away. The likelihood was that he would perish in the wild, but I would much sooner that happen than leave him ensnared to be butchered by drunken yobs.

When we were given the nod to leave, the thirty or so

families ran out of our houses, piled into the vehicles and sat there with the doors and windows locked waiting to drive the forty kilometres from Fahaheel to Kuwait City. Peter had still not flown away and Stuart became very distressed, but then Craig had a brainwave and showed again the level of maturity that had been forced on him so suddenly. He told Stuart that as soon as we had left, Peter would fly off either to find his mummy or to go to England where he would wait until we returned there to look after him. Stuart seemed much happier at this piece of news.

All the cars were lined up ready to move off, and suddenly dozens of Iraqi soldiers with a large number of officers seemed to come out of the woodwork. They were everywhere. The British Ambassador also arrived and we were instructed to follow him in convoy to Kuwait City where our destination was to be the Kuwait International Hotel. Stuart must have found it all quite bewildering because he was leaving for the last time the only home he had ever known. Although he had been born in England, he had been little more than a baby when Derek went to work in Kuwait and could remember nothing about his native country. This was the first time we had been outside the small, closed world of our housing estate since before the invasion nearly a week earlier, and as we drove along we gazed in amazement at the changes that had taken place. Tanks and soldiers were dug in all the way along the coastline in Fahaheel. Traffic on the roads was very light and most of the motorists were Iraqi soldiers in cars they had illicitly acquired. Our convoy certainly turned a few heads – I suppose the sight of a line of a dozen or more cars full of Western women and children took a bit of believing. A fair number of people appeared to be out and about as normal, most of them Indians or Bangladeshis.

Throughout the journey we saw many signs of damage, particularly of abandoned, crashed and looted vehicles, but nothing prepared us for the devastation we saw in Kuwait City. We had heard that it had been hit pretty badly by shells and bombs during the fighting, but we could hardly believe the extent of the damage we found waiting for us as we drove into the shattered remains of what had been a fine, affluent city.

*

When we arrived at the International Hotel shortly before lunchtime, we were told to park our cars in the outside car-park and quickly to meet up in the reception area. As soon as we were inside the building, many of us burst into tears, partly out of relief at having reached comparative safety but also because of our concern at what lay ahead. We were ordered to surrender our passports to an Iraqi soldier at the reception, but I was reluctant to do so at first. I turned to the British Embassy official who had remained with us and said, 'I don't like the idea of having to give him our passports,' but he replied, 'My dear, I can issue you with another within fifteen minutes.'

We were all allocated bedrooms; Cassie asked if she could share with us rather than be in a room by herself, and naturally we did not mind. As we started making our way to the lifts, two English members of the hotel staff, whom I knew from past visits there, approached me and asked if I would take their families' telephone numbers and make contact with them if we got back to London before they did. They were very grateful when I agreed to their request, though the whole incident was a little upsetting for everybody because it really brought home how none of us knew what our future destinies would be. I often wonder where all these people are now and, more importantly, how things turned out for them.

After a week of being trapped and confined to our own homes, the International was wonderful, particularly for the children, who now had a bit of space in which to move around. Our rooms were very nice and quite luxurious and we were allowed to roam freely about the building, although we were forbidden to go outside. The hotel and its grounds were patrolled by armed guards, and there was a security guard on every occupied floor as some high-ranking Iraqi diplomats were also staying there. Although this made it impossible to forget the Iraqi presence, we felt a lot easier now we were out of the nightmare of the previous few days, and we just counted ourselves lucky still to be alive.

After settling ourselves in, we decided to have a look round the hotel. Normally, it was very popular and crowded, but now it was dead. There were a few people around but they, we discovered later, were mainly Iraqis; the only other guests besides our party appeared to be a French couple with two small children, who had been caught up in the invasion *en route* to Luxor where the man had been due to start a new job.

The hotel management told us that dinner would be served between 7.00 p.m. and 9.00 p.m., and they went out of their way to help us keep the children entertained. They had erected one of those blow-up bouncy castles, and the younger children started jumping madly all over it to release a week's worth of pent-up energy. Craig was delighted to find the hotel's bowling alley was still open and, even better from his point of view, you did not have to pay to use it!

After about an hour, we went back to our room where we had a rest before having a wash and brush-up in readiness for dinner. In the meantime, Cassie had got together with two of the other girls in our group who did not have any children, and I pointed out that she might get a little more peace and quiet if she teamed up with them. We both saw the sense of this, as we had all had virtually no sleep during the past few days, and so she moved down a floor to their room.

During the next hour, all the adults in the party started drawing up a new method of staying in touch with one another and with the outside world, now that we no longer had our own private telephone system. We decided that all telephone messages from the Embassy should come through to a single point and that two people on each floor should then be responsible for passing on the information. The ballroom was commandeered for a special meeting to be held each evening after dinner when the hotel manager, Mr Simon, would keep us up to date with the general news on what was happening in Kuwait and hand out useful information about the hotel.

After the boys had enjoyed another session with the bouncy castle and the bowling alley, we met up in the restaurant with the rest of our party for the evening meal. Everyone's mood had lightened considerably and we were more relaxed than we had been at any time since our husbands had been taken to Baghdad, although we were still nervous. Our settling-in period at the hotel had been slightly bizarre in the circumstances, being more like an annual outing arriving at a holiday camp than a group of refugees being placed under house arrest.

Yet the armed and uniformed guards, who could be found everywhere throughout the hotel, were a continual reminder of the real peril and uncertainty in which we stood, and we were anxious to make sure the children were on their best behaviour in case they upset the Iraqi diplomats staying in the hotel. Thinking about it later, we saw that we were being naïve because everybody knew who we were and what we were doing there. Food supplies in the hotel were still good, but we could not get out of the rationing habit that had been forced on us while we had been trapped in our homes, so we kept telling the youngsters not to take more than they knew they could eat.

After dinner, I settled Stuart in bed and Craig stayed to keep an eye on him while I went to the inaugural meeting in the ballroom. We were told that, in the event of an air raid or some other military attack on the city, an alarm would be sounded and that would be the signal for us to seek shelter in the hotel's underground car-park. All the vehicles there would be drained of fuel to lessen the risk of an explosion, and supplies of bottled water would be put there to enhance our chances of survival if the hotel were damaged and we became trapped. The management had obviously thought the whole thing through and we were very impressed with their efficiency, though the implications of what might happen frightened us. It seemed that, every time we started to feel a bit safer and more confident, there was always some worry waiting to bring us back down to earth with a bang.

We were also advised to fill up the baths in our rooms each evening in case of a sudden water shortage. At the end of the meeting, Mr Simon suggested that we should all go down to the basement to familiarize ourselves with the lay-out of the car-park, and we were taken there with a guard to keep an eye on us.

When I returned to my room, I found Stuart fast asleep with Craig watching over him. I explained to Craig everything I had been told and promised to take him to the car-park the next day so that he could see it for himself – it was only fair if he was to be the man of the house while Derek was away. When

I look back now from my safe home in England to those awful, dark days, I can hardly express the pride I feel at the way he behaved. Yet he was not the only one – all the kids in our group had seen their fathers dragged away and had had their worlds turned upside-down, yet throughout they showed a fortitude that had to be seen at first hand to be understood and appreciated.

Thursday 9 August

Our first proper night's sleep since before the invasion was long but fitful, and, although we awoke fairly early, we found it difficult to get out of bed and face another day. It was therefore 8.30 a.m. before we got down to the dining room for a breakfast which, although somewhat plain by the International Hotel's normally lavish standards, was still more than ample. The children in our party tore into their meal with the natural voracity of young healthy appetites, but the women could eat very little – we seemed to fare better by surviving on our nerves. One of the waiters told us of the arrangements for getting our laundry cleaned and so, after breakfast, I went to get our few bits and pieces together while Craig took Stuart to explore the building. Having done that, I suddenly realized that my day had ground to a halt; there was simply nothing left to do but look forward to lunch.

If the problem of boredom was affecting the adults, the chances were that it would not be long before the same thing happened to the children, so some of the other girls and I got together at the bouncy castle and decided that we had to try and organize ourselves a bit. We agreed that keeping the children content and occupied would have to be our main priority, and at the same time we would make ourselves too busy to be bored. If we were to avoid brooding about what was happening to us and our husbands, it was vital that we did not find time weighing heavily on our hands. It was exactly a week since our nightmare had started, and today, of all days, was not the time to let ourselves fall into a downward spiral of unhappiness and regret. Accordingly, we started making plans and putting them into operation. Like me, one of the other girls had experience of working with playgroups, and she and I decided to try and find some toys from somewhere and then get all the children together for supervised play sessions in the mornings and the afternoons. The morning passed quite quickly as we busied ourselves in getting this off the ground, and the hotel management also came to our rescue again. They set up a television and video in one of the downstairs rooms, but as there were only a couple of tapes with the machine, we undertook to scout round for a few more.

Meanwhile, a number of messages from friends and well-wishers had come in to the unofficial office we had established in an upstairs room with a continuously manned telephone. Everybody just wanted to check that we were all right and to tell us how pleased they were that we had managed to escape from our housing complex safely. But soon even these expressions of concern were to assume a chilling significance. Later in the day the Embassy warned us not to contact our friends and colleagues in the British expatriate community, because the majority had not yet been captured and were in hiding, and it was feared that the telephones might be tapped. I very much wanted to speak to my boss and to a woman with whom I had been friendly for several years, but I was too frightened to do so: I did not want to risk putting them in jeopardy by revealing their hiding places to the listening Iraqi secret police. This, together with the rumours that were beginning to filter through about some of the atrocities being committed against the ordinary Kuwaiti people, made our spirits sink and once again stirred up our concern for our own and our husbands' safety.

During the afternoon, we went into the hotel's coffee shop and sat in a window with a panoramic view of the whole sea front and the main road running along the coast into Kuwait City. Wherever we looked, we could see Iraqi soldiers dug in all along the shoreline, and the traffic on the coast road was made up mainly of military vehicles driving up and down. It was very hot outside and the distant horizon was lost in a haze where the light blue of the cloudless sky merged gradually into the darker marine blue of the Gulf itself, but we were cool and comfortable as we sat in the air-conditioned cocoon of the hotel. Ironically, the scene somehow looked very peaceful and we felt as if we were viewing it from afar – detached, safe and completely removed from it. Yet in reality we were very much involved, and we had almost consciously to remind ourselves that what we were watching was not a half-hearted military manoeuvre set against the backcloth of an innocent seascape, but the outward signs of the brutal suppression of a small, independent country by ruthless, battle-hardened troops.

The interior of our hotel had taken on a peculiar mixture of atmospheres as the outward signs of military security rubbed shoulders with scenes of pure domesticity created by ordinary British families who could quite easily have been on holiday. The Iraqi soldiers were prominent as they patrolled the whole building, but they did not really interfere with us at all. Then, in the middle of what could have been a clip from a war film, two table-tennis tables were erected in the main lobby upstairs and were suddenly surrounded by Western teenagers all clamouring for a game just as if they were at a Friday night youth-club or a sports centre in the heart of England. Just before the evening meal, the French gentleman approached us with an idea for arranging simpler meals for the younger children at noon and 6.00 p.m. This seemed to be a very good idea because it meant that the adults would be able to relax more over their own lunches and dinners, and the Frenchman promised to arrange it with the hotel management.

When the time came for our evening meeting in the ballroom, we received the important information that, no matter what else happened to us, we would not starve in the immediate future. This was thanks to the good offices of the Iraqi diplomats who, being anxious to maintain the standard of their own diets, had promised the hotel management that they would ensure that regular and plentiful supplies of food were delivered to the building. We were also unlikely to be bored the following day because one of the other guests was organizing a treasure hunt, and Craig seemed quite excited at the prospect when I got back to our room and told him about it. Bless him! After all he had been through, it was good to see him suddenly show so much interest and excitement in such a simple pleasure. He deserved the chance to be young and carefree again, even if it was only for a few hours.

We were amazed to find that the television station was still transmitting ordinary programmes, and the boys and I watched a couple before going to bed for the night. Before we went to sleep there was one last safety precaution left to make: I and a friend called Jean, from the room on the opposite side of the corridor, agreed that in the event of an air-raid warning she would make sure that we had heard it and were making our escape, and I would do the same for her. It was scant protection against the horrors of twentieth-century warfare, but it did make our tense minds just a little easier.

Friday 10 August

The first sign of a real breakdown in our health caused by the stress and tension of our predicament started to manifest itself as two of the women were taken ill. One of the girls was in the early stages of pregnancy and had already on several occasions come close to suffering a miscarriage, and we begged the hotel management to see if our captors would allow a doctor into the building to examine her. This was arranged later in the morning, and he immediately confined her to bed for a few days. He also examined the other casualty, who had been very poorly and was in a lot of pain. He diagnosed a possible stomach ulcer and she was put on a completely fat-free diet. Everyone was already a little low-spirited because of the uncertainty over how long we were to be kept prisoner, and these medical emergencies only served to exacerbate our anxiety.

Thank heavens, therefore, for the treasure hunt. For the first time, the hotel actually seemed to be busy as everybody rushed about the corridors looking for clues. The children really enjoyed themselves and took it all very seriously, and suddenly it was midday and time to experiment with the younger children's new meal. This proved to be a big success and the youngsters thought it was more like a party. Our preoccupation with keeping to a routine, which we worked out for ourselves, may seem petty and frivolous to anybody who has not had the misfortune to undergo an ordeal like ours, but at the time it was vitally important because it kept us busy, stopped us brooding about what might happen and helped us to get through a few more tedious hours without losing our sanity. Although we were being physically well cared for, we could now intuitively understand something of what prisoners of war and other long-term detainees have to come to terms with, particularly if they have to exist in circumstances of great personal danger. Boredom and fear can kill just as surely as a bullet, and they do so far more slowly and painfully.

We also experienced for the first time an understanding of the fact that many of the Iraqis were pleasant, ordinary people with the same sorrows and regrets as ourselves. A uniformed guard asked one of the teenagers in our party where his father was, and the boy replied, 'Your lot took him away.' The guard looked at him for a second or two before saying, 'I'm very sorry,' then turned on his heel almost shamefacedly and walked away. When the guards were off duty, they used the same facilities in the hotel as we did, and a number of them tried very hard to be friendly and talk to us. It was a pattern often repeated throughout the following weeks, even after we had been taken to Baghdad. We found that they are just like people the whole world over – some happy, some sad, some kind and some cruel. Please do not judge the whole Iraqi nation by the standards of Saddam Hussein.

As we got to know the hotel better and to sort out in our minds exactly who was who, we discovered a number of other guests who had been innocently caught up in the war just as we had been. I suppose this type of thing is inevitable in times of warfare and has always happened. It seemed that everyone we met had a sad story to tell, and I felt particularly sorry for some Americans who had been due to leave Kuwait for good on the very day the invasion started.

During the afternoon, the uniformed guards were replaced by plain-clothes minders wearing safari-style suits. They were still armed and patrolled the hotel, but their more casual appearance meant there was less of an obvious military presence always breathing down our necks. The first playgroup session started for the younger children at 2.00 p.m. and was quite a success. There were plenty of volunteers to run it and quite a selection of toys pooled by the hotel and the different families so, after helping to sort out a supervisors' rota and leaving Stuart there, I was able to meet up in the coffee shop again with some of the other wives. We talked at length about the political situation and the increasing pressure being exerted on Iraq by the Western powers, and we were all worried about where and how it would end. Naturally, we all had different views on the subject and we expressed them with vigour, but the only useful purpose our debate served was to act as a safety valve through which our tension could escape, as we were powerless to affect the issue one way or the other. In the middle of our heated discussion, we were joined by one of the men from the Embassy. He did not have any news for us, but he was accompanied by two female colleagues who, we hoped, would be able to get hold of various feminine creature comforts which were difficult to discuss with men. They also brought some books and more video tapes with them, and these were very welcome.

After I had rounded up Stuart and Craig, we went back upstairs to our room, but half an hour later we received a message that the Embassy official wanted to see all the women immediately at a meeting in one of the other rooms. I almost ran there, fearing that we might be about to receive some bad news, but I need not have worried. Most of the meeting was taken up with updated information about the war as well as a new report about our men who were apparently in good spirits in Baghdad, but we were told nothing to indicate when we might be moved or where to. The most positive development was that we were each to be allowed to send a short message home to the UK through the Embassy, and we were soon giving the necessary telephone numbers, and transcripts of what we wanted to say, to the two female officials.

Afterwards we returned to our rooms, because we all had

some chores to do – we might have been staying in a luxury hotel as guests of the Iraqi Government, but we still had to do our own cleaning. Because the hotel staff had been reduced to an absolute minimum, the management provided us with cleaning materials, as well as clean towels and bed linen, and we got down to our new-found calling as chambermaids. At least it gave us something to do. My work was hampered a little because, for once, both Stuart and Craig were very irritable. I think the tension of our strange mode of living had finally got to them and they were exhausted. The three of us had a hot bath and went to bed early, and I ducked out of the evening meeting in the ballroom. My friend from the room on the opposite side of the corridor promised to knock me up if there was anything of importance to tell me, but my sleep remained undisturbed.

Saturday 11 August

I awoke very early and found it impossible to get back to sleep. I tossed and turned and could not settle, so eventually I got up and sat at the window looking at the scene outside. Smoke drifted across the sky from a couple of fires which were still smouldering on the outskirts of the city, and a few vehicles were driving along the nearby road, yet everything seemed strangely quiet and peaceful. My thoughts were a confused jumble as I looked at the two boys still sleeping in their beds, and I kept pondering on how we had all got into this mess and how we would get out of it. It is an awful feeling to go to sleep each night wondering if you are going to wake up in the morning, and I felt guilt-ridden that my children should have been put through such an ordeal. They were only in Kuwait because Derek and I had been working there; they had had no choice in the matter. Then my thoughts flew to Baghdad and I wondered what Derek was doing. Were he and the other men okay and were they being well-treated?

This, I decided suddenly, was getting me nowhere. Eating my heart out in this way was self-indulgent and would only make me miserable and leave me with less strength with which to support my boys, so to take my mind off things I started reading a book one of the other women had given me.

Eventually, Stuart woke up and straight away I thought that he seemed flushed and a bit off-colour. I fished out of my handbag a thermometer I had managed to bring with me and, when I took his temperature, it came as no surprise to discover he had a fever. I contacted Maggie, one of the nurses in our party, on the internal telephone, and she came up to have a look at him. She said that I should keep an eye on Stuart and she would come back to see him again if I was at all worried, but he seemed to rally a little after he had been up and about for a short while.

When Craig awoke, we got ready and went down to breakfast to find that the food was not as plentiful as it had been. There was still enough to eat, though, and I think it was a case of the hotel management being sensible and cutting down the portions to make sure that supplies would last. One thing that had not altered, however, was the attitude of the hotel staff, who were absolutely superb; they always had smiles on their faces and could never do enough to help us. A few of the other families in our group were also in the dining room and, although everyone seemed to be generally all right, it was noticeable that morale was dropping daily.

The new guards seemed a little more pleasant than the first lot and sometimes tried to communicate with us – usually through the children – while they ate their meals in shifts in the same restaurant. We saw the Iraqi diplomats only infrequently, usually at about 4.00 p.m. when they returned to the hotel and strode in with their assistants and other underlings scuttling about them. There were usually a couple of them at our evening meetings with the management in the ballroom, and there was one particular man who always sat in the front row and monitored everything that was said.

During the morning, a new notice appeared on the notice-board asking people interested in taking part in junior and senior bowling competitions to put their names forward. Craig volunteered straight away, and I put my name down a bit reluctantly after being talked into it by the other women.

Shortly after lunch, a personal call came through for me from outside the hotel. As I walked to the telephone I wondered who on earth it could be, and I was amazed to find that it was Miriam, one of my closest friends who had been in Kuwait for a couple of years and had worked with me at the playgroup until her midwifery job came up at the Ahmadi Hospital. The Iraqis had at this stage put a news blackout on our precise whereabouts, but this tremendously courageous woman had found out from an unofficial source and had taken the risk of ringing me from Salwa. I was very fearful of talking to her in case any eavesdroppers managed to locate her and sent the police round to arrest her, so I cut the conversation short even though I was aching to have a good, long chat with her. During the next hour or so, I made discreet enquiries with the hotel management about whether our calls were being monitored, but they vehemently denied that any tapping was going on, so I took my courage in both hands and phoned her back. It was wonderful to be able to talk to someone from the real world outside the hotel, and my friend spent ages telling me about some of the things that were going on and making sure the boys and I were all right. She even asked if she could come and visit me, but I said definitely not as my conscience could not have coped with her placing herself in such danger just to make me a bit happier.

After we had finished talking, I decided to take another risk and telephone my bosses at the playgroup. They were delighted just to hear my voice again because they had been so worried about what had happened to me. They asked where we were being held, but for their own protection I refused to tell them. If the Iraqis had found out, they might well have decided that they posed some sort of security breach and taken steps to eliminate them. It was lovely to hear them again and to know that they were safe, but the general news they had to tell me was very depressing. Food was becoming scarcer and more expensive every day, the Iraqis had completely swamped the country and there was a chronic shortage of money caused by the closure of the banks and the massive devaluation of the Kuwaiti dinar. After we had said goodbye, the door that had opened briefly between me and the outside world seemed to slam shut again, and, as I put down the receiver, I burst into tears and wept until I thought my heart would break.

After pulling myself together, I saw Stuart off to playgroup and went to the coffee shop to have yet another debate about our crisis with some of the other women. I knew they would have congregated there because there was very little else to do. At about 3.00 p.m. a major event took place when the hotel management persuaded the owners of one of the little shops in the complex to open for an hour so that we could buy a few bits and pieces. News of the sudden appearance of this Aladdin's Cave spread so quickly that within minutes a queue formed as people rushed from the four corners of the building. Less than a fortnight previously, the shop would have been just one more retail outlet that we lucky consumers, with our pockets bulging with valuable dinars, could afford to ignore, but now it was a veritable treasure house. It was wonderful to savour briefly some of the little luxuries we had feared we might never sample again, and I bought some chocolate for the children and 200 cigarettes for Derek in case we saw him in the near future.

Life seemed rather flat again after the shop had closed, even though the shopkeeper promised to reopen in a day or two when he had replenished his stocks, and we just wandered about the hotel trying to waste a bit more time. One interesting snippet of news that filtered through to us from our outside contacts was that many people were making quite elaborate plans to avoid the fate that had befallen us. People of all nationalities were lying low together in different houses and were pooling their food and hunting around for further supplies.

At least two of the younger members of our party were happy because they were at last reunited with their parents who were elsewhere in Kuwait. A little boy called Danny from Ahmadi and a teenager called Glen had both been stranded on our housing estate when the invasion took place, and it had been too dangerous to try to return them to their families. Danny had been staying overnight with a schoolfriend and Glen had been baby-sitting. We did not think about it at the time, but their parents must have been frantic with worry. It was a great consolation that officials from the Embassy had found a way of returning them to their families safely. Craig also enjoyed a brief moment of delight when the prizes were presented for the treasure hunt just before dinner, as his team came second.

During the evening meeting in the ballroom, the Iraqi diplomats issued a statement all about how Kuwait was getting back to work: the telephone system was said to be being repaired, the slaughterhouse becoming operational once more and some of the banks being reopened. Although the statement was read out by the hotel manager, it was something of a propaganda rallying call by the new rulers of the country, and we shall never know whether its claims about the progress being made were true. Every evening, the news from the country generally was very mixed, with some aspects of daily life showing a definite return to normality and others being disrupted almost beyond recognition.

When I returned to our room, Stuart was asleep, but Craig told me he had been very restless and was obviously not well. It was just one more worry for me to face and I telephoned downstairs to ask Maggie, the nurse, to come and have a look at him. She checked him over and left behind some antibiotic syrup to dose him with for a day or two. She emphasized that I must return the bottle to her when I had finished with it because our meagre supply of medicines was dwindling fast and someone else might need it. In our situation all these little things had now become very important. I sat up for a long time after she had gone, worrying about whether Stuart was just suffering from some minor childish ailment or whether he was on the verge of a serious illness, and Craig dutifully sat up with me to give me what comfort he could.

Sunday 12 August

This was the fourth day of our incarceration in the hotel and by now the walls were beginning to close in on us. In a place like that, there is absolutely nothing to do and nowhere to go after a couple of days. When we had first arrived, there had seemed to be so much space and luxury after we had been cooped up in our houses for so long, but by now we had seen it all and done it all. The management told us the children could use the swimming pool in the garden if they wished, and some of them actually did so, because it was enclosed and seemed fairly safe from the outside world, although I was by no means certain and would not let my boys go. But at least Stuart seemed to be better, so I had something to be grateful for.

The bowling competitions got under way during the morning, and Craig got off to a good start by winning his first match. Most of the junior preliminary matches had been played by lunchtime, leaving only the semi-finals and the final for the afternoon. Craig got through to the final in which he took on his friend, Steven, and emerged as the overall champion. He was delighted, and for a glorious half-hour had something to take his young mind off his troubles. My first match was at 3.00 p.m. and I had been teamed up in the draw with a man called Rob, who was with another party of stranded Britons. We did not think we stood a chance, but we surprised ourselves by winning our way to the second round on the following day. It was also my turn to help on the playgroup rota, so for a time my afternoon fairly flew by because I was so busy.

The straight-faced coldness of most of the guards in the hotel was beginning to melt a little by now, and they were making increasing efforts to talk to the children. I suppose they were all married with wives and children back at home, and understood what we must be going through.

Later in the afternoon, the sports shop in the hotel complex opened for a short time and was immediately besieged by crowds of captive shoppers who were anxious to add to their scant wardrobes. We had all had to leave our homes so quickly and with so little luggage that we owned only slightly more than the clothes we stood up in. Everyone was in the same situation, so any extra clothing they could get hold of was a real bonus. As a result, the shop filled up very quickly and people were buying everything – it was a bit like the first day of the January sales. A lot of the women bought T-shirts and tracksuits, trainers were another very popular line, and I managed to buy a few things for Craig whose shortage of gear was becoming a real problem.

After taking the precious purchases back to our room, we went down to the video room and killed another hour by watching a cartoon. We returned upstairs but only got as far as our door because Jean from the room opposite invited us in, and she and I had a chat while the children played together.

We took our time over dinner that night because it gave us something else to do, and then went for a walk for a few minutes before going upstairs to settle Stuart down for the night. I had been back in our room for half an hour when there was a knock at the door and I found Jean bursting to tell me something.

While she had been in the corridor getting a cup of tea, a guard had come out of the lift and said to her, 'Have you heard the good news? Our President has said that we must help all foreigners to leave if they wish, but we have to wait for further orders.'

She replied, 'If that's true, it's wonderful news. Maybe it means that you will also be able to return home to your family.'

'In Iraq, we say *inshalaa* [God willing],' said the guard.

'We say the same in Kuwait,' she said, and they smiled at each other as they finished their conversation and parted company.

Although this piece of news was totally unofficial and tenuous, it was very welcome and was the best thing we had heard since our problems started. If only we had known! We could not realize it at the time, but this was the first example we encountered of the cruel type of deception the Iraqis were to use against us time and time again. They would tell us that something pleasant was definitely going to happen, then that it would not happen and then that it *might* happen. It was a deliberate policy of confusion and uncertainty, an emotional version of the 'divide and rule' ploy used in international politics and industrial relations, and it was meant to break our spirits by raising us from the depths of despair to the heights of elation before plunging us into misery once more.

I prefer to think that the guard who had helped perpetrate this particular rumour had done so quite innocently and actually believed he was telling my friend the truth, and it is very likely that this was the case. The system of bureaucracy and command in Iraq works by a deliberate system of ignorance and fear. Everybody in an official position knows only his immediate superior and the person just below him, and therefore, when he tells you he does not know what is happening, he is almost certainly telling the truth. The system means that nobody is given any autonomy or freedom for innovative ideas, that nobody dares criticize the Government because they do not know the importance of the person to whom they are speaking, and that all orders, decisions and rumours can come from only one source – Saddam Hussein himself.

It was fortunate that my friend and I had the sense to discuss this piece of hopeful information thoroughly and agree to say nothing to anyone else until we had official confirmation. We felt intuitively, even then, that if our party believed they were about to be freed and then had their hopes cruelly shattered, our communal morale would hit rock bottom. Although many of us would have coped with such a let-down, a number could not have sunk any lower, and the disappointment might have broken them. We went down to the usual evening meeting hoping that there might be some statement to confirm what the guard had said, but it was not even mentioned.

When I returned to my room afterwards, Craig was still awake. The joy of his victory in the bowling tournament had completely worn off and he was having problems sleeping as his mind kept churning over with fears of the dangers we faced. To try and pacify him, I told him what the guard had said to Jean and suggested that our position sounded a bit more hopeful, but I also warned him that we had received no confirmation so he should not mention it to anyone else. The two of us watched television together for a bit and he actually dozed off in front of the screen. I shall never know whether sleep came to him at last because his mind was a little easier or because he was simply exhausted.

Monday 13 August

Stuart and I were woken very early by the noise of children in the corridor outside our room, but Craig slept through it all as his tired mind at last found the deep and peaceful slumber it so desperately needed. I got up and, taking Stuart with me, called in at the laundry with our dirty washing before going into breakfast. When we returned after our meal, Craig was still asleep, so we left him in bed and went for a wander before ending up – inevitably – at our unofficial debating parlour in the coffee shop.

I was paged at about 11.30 a.m., and hurried to reception fearing that something was wrong with Craig, but it was a message from my friend Miriam in Salwa asking me to phone her back. When I did so, I was distressed to find her much lower than when I had spoken to her only a couple of days before, yet it was little wonder when I heard some of the stories she had to tell me about what was going on outside the cloistered world of our hotel. Shops and supermarkets had been looted of their last remaining food stocks before being burnt to the ground, and the Iraqi troops were on the move once more. She herself was living in a house with thirteen other people; they shared all the chores and rationed the food among themselves. She also told me of groups of mutual friends who had tried to escape into Saudi Arabia at various points on the border, but had been turned back. There was one party which was believed to have made it by paying 500 Kuwaiti dinars to some wandering Bedouin who smuggled them across the desert. Considering what she was going through, Miriam still sounded undefeated, and she kept insisting that she should come and visit me, but I repeated that the answer to this was a definite 'No'.

After lunch, it was time for Rob and me to try and continue our winning run on the bowling alley, but our beginners' luck of yesterday deserted us. We gave our opponents a close fight but it was not quite enough, and we made a graceful exit from the competition. It was very good fun while it lasted, but our defeat was probably for the best – one bowling champion in the family is quite sufficient. The rest of the afternoon really dragged, and we went back to our rooms at about 5.15 p.m. to get ready for our evening meal.

About an hour later, there was a knock at the door and one of the other girls told me that we had to attend a meeting in five minutes' time. We all gathered very apprehensively, not knowing what to expect, but for once the news was apparently good and positive – and just what we had been awaiting for nearly two weeks. We were told that our men were still in good health and that the British Embassy was trying to organize a convoy to take us the 800 kilometres to Baghdad to join them.

A final decision would be made the next day. Although this sounded very hopeful, we were reluctant to put too much faith in it in case it failed to materialize. Luckily we could not foresee the discomfort, deprivation and danger we would have to face on that convoy we wanted so much.

We spent the rest of the day talking excitedly about the possibility of seeing our husbands again; it was the only topic of conversation all through dinner. Disappointingly, our reunion was not mentioned during the evening meeting which was concluded in five minutes without anything of much import arising, so afterwards we all went to the coffee lounge and talked about it there instead. Sleep eluded me that night as my mind became active with the unknown which lay before us. Would we make it to Baghdad for the meeting of which we had dreamed, and if so, when? What would happen to the children? I was enveloped by a heady mixture of hope and fear, and it must have been 2.00 a.m. before I fell into a fitful doze.

Tuesday 14 August

I awoke with a start to hear someone knocking at my door, and leapt out of bed with my heart racing as I feared there had been an air-raid warning. I need not have worried because it was daylight, we had overslept and the caller was just my friend Jean, who had dropped in to check on how we were. Apparently there had been some excitement during the night, and we had slept right through it, so Jean stayed and told me what had happened. Just after 2.30 a.m., there had been a number of loud explosions and some gunfire so close to the hotel that it had woken many of those in our party. I think it had not disturbed me because I had lain awake for so long the night before that when I did eventually drop off, I was for once in a really heavy sleep.

The boys and I were so late that we had missed our breakfast, and when we eventually got downstairs at about 10.30 a.m. we found the whole place buzzing with excited conversation about the dramatic events in the early hours. There was speculation that it had been caused by the Kuwaiti resistance which was still very strong and seemed to be causing the Iraqis quite a bit of bother. It seemed that reliable information had filtered into the hotel from friends outside who said that the resistance had attacked the port down at Shuwaik and caused a lot of damage. We had heard very little gunfire since we had been moved to the hotel. I do not know whether this was because it was getting less or because we were so isolated from the outside world, but the sudden presence of it now had a very unsettling effect upon many of the girls.

I was paged by the hotel staff at about 11.15 a.m., and when I arrived in reception I was amazed to find Miriam standing there. My first reaction was to burst into tears, but then almost immediately I was angry with her for risking her own safety by coming down to visit me after I had expressly told her not to. I was wasting my breath, however, because she was totally laid back as usual, ignored my protests and started telling me about her adventures during the drive over from Salwa. She had been stopped a number of times at road blocks, and Iraqi soldiers had kept trying to thrust pictures of Saddam Hussein into her hands, but she refused them, explained that she was Irish and made out that she could not speak Arabic – even though she spoke it very well – and could not understand what they were on about. I asked if she had had any problems getting into the hotel, and she said that the guard on the door had not wanted to admit her, but had at last let her through when she spoke to him in Arabic and explained she had come to see a friend.

Miriam had lots of stories to tell me about what was happening outside. Being full of daring and not easily frightened, she had ventured up to Ahmadi a few days before to visit another friend, and discovered that Iraqi soldiers were knocking at the houses and begging for food. Some people were even agreeing to feed them, despite the shortage of rations, but at that stage, if anybody refused to help them, they just left without causing any trouble. There was also a rumour that three youths had been caught looting and taken back to Baghdad to be shot. She said that the Iraqi troops were everywhere, although the Kuwaiti resistance was still very active and there was a large number of burnt-out Iraqi trucks abandoned along the roadsides.

Miriam stayed with me at the hotel for a large part of

the day, and she was amply and unexpectedly rewarded for her thoughtfulness. During the morning, the gift and sweet shop opened again. Miriam was delighted because she was a chocoholic who had been unable to get hold of a single square of chocolate since the emergency started two weeks before, so she immediately went into the shop and bought several bars of her favourite treat. She stayed at the hotel for lunch, and over our meal I told her about the possibility of our party travelling to Baghdad. She was very dubious about the whole business. She told me that quite a few of her friends had tried to escape from Kuwait over various borders and, although some had got through, most of the attempts had ended in failure.

We talked about the dilemma facing everybody, but finally agreed that our party had little choice but to seize the opportunity of going to Baghdad to rejoin our husbands. Miriam's husband had actually been safely working in Germany when the invasion took place, so she was more of a free agent than me and was better placed either to stay put or to make a break for it, depending on the circumstances in which she found herself. It was lovely seeing her again, but after she had bid me a tearful farewell at about 3.45 p.m. I was very worried about whether she would get home safely. I waited for about an hour after she had left, then rang her at the house where she was living and was relieved to hear her voice on the other end of the telephone. She had not encountered any problems except for a few more road blocks, and we agreed we would not make contact with each other again until we were safely home in Britain. I also called my boss again to make sure he was still all right, but said nothing about the possibility of our going to Baghdad.

The children were becoming very fed up by now as there was really nothing new happening to keep them occupied. There was a flurry of excitement elsewhere, however, because there seemed to be a large delegation of Iraqi diplomats walking round the hotel and the guards were in a flap. Later in the day we received confirmation that we would be joining a convoy to Baghdad, and we were suddenly in a flap ourselves because we became caught up in making the necessary arrangements to ensure that there was enough transport at the hotel to get us there. All our vehicles had to be checked so that we could be certain they were capable of making the long journey, and we were given some information about the proposed trip. We were told that it was being organized by the British Embassy although it was expected that an Iraqi military guard would accompany the convoy; the final details were to be announced the following day. We were all relieved that at last concrete steps were being taken to reunite us with our husbands, but at the same time we were apprehensive about what lay ahead of us.

Nothing had gone smoothly for us since the invasion, and it seemed that our ill-luck was destined to remain with us. This became apparent when we were asked to move all our vehicles from outside the hotel into the underground car-park. I handed the keys of my jeep in at reception and a member of the hotel staff promised to drive it in for me, but about ten minutes later he brought the keys back and informed me that the vehicle had been broken into, a window had been smashed and all the electrics had been pulled loose. I quickly arranged to be taken down to the car-park under armed guard and two of my friends came with me. I nearly wept when I saw the jeep and I kept thinking of how it had survived for a week on our housing estate only to be wrecked in a hotel car-park! Even the Iraqi guard who was with us was devastated and really upset that this could have happened, though I felt at the time that he must have been living on a different planet for the past two weeks. I was assured that someone from the hotel would have a look at the jeep later and see if it could be patched up, and as there did not seem to be anything else we could do at that moment we returned upstairs.

There, more bad news was awaiting us: we met up with some of the other girls and heard that their cars had also been broken into. One of my friends, Elaine, had a brand-new Pajero which had been absolutely wrecked, and yet again our newly-raised spirits plummeted. It would have been more than we could have endured if, just as we had been given the all-clear to travel to Baghdad, Fate had stepped in to rob us of the means of getting there. A member of the hotel staff, who knew something about cars, had a second look at my jeep and said that it was not advisable to attempt such a long journey in it. When all the cars had been checked, we discovered that something like five of them were unusable, so we immediately contacted Kuwaiti friends and told them about this latest problem. They promised to try and help us find alternative transport, but stressed they could not let us know definitely until the following day.

After the meeting in the ballroom, which was extremely short, I sat in Jean's room for a time talking to her about our coming journey. When I eventually went to bed, I lay awake for hours with thought after thought rolling round in my mind. I was haunted by the possibility of not now being able to make the trip and by doubts about whether, even if I could, it was necessarily the right thing to do. Above all, my main concern was for the safety of my husband and children. Sleep was a long time coming, yet when it arrived it was surprisingly deep and refreshing.

Wednesday 15 August

I realized properly for the first time what stress Craig was under and how much I was relying on his ability to behave like an adult. We both awoke very early and sat talking together about our journey to Baghdad while Stuart was still asleep. I told him everything I knew at that stage and he was a little concerned about the jeep's being out of action, but I reassured him we would probably just be found seats in someone else's car after all the problems had been discussed and resolved later that morning. He asked me lots of questions to which I did not have the answers, such as whether we needed new passports, how we could refuel the cars during the journey and what would happen if anyone in the convoy got lost. He seemed to have thought of everything and the list of his questions seemed endless.

After Stuart had woken up, we went down to breakfast and found a lot of long faces waiting to greet us. I think the enormity of the expedition we were about to undertake had by now hit everyone. Messages were flying round the hotel all morning as we became involved in planning the journey, and the time passed quite quickly. Our sources outside the hotel had managed to get hold of some spare cars, though goodness knows where they found them. All of us who could drive gathered in one of the upstairs rooms and we started trying to sort out a passenger list for the various vehicles. We managed to put two drivers in most of the cars so that they could relieve each other behind the wheel when necessary, though this was not possible in every case. We were also unhappy about the fact that some families had to be split up and would be travelling in different vehicles, but we really had no option because we had barely enough cars or drivers to go round. If we wanted to go on this convoy, we would have to manage as best we could. The two boys and I were quite lucky, because there was a lady called Angie who had a jeep the same as mine and as she did not drive I was asked if I would take over the wheel. Angie had two teenage children and the six of us could be accommodated in the vehicle, although it did mean that I had no relief driver.

No one in an official position seemed to go out of their way to help us, and we would have been in severe difficulties if it had not been for our Kuwaiti friends who really rallied around us. Many of the women would have dearly loved the facility of a bus to get us to Baghdad, but we were left in no doubt by the Iraqis and the British Embassy that this was not possible. As more details of the convoy emerged, there was an equal number of doubts about what would happen if anything went wrong. We were told that in the event of one of the cars' breaking down, we would just have to double up in the other vehicles which were already bulging at the seams.

By lunchtime the children were beginning to get bored, and after we had eaten one of the girls, Sheila, said she would take her daughter outside to the swimming pool. Despite my earlier worries about safety, I said that Stuart and I would join her and I volunteered to take Stuart's special friends, James and Thomas, with us. Their mother, Elaine, readily agreed because she was busy finalizing some of the details for the convoy, and Craig and his friend Mark also joined the party. When we got out to the poolside there was no sign of Sheila and her daughter, so my lot plunged in without them as I sat and watched. While the children were swimming, there seemed to be a commotion outside the hotel grounds, with sirens wailing, but just as I was starting to get edgy the racket ceased as suddenly as it had started. Sheila had still not appeared by the time I decided to return to the hotel, and when we got back inside and I saw her there, I asked her where she had been. She explained that she had been stopped by an Iraqi guard who said it was not advisable to go into the garden as there had been a shooting outside. I nearly had a fit when I heard this and realized how close we had been to danger. My original fears had obviously been well founded and I was amazed that no one from the hotel had known we were there. The children were oblivious of what had happened, and settled down in the video room to watch cartoons.

Another meeting was called at 6.00 p.m. to discuss some more details of the convoy on the following day. We were told that everyone had to be down at their vehicles and ready to load up by 5.45 a.m. when we would receive lunch-boxes and bottles of water provided by the hotel. We asked a number of questions, such as how long the journey would take and what we would do for refuelling points. The Embassy staff thought the trip would take between twelve and fifteen hours, and they were not sure whether we would come across any new petrol supplies *en route*; the best idea they could offer was that we should not use the air-conditioning systems in our cars so as to cut down on fuel consumption. In the event of a vehicle's breaking down, the driver would have to summon help by flashing her headlights at the car in front. We were told that we had to be ready to leave the hotel at 6.45 a.m. and must arrive at the Embassy at 8.00 a.m. in time to start the journey proper. There seemed to be a number of loose ends in the way the convoy had been planned, and none of us was very happy about the situation.

After dinner that evening, we met the hotel manager, Mr Simon, and thanked him for all the kindness and consideration he had shown us. He wished us a safe journey to Baghdad and a speedy return to Britain. I went back to my room afterwards because there were a couple of telephone calls I wanted to make. First of all, I rang my boss at the playgroup to let him know we were on the move and to say goodbye, but I found this very upsetting. He was a true Kuwaiti in every sense, and I knew that deep down he had no intention of leaving the country he loved so much, despite the uncertainty of what might happen to him. He seemed in surprisingly good spirits when I spoke to him for that last time, and I hope with all my heart that when this whole sad business is finally over and the shattered remains of Kuwait have been restored to their former grandeur, he emerges unscathed and I can meet him again. I heard later that he survived the early days of the occupation, moved from his own apartment to a safe house and surfaced unharmed after the war was over.

I also telephoned an Indian woman named Nandi who had been a very close friend and work colleague from our early days in Kuwait, and who had a husband called Chopun and two teenage children, Shaugat and Gargi. She was very upset to hear that we were leaving because she was concerned about the danger of our trip to Baghdad, but she hoped that we would soon be reunited with Derek. We both burst into tears as we said our goodbyes and she asked if I would telephone her brother in Bombay and let him know how she was as soon as I was free to do so. She had to stay in Kuwait – initially out of choice but eventually because it became too dangerous for anyone to try and leave. She also gave up her apartment, and went to live in the same safe house as my boss; eventually she made it safely back to India.

I received one final call from Miriam shortly afterwards, and I told her about everything that had happened, including how my jeep had been vandalized. She asked me if she could have the vehicle, as there were several men living at the house where she was staying and she thought they might be able to repair the electrics enough for it to provide them with a means of escape across the desert. I did not mind in the slightest, and in a strange sort of way I even felt easier about leaving it with her. I told her where it was parked and said I would leave the keys with the hotel manager, then yet again we said goodbye. Despite all the practice we had had at parting, it was becoming harder rather than easier. After she had rung off, I went to find Mr Simon to explain what I wanted to do, and I left with him the ignition keys and a hastily scribbled letter authorizing Miriam to take the jeep.

Then I went straight back upstairs and put together the last of our things in readiness for the journey. It did not take long despite the recently purchased additions to our wardrobes. Craig and I talked for a time about our trip and then started watching a film on the television, but we both fell asleep in front of the screen. I was woken just before 2.00 a.m. by the buzz of the television, which was still on although the station had obviously closed down for the night some time earlier. The two boys were both sound asleep and, surprisingly, it was not many minutes before my heavy eyelids started drooping and I joined them.

Thursday 16 August

I was out of bed and in the shower by 4.30 a.m. and then I uselessly packed and repacked our bag a number of times, probably more out of nervousness than for any practical reason. I got the boys up and dressed and we went downstairs to stow our belongings in the jeep. Many of the other women were also up and about and anxious to get moving, and you could feel the tension in the air as they milled about in the hotel foyer. Their mood affected the children who all looked tired and strained, and even two of the guards could sense the anxiety and seemed to trail us everywhere. We loaded the cars and then went in to breakfast where we did our best to encourage the children to eat well so that they would not start fading on the long journey. During the meal, two of the Indian waiters asked me if I would post letters to their families for them when we returned to Britain so that their relatives would know they were safe. I said that of course I would, although I pointed out that they might well return home before I did – but they still wanted me to take the letters. They were very grateful, said they would miss us all and wished us good luck for the future.

After breakfast, we all went down to our cars, drove them slowly in line out of the underground car-park and queued in a side street while the hotel staff handed out lunch-boxes and jugs of water to go with the bottled water and fruit we had managed to acquire for ourselves. At last the time came to begin this momentous trip which we hoped would reunite our families once more, and we drove off to our prearranged meeting point in the car-park of the British Embassy, where other refugees from various parts of Kuwait were scheduled to join the convoy. As we drove through the city, we could hardly believe the destruction we saw – burnt-out cars and military vehicles, and buildings that had been virtually demolished. We arrived fifty minutes early at the Embassy, at 7.10 a.m., and discovered we were the first group to have got there, so we parked and got out of the vehicles to stretch our legs. Craig spent the time looking around by the front gate of the Embassy, and he returned to the car after a few minutes carrying a bullet he had found on the ground.

Gradually, other cars started to arrive, and we were absolutely amazed when we saw the number of personal belongings that had been crammed into them. We had been told by the Embassy staff to pack only one bag – one that was small enough to run with if necessary – and the advice had seemed to us sensible, yet many of the newcomers had turned up with virtually everything including the kitchen sink. When most of the families had gathered, the padre, Michael Jones, said a short prayer asking for a safe journey for us, then he and his wife joined the convoy. The Iraqi guards who were supposed to accompany us were still missing, however, and we found ourselves in the bizarre situation of having to drive round to the Iraqi Embassy to enquire where they were. When we got there, the British Ambassador went inside while the twenty-nine cars in our convoy parked and waited. It was the first of many long, trying waiting periods we were to spend in the searing Middle Eastern heat during the next twenty-eight hours. I suppose we must have waited for about an hour but it seemed more like three, and we filled the time by gazing at the Iraqi troops camped along the sea front and the many lorries full of soldiers that drove past us. The temperature was increasing all the time as the sun rose in the sky, the children quickly got fed up and we just wanted to get going.

After what seemed like an age, the Ambassador came out again with the escort he had managed to arrange for us, and we all heaved a sigh of relief as we got moving properly – or so we thought. At every set of traffic lights, one of the soldiers climbed out of his vehicle and tried to ensure that we all got safely over the junction before the signals changed, but we had travelled only three kilometres when we were pulled in to the side of the road. Jackie, who was travelling in the car in front of us, told me we were stopping for 'rations', and I was just wondering why we needed more rations – we still had uneaten lunch-boxes with us – when a quick count of the cars revealed that six of them had already got lost. We waited and waited for the truants, but in vain, so a couple of the official cars were sent out to try and find them. They were nowhere to be seen (the mysterious extra rations also failed to materialize) and eventually we had to move off without them.

This time, we managed to travel one whole kilometre before being stopped again by a crowd of people with cars outside a housing complex. We did not know exactly what was happening, but it appeared that some new arrivals were planning to join the convoy in a whole range of vehicles including vans and campers which seemed to be packed with all their belongings. By the time this latest confusion had been sorted out, another hour had passed, we had been on the road for something over three hours and we were still in Kuwait City. In addition, six of our cars were still missing and the only information we had received about them was some vague rumour that they might try to catch us up as we crossed the Iraqi border. This much-vaunted, historic convoy was fast taking on a nightmarish, farcical quality.

We got moving again, drove out of the city at last and travelled for ten kilometres before being stopped for another car count. This particular stoppage was notable because I finally uncovered the mystery of the missing 'rations'. It appeared that we should actually have been picking up some Russians, and I had misinterpreted Jackie's strong London accent. We all collapsed with laughter and it was just as well – this was the last decent laugh we were to have for a long time.

We started off again after about ten minutes. By this time, the weather was really hot and the insides of our vehicles without the benefit of air conditioning were sheer hell. There were burnt-out vehicles all along the main highway out of Kuwait and we were passed by lorry after lorry packed with plundered personal Kuwaiti belongings on their way to new owners in Iraq. Any private car left on the roadside had been stripped of everything including the doors, and were now just metal shells. The military presence was very prominent, and as we drove through Jahra, which had been hit very badly during the invasion, the scale of the destruction noticeably increased.

We were pulled in another couple of times for car checks and reached the border at about 2.00 p.m. The temperature was by now close to fifty degrees, and the heat was so fierce that it was like the overpowering blast that hits you when you open the door of a very hot oven, and we were completely fed up and exhausted. To make matters worse, a new problem was waiting for us at the border checkpoint. After a twenty-minute delay, we were told to go into an office building, and there we discovered that the Iraqis were concerned that our Embassy had not issued us with new passports. At length, it was agreed that we should give our own and our children's names to one of the British officials who in turn passed them on to the Iraqis.

At this point occurred one of the most disgraceful incidents on the whole journey. One of the women, who was travelling with her two little girls, became very upset because she had been separated from her seventeen-year-old son who was in one of the six 'lost' cars. When she enquired of a British official what might be happening to him, he callously replied, 'Oh don't worry about him – they will be back at our Embassy in Kuwait by now and will probably be on the next convoy out next week.' The poor woman was distraught, and other people were also starting to get angry. What happened next was unbelievable in the circumstances: one of the British officials started singing the *Music Man* song, complete with actions, and, amazingly, nearly everyone in the convoy joined in. At first, the Iraqi soldiers looked out of the windows at us completely astounded, and then their faces split into broad grins – they probably thought we were crazy.

We were kept waiting there in the unbearable heat for one and a half hours. The border guards brought water round to us every so often; I suppose they were trying to be kind and were worried about the risk of us dehydrating, but it was hardly refreshing because it was warm and not very clean. When we were eventually given clearance to cross the border, we got outside and found to our delight that our six lost cars had turned up. It transpired that they had been found by some Iraqi soldiers who had taken them on a grand tour of Kuwait City looking for us and, having failed to find us, had then brought them straight on to the border. It was a complete fluke that we had met up and the whole episode was yet another example of the haphazard planning by the British Embassy.

We started off on our journey across Iraq, but we had travelled only a few yards before we made another stop. This time the delay was caused by our spotting a petrol station; we all pulled on to the forecourt and topped up our tanks because we did not know how long it might be before we saw another. This took half an hour, and then we travelled for twenty-five kilometres before halting again when one of the cars broke down and its occupants had to be squashed into other vehicles. After that we fell into a pattern of stopping every twenty-five kilometres so that the new shift of guards, who had joined us at the border and were doing their best to hurry us along, could make sure that nobody had escaped. During our next stop, the Embassy official insisted on having a meeting at the rear of the convoy of all the drivers, because darkness was falling and he felt that we would have to stop at some point for sleep.

The convoy was being led by a guard in a military vehicle, there were another couple of guards driving at the rear, and a third Iraqi vehicle kept driving up and down alongside us to make sure that everybody kept together. Our jeep was towards the front of the procession. The children from our two families were bored and exhausted by the sticky heat, and although Stuart managed to doze off for a time, the rest were wide awake because they were crammed together and did not have enough room to sleep properly. Suddenly Sheila, who was driving the car in front of us, pulled off the road and announced that she was exhausted and could not drive any further. One of the guards actually took over the wheel for her so that she could get some rest, and we ploughed on until we came to a kind of camp, which was little more than a large car-park with a few scattered buildings and a huge poster of Saddam Hussein giving us a welcoming grimace. We were told that we were stopping for a two-hour sleep-break, and some people got out of their cars to stretch their legs while others just settled down to sleep in their seats. My two boys fell asleep on the ground outside the jeep, and one of the guards kindly brought a seat cover from his vehicle for them to lie on.

We now had a new problem because Angie's teenage son, Gregg, had become very sick during the journey and the guards were concerned about him as they thought he was becoming dehydrated. They insisted on taking him to a hospital near the camp, and he was given injections and made as comfortable as possible. I did not manage to sleep at all and it did not seem long before everyone was being roused and we were travelling once more. When we stopped to refuel at a petrol station again, Gregg was still very ill and one of the guards took him, Angie and his sister, Lindsay, on ahead of the convoy so that he could be treated in a second hospital. We were all extremely worried about him, though I will not pretend that the extra room in our jeep was not welcome. Stuart stretched out on the back seat and Craig came in front with me, and we made the most of our unexpected added luxury until Angie and her children rejoined us when the convoy stopped to use a toilet block. Gregg had been given another injection and the Iraqis hoped they had patched him up enough to complete the journey. We now heard that he was not the only person in the convoy to have been taken ill. Elaine and Caroline had been rushed on ahead to Baghdad because their two small children had gone down with the same complaint.

By now it was the early hours of the morning and tiredness was really beginning to set in. The six of us were crammed together again and the strain of the long, hot, uncomfortable journey was beginning to catch up with us all. Although Stuart had shed a few tears when the sun was at its highest in a cloudless sky during the afternoon, the children had been tremendous considering what they had been through. The guards were trying to quicken the pace of the convoy, but

I was so tired that I found it difficult to concentrate and was afraid of falling asleep at the wheel. One of the drivers in front of us was having the same trouble, and when she pulled in and said she could not go any further, I said I needed some sleep as well. Maggie, one of the two drivers in the car behind us, took over behind the wheel of our jeep and almost immediately I fell asleep as we continued across the desert.

Friday 17 August

Dawn was breaking when I awoke about an hour later, and at 6.30 a.m. we pulled in at a little roadside café and shop where we were able to stock up with soft drinks for the children. Maggie returned to her own car while Angie, who had been travelling in Maggie's place, came back to us, and I climbed wearily into the driving seat once more. We all felt that the journey had been going on for ever and that we would never get to Baghdad, and I was still so exhausted that I felt as if my hands were almost welded to the steering wheel and that I was driving only half-consciously on automatic pilot. Tempers were also becoming rather frayed, and I nearly snapped at poor Angie when she came up with the apparently ridiculous idea that rubbing toothpaste over your teeth and gums helps you to stay awake. Keeping my temper with difficulty, I tried it as we drove along – and found to my amazement that it worked! I recommend it to anybody who finds themselves in similar difficulties.

At last we saw the outskirts of Baghdad approaching, though I think we were all afraid that they might turn out to be a mirage. Our next stop was at a police post in the city itself where we had to wait for yet another half an hour until some plain-clothes police arrived to take charge. They came round to each individual car asking for the names of all the occupants, and again there appeared to be a lot of fuss about the fact that we had no passports. One of the officers was even overheard saying to a British official, 'How can we book them into a hotel without passports?' There is not the slightest doubt that not having these documents – which I had been assured back in Fahaheel could be issued to us within fifteen minutes if necessary – caused us problems right from the moment the convoy set out on its 800-kilometre journey.

We sat helpless and infuriated in our cramped vehicles for another one and a half hours before the officials decided that they could get round the problem. Our convoy was split up into different groups and we had no idea what was happening, yet the British Embassy staff just drove off and left us. It was probably as well for them that they did, because we later discovered that our nightmare twenty-eight-hour journey could have been completed in less than one quarter of the time. Our Embassy experts had apparently been unaware that a new motorway had opened between Kuwait and Baghdad. The Iraqi guards who had escorted us across their country – professional soldiers in smart, dark green uniforms – showed more kindliness and concern for us at this moment than our own British officials. They came round to all the vehicles to say goodbye and we thanked them because they had been truly wonderful and always very helpful and friendly. Several of them said they were very sorry we had been put through such an ordeal, and you could see that they really meant it.

One piece of good news was that our group from Fahaheel was to be lodged in the Mansour Melia Hotel, and this really lifted our spirits because we knew this was where our husbands were staying. The special police now took charge of us and led us quickly through the streets of the city to the hotel. We all felt very excited and relieved to be there because we thought we were only minutes away from seeing our men again for the first time in more than two weeks. But Fate and the Iraqi hierarchy had other plans for us.

We were told to leave our bags in the cars and were ushered into the lobby of this smart five-star hotel and through to a large dining room where all the tables were laid for lunch with sparkling white tablecloths. We sat down, all of us fidgeting anxiously as we watched the doors at the end of the room, waiting for the first sign of the men. The police who were escorting us also came in and sat down round one of the tables.

After about twenty minutes of impatient watching and waiting, Paul, one of the teenagers in our party, came over and said he had just heard a conversation between the Iraqi officials suggesting that the men had been taken away from the hotel the night before. This sudden shattering of our dreams was too much for one of our girls; she broke down completely and sobbed uncontrollably, and the padre, who had accompanied us, rushed over to comfort her. In the middle of all the confusion, Elaine, who had travelled on ahead of the convoy after her children had been taken ill, suddenly walked into the room followed by her husband, Mike, and three of the other men. Seeing our distress, Mike had a word with the police guards and then stood in front of us and told us what had happened. It appeared that all the rest of the men had in fact been taken away, and the only reason he and the other three had not joined them was that there had not been enough room on the coach. We were told they had been accommodated at different hotels around Baghdad, and we were given the impression that it was all a big mistake and would soon be rectified. We did not know it at the time, but it was nothing of the sort. The Iraqis were once more up to their dirty tricks of trying to break our spirits by continually promising one thing but doing another.

Everybody in the group was very low and several of the girls burst into tears. Shortly afterwards, a huge curtain was drawn open at the bottom of the room to reveal a table laden with food from which we could help ourselves, but hardly anybody did. We all felt devastated, and food was the last thing we wanted. After sitting around uselessly for a time filling in forms brought to us by the guards, we were led back to the lobby where we were told that we were being given rooms in which to rest until arrangements could be made to take us to our husbands. We were then taken up to the eighth floor and it was here that we realized we were not being entertained in a luxury hotel so much as being confined in a costly prison camp. There were corridors to both left and right leading to the bedrooms, and separating them was a lobby area with two lifts and seating for four guards. We were allocated our rooms and then told that only one person from each car was to go back downstairs and collect the bags from the vehicles. I went down with a guard breathing down my neck as if he was afraid I was about to make a run for it, collected the bags and was then forced straight back upstairs. We were told we could go up or down one floor, but apart from that we had to stay in and around our rooms. This came as a shock after the comparative freedom we had enjoyed at the International Hotel in Kuwait, and as we were so crowded together, it was a very good thing that we all got on so well. We ordered coffee and tea and sat drinking it on the floor in the corridor outside our rooms just to get a change of scene. The guards seemed to find this amusing.

Later that afternoon, Gilly came round with a list she had been given of fifteen names of people who had to be packed and ready to go by 6.00 p.m. My name was not on it and at first I was very disappointed, but I overheard a conversation between two of the women who were due to leave and they were clearly very apprehensive about being parted from the rest of the group. After talking it over, none of us liked the idea of their being split off from us because we would not know where they had been taken, whether they had got there safely and whether they had met up again with their husbands. When those due to leave went reluctantly to meet in the central lobby by the lifts as they had been instructed, we all went with them to demand answers to the questions that had been raised over their safety, but the Iraqi officials would tell us nothing. Someone then asked whether they had to drive their own cars because, if so, most of them needed petrol, and someone else demanded to know whether there would be any bottled water for the children travelling on the trip. That flummoxed the officials: it was obvious that no proper thought had gone into this at all, and they became very embarrassed and told us all to go back to our rooms while they sorted it out. Some of the little children who had been expecting to see their daddies again very shortly started crying. About an hour later, the girls who had been due to leave were told they would not now be going until early the next day.

At about 7.30 p.m., the guards knocked on the doors of our rooms and then escorted us down to the dining room for our evening meal. Stuart was very grumpy because he was shattered and there did not seem to be anything he particularly wanted to eat, which worried me as he had eaten virtually nothing for the past thirty hours. I managed to get him to eat a little bread and butter, but he was so tired that all he wanted to do was sleep. Craig also ate something after a little persuasion, but the worry and disappointment of not seeing Derek again was affecting him badly, too. After dinner, we were ordered to go straight back up to our rooms, and my two boys both settled down to sleep very quickly.

Some time later, there was another knock at the door and I was given a message that a meeting would be held at the end of the corridor at about 9.00 p.m. When I got there, I found that the four men who had rejoined our party had gleaned a few extra scraps of information. One of them had managed to smuggle into captivity with him a little short-wave radio set which the Iraqis knew nothing about, and he gave us the latest details from the BBC World Service about the situation in Kuwait and the world political reaction to our plight as hostages. The men also told us that the fifteen women on the list would be going to join their husbands the following day while the rest of the men would come to meet us at the Mansour Melia.

Inevitably, after all we had been through, some of the women had vented their anger and frustration on the Iraqi guards, but Mike and his friends advised us not to do so because the guards could sometimes be useful and helpful. We were also told that we were being allowed to use the outdoor swimming pool for an hour in the morning, although the guards would be there to keep an eye on us. We complained that none of us had any swimwear, but they said we could wear T-shirts, pants, anything. At the end of an hour, a whistle would be blown and we would all have to go back indoors. Isn't that how daily exercise periods are ended in Her Majesty's prisons? Another point raised was that the British Embassy staff had been refused access to us and we did not know if they would be able to get in and see us again. This was particularly worrying because they had not been told that our husbands had been moved or, more importantly, where they had been moved to.

Both the boys were asleep when I got back to my room, and I lay in bed for some time thinking over the traumatic events of the past forty-eight hours and wondering how we had got through them. The heat and the conditions in the cars had been worse than we could have imagined, and the children particularly had been magnificent.

But the most remarkable and significant thing was that, considering the convoy had been organized through the British Embassy, it had been an absolute shambles from start to finish. I hope that no one else ever has to endure what we went through and that every British Embassy in the world is properly instructed on how to handle any future hostage crisis efficiently. The mistakes of Kuwait must never be repeated.

Saturday 18 August

Despite our lack of sleep during the journey from Kuwait, we awoke surprisingly early this morning, at about 7.15 a.m., although Stuart was a bit cranky because of the after-effects. About an hour later we were all taken under guard down to breakfast in the dining room, where we found the first unpleasant shock of the day waiting for us. We quickly learned that the fifteen women whose names had been on a separate list had already been taken away from the hotel and no one knew where they had gone. The news left a sinking feeling of anxiety in the pits of our stomachs and brought home to us how helpless we were and how vulnerable to the merest whim of our captors. One or two of the guards seemed inclined to be friendly, so we asked them what had happened to the women, but they said they did not know. We had little appetite for the food that was put before us, but we dawdled over it for as long as we dared so as to delay our inevitable return to the confines of our rooms.

When we eventually returned upstairs we were told that we could use the swimming pool as promised, and we gathered together what swimming things we could muster. I had actually managed to pack two pairs of trunks for the boys and I found some bikini briefs and a long white T-shirt for myself, so we grabbed some towels and went down to the pool. The guard who shadowed us this time was carrying a newspaper. During the days ahead we were to find that many of the guards did the same, the paper being used to hide either a gun or a walkie-talkie.

When we reached the pool, the children were very excited

and plunged straight into the water as if they wanted to wash themselves clean of the last dust from their trip across the desert. We women were far more inhibited and shy because there seemed to be guards everywhere, so we just sat around watching the youngsters. I sat on a sun lounger next to Mike and asked him quietly if he had heard any World Service news on his short-wave radio, and he told me that we were now being officially referred to as 'hostages'. This gave me a bit of a shock because we had not really thought of ourselves like that before. The Iraqis refused to use the term and kept insisting that we were 'guests', another word that was to become very familiar to us.

Our hour of comparative freedom seemed to be over in just a few minutes, the whistle was blown and we were all ushered back inside. It was very odd to be lazing by the pool in the sun with the children happily playing nearby, just as we had most afternoons during our life in Kuwait, and then suddenly to have to return to the reality of being prisoners. We all went inside and found ourselves in a crush of people outside the lifts as the anxious guards tried to hurry us along. I do not know where they thought we would go if we escaped from the hotel, because Westerners tend to stand out in Baghdad. It took nearly forty-five minutes to get back to our rooms and then, after we had changed, a few of us gathered in the corridor and asked if we could have some tea. Our guardians agreed to our request, but it would not be long before even this ordinary drink was rationed.

The spirits of our group sank very low after this, because once we were back in the hotel with time weighing heavily on our hands, we started brooding about the fate of the missing women and wondering whether we would ever see our men again. One or two of the guards seemed quite friendly and we constantly asked them if our husbands were coming – and when – but they kept saying they did not know. We did not believe them at this stage because we had yet to understand the Iraqi system of retaining command by keeping people ignorant, and it was not until much later that we realized they were probably telling the truth.

Lunchtime arrived and we noticed that the standard of the meals being put before us had deteriorated sharply and the portions had become very much smaller. I was also becoming concerned about Stuart because he had eaten almost nothing since the convoy had started its journey. I eventually coaxed him into eating a bread roll after begging for some butter and jam to go with it. Again we took as long over our meal as possible because the thought of being hemmed in by the four walls of our bedrooms was terrible, but there came a point when we had to return upstairs.

Amazingly, Stuart and all the other little children around his age seemed to accept our new situation without question and to come to terms naturally with our confinement from the start, even though it was in stark contrast to the freedom they had always known throughout their short lives. The two children of a woman called Sue, whose room was just down the corridor from ours, were a case in point. Kayleigh was only three and her brother, Ben, not yet two, yet they wandered up and down between the rooms without ever getting really fractious. It was almost as if they knew that our safety depended upon their being quiet and good, and that it would be pointless to ask if they could go outside to play.

The big event in a long, boring afternoon was that we acquired a new neighbour. Nikki, my friend who was pregnant and about whom we had been so concerned back on the housing complex in Fahaheel, asked if she could move into the room opposite ours from the floor above because her closest friends were among those who had been taken away that morning. Her arrival gave Stuart something to be happy about because she brought with her two more of his playmates, Shaun and Daniel. Later, a guard came round and took down all our details yet again. This particular man seemed quite kindly and was to become as close a friend as it was possible for us to have, given that he was a gaoler and we were his prisoners. We asked him our usual questions about our husbands and the missing women, but even he said he did not know where they were.

By early evening, we were all sinking lower and lower into depression, several of us were close to tears and we just did not know what or whom to believe any more. Then, as Sue,

Nikki and I were talking in the corridor at about 6.20 p.m., one of the guards came up and told us that our husbands were downstairs. The news shook everybody out of their lethargy in seconds, but the next five minutes ticked by in slow motion as we all gathered at the end of the corridor and stared in agonized anticipation at the closed lift doors. Then we heard the whirr of the lifts stopping at our floor, and one set of doors opened to show half the men standing there; moments later the other doors slid back to reveal the remainder. The men strode hastily out of the lifts and almost melted into the waiting crowd as families were at last reunited, and suddenly more than two weeks' worth of tension and hidden emotion exploded like a safety valve blowing. In every corner of the room people were almost ferociously hugging each other as if they feared someone might disappear again. Tears flowed freely, and they did not all come from the women and children.

There was just one unhappy corner – and it was ours, because Derek and three of the other men were still missing. The boys and I broke down and wept as the unthinkable and the unspeakable, which we had so dreaded, seemed cruelly to have come to haunt us. The growing conviction that we would never see Derek again had completely taken root by the time one of the lifts returned, and Derek and two of the other men stepped out of it; they had been taken by mistake to the wrong floor. Stuart just clung to his father as if they were glued together, and Craig was completely overcome. You could sense the communal feeling of relief hanging in the air, and the various families drifted back to their own rooms to enjoy talking together in the only bit of privacy available to them. In the middle of so much joy, however, one of the girls, Theresa, sat alone in her room and cried as if her heart would break. Her husband, Alan, was the only man who had still not returned because for some reason he had ended up at an installation away from the others. They were not reunited until the following day.

When we were alone, Derek told me that the night before we arrived in Baghdad, he and the other men had been moved out of the hotel and taken to a camp a three-and-a-half-hour drive away to the north, so the impression we had been given – that they had been dispersed to a number of different locations – had been completely false. The fifteen women who had left the hotel that morning had been reunited with their husbands at the camp, but then the Iraqis had continued their game of emotional blackmail by leaving Derek and the other men to stew in a room by themselves for a time before telling them that they were being brought back to us. Throughout our captivity, we found time and time again that groups of Westerners were treated differently to one another and were kept in the dark about what was happening, and despite the innocent-sounding assurances we received, we quickly discovered that it was all part of a deliberate plan, hatched at the highest level of government, to try and break our spirits and divide us.

I knew there was much more of a serious nature that Derek wanted to tell me, but now was not the time when the children were around. He also wanted to hear about what had happened to us since he had been forced to leave us, and anyway Stuart would not leave his side and Craig had umpteen questions to ask and lots of news to tell his dad. We were disturbed after about an hour by a guard who knocked at the door to tell us that it was time to go down to dinner. Everyone in the dining room looked and felt much more at ease, though for once we hurried our meal so that we could get back to our rooms and continue catching up with the news we had for one another.

Later that evening, Derek and I settled the boys in bed and then walked along the corridor for the 9.00 p.m. meeting that had become such a part of our lives. Everyone was very concerned about the fact that we had now completely lost contact with our Embassy, but the meeting ended after only ten minutes, and after the boys had gone to sleep, we sat in our room and talked and talked about the things we did not want them to know about.

Derek began by giving me a blow-by-blow account of what had happened when the men had been taken away from us back in Kuwait. They were driven to Ahmadi for questioning, and were told that if they just gave their names and addresses, they could return home within half an hour. It quickly became apparent to them, however, that this was a lie made up by the Iraqi guards, who did not really know what was happening to them. After a few hours, they were told that they were being taken to Baghdad 'for their own safety', and this phrase really stuck in Derek's mind. All the men were immediately up in arms about being parted from their wives, who they knew would be in danger if they were left by themselves in Fahaheel, and after a long, heated argument the guards agreed that they could call at our housing complex on the way through and pick us up. Unfortunately, they only got as far as the town's fish market before being turned back by an officer who would have nothing to do with the new arrangement, and despite their protests they were taken straight away to begin their journey to the Iraqi capital.

Their trip in an oil-company bus turned out to be as horrific as in our convoy, and it got off to a bad start when the driver became visibly ill on being told where he was driving to and had to be replaced behind the wheel by a soldier. The new chauffeur gave the impression he had never driven before – he had to be shown how to depress the clutch to engage gear – and the way he drove the vehicle may have been responsible for the fact that it eventually broke down.

As they travelled, they could see something of the carnage and destruction that had been wrought during the invasion. All along the road there were burnt-out cars and Kuwaiti military and police vehicles which had been shot at and which had bodies still inside them. At the border, they noticed how many Iraqi military vehicles were still pouring into Kuwait and it was obvious that the invaders were planning to stay for a lot longer than a few days.

Their journey was very uncomfortable because there were twenty-eight of them in the sixteen-seater coach, and they had no food or water. They were driven as far as Basra in southern Iraq, herded on to a freight plane and flown direct to Baghdad where they were lodged in the Mansour Melia Hotel. They were as worried about the women and children as we were about them, but they were equally powerless to do anything.

For the first two days they were restricted entirely to their rooms, but once they had been questioned again and their photographs and other details taken, the atmosphere relaxed a little. The hotel had by this time been filling up with new hostages who were being picked up on a daily basis, and British Embassy representatives were allowed in to see them and make sure they were all right. Food was apparently plentiful, and after a few days they started organizing activities such as quizzes, Trivial Pursuit, chess and Scrabble to keep everybody occupied. They were allowed to keep fit by using the swimming pool at set hours during the day, and some of them also burned up a lot of time and surplus energy by running round and round a small garden in the hotel grounds. Nearly all the other men in the hotel eventually started joining in these activities which helped to keep everyone sane, and a doctor in residence there examined everybody and had a ready supply of pills and medicines with which to treat the inevitable cases of sickness and stomach upsets.

There had seemed to be a very international crowd at the Mansour Melia at this time, including French, Germans, Japanese, Britons, New Zealanders and Australians. Many of the Brits had been taken off the British Airways flight BA149 which had landed at Kuwait at the time of the invasion to refuel. These people had barely set foot on Kuwaiti soil, but had found themselves innocently caught up in this impossible situation. Some of those living in Kuwait had made a dash for the border in an attempt to escape but had been caught and escorted to Baghdad, while others had literally been kidnapped off the streets of Kuwait City. No matter where these people had come from, they were all now part of a complicated plan with their destiny in the hands of just one man.

Derek then told me how, the day before our arrival, he and the other men had been forced on to coaches by the armed special police and taken to various installations. At first they thought they were being taken home because they saw the signs for the airport and then appeared to be heading for the Jordanian border, but they were disappointed when the coach turned northwards and drove for four hours to an oil workers' camp. The men became very angry and demanded to know why they could not have met their wives before being moved. They received the stock answer that the official in charge was only following orders and that the matter would have to be raised with a higher authority *boukra, inshalaa* - tomorrow, God willing. The problem was that tomorrow never came and God never willed it.

At the camp, which was filthy and crawling with insects, they were marched around for meals under the constant supervision of the armed police, who looked menacing, always seemed suspicious and could not speak any English. Our men felt that they might have been killed at any time and nobody would have known anything about it because the camp was in the middle of nowhere. The rooms they were given had not been inhabited for years and were full of mosquitoes and bugs, and they had no personal belongings or comforts. Oil workers and engineers, who were obviously used to mixing with foreigners, acted as translators and, in stark contrast to the guards, were friendly and understanding. They said they had no idea why the men were being kept as prisoners and they seemed to be telling the truth.

The second day started badly for Derek, who awoke to find himself and his bed covered in ants. He jumped into the shower to get rid of the insects and then found he had nothing with which to dry himself, so he took down the tatty curtain in his room and used that. After breakfast, a few new faces appeared amongst the guards and it was clear they were special police because they could speak English quite well. Derek heard one of them telling a hostage that Mrs Thatcher and the British Government did not care about the prisoners and that he would shoot anyone if he were ordered to do so. The senior officer in charge took his job quite seriously. He was wearing a new leather holster for his pistol, and he kept striding up and down the room as if he were John Wayne, stopping every so often to retie the leather strap that held the holster to his leg. Every nation obviously has its poseurs. Two of the new guards incessantly told tales of the glories of the Iraq-Iran war and of how they had killed people in battle. This was the start of an attempt to break the men psychologically, but they coped with it by ignoring their tormentors.

Derek spent a miserable day and a sleepless night worrying about the future and about whether he would ever see me and the boys again, but there was something of a cabaret after breakfast the following day. The senior official was now sporting a new green uniform and brown boots, and he had tied his sparkling holster a full six inches lower down his leg. He read out a list of names of some of the men who were at last being taken to see their wives and families again, and they were marched away leaving Derek and the others wondering what was to happen to them. There was no one around who could speak English and they were left to worry about the fate of their wives, but after thirty minutes of mental agony the officer returned and said that they were also being taken to join us in Baghdad. The thought went through their minds that this was just another psychological trick or even that they were being taken away to be disposed of, but this time the official was telling the truth.

The hostages picked up some fascinating details of the invasion of Kuwait from some oil workers who had found themselves in the middle of it and had been captured in the dark on the rigs. One man called Taffy told how the Iraqi soldiers took watches and jewellery from him and his colleagues, and then forced them to lie face down in the sand in the lights of armoured vehicles while machine-guns were pointed at them. They lay there for ages expecting their lives to end there, in the middle of the desert, with no one ever hearing of them again, but eventually they were loaded on to the back of an open truck which then followed the Iraqi tanks as they charged down to attack Kuwait Airport.

One of Taffy's friends had discovered that the Iraqis had been able to overrun Kuwait so quickly because they had been smuggling soldiers over the border in large grain lorries, which regularly passed between the two countries without being properly checked by the border guards. This man had been captured while working near the border and had seen hordes of troops jump out of the lorries. He had only just escaped with his life, because while he was sheltering behind a lorry, the vehicle next to him had exploded after being hit by a Kuwaiti shell.

Some American oilmen told how the Iraqis had burst into their sleeping quarters on the rigs. They were convinced they would be shot, but found to their relief that the invaders were more interested in finding food and water as they had been stationed near the border without rations for several days before the invasion.

I recounted some of the things that had happened to us, and Derek was shocked and furious when he heard how the British Embassy had left us to fend for ourselves for nearly a week on our housing estate in Fahaheel surrounded by those troops. Although he did not say so at the time, he felt that we had been very lucky to get out of there in one piece.

After talking for ages, we settled down in bed for the night. At one point, I remember hearing the chanting of anti-Western demonstrators marching down the street outside the hotel, and the seriousness of our present situation dawned on me completely for the first time. Derek found it difficult to settle, and when I awoke at about 2.00 a.m. I could see him standing at the window, smoking a cigarette and looking out across the darkened city deep in thought. I have no idea what time he came back to bed or whether he managed to get any sleep.

Sunday 19 August

It was wonderful to be with Derek again, yet ironically it led only to the worst feeling of fear I had yet experienced, as at last I fully understood the appalling danger confronting us. When the women and children had been left by themselves in Kuwait, our fight to be reunited with the men had become our primary aim and had kept us going from day to day until it had almost become an obsession. Now we had achieved that ambition, we had to stop and ask ourselves, 'Where do we, as a family, go from here?' The answer was that we were going nowhere. Instead of being separated by captivity, we were together in captivity, but we were as far as ever from gaining our freedom, and the international political quarrel about us was getting worse almost hourly.

The boys and I turned to Derek for reassurance, just as we always had done whenever we had a problem, and I realized with horror that, for the first time ever, he did not have any answers. Although he never told us so then, he was convinced in his heart that we were all going to die. He became very frustrated at not being able to answer the boys' questions about what was happening, and Craig, particularly, understood that here was something that not even his trusty, reliable Dad could do anything about. The fact that we were now together effectively in the front line of a fast-approaching war made Derek gravely concerned for our safety, and the boys and I were an added pressure and responsibility for him. He wished that he were by himself and that we were safe in England, and he became very quiet and thoughtful. This morning, like every other morning during the rest of my stay in Iraq, when I woke up I found him already up and about and deep in thought, and it became more and more obvious to me what he was thinking about.

He took his first decision for us very early while the boys were still asleep, and I was happy to go along with it because he had been in Iraq longer than me and knew what he was talking about. He said that we should pack the few things we possessed, because he thought we would shortly be moved out of the hotel and the Iraqis apparently gave you absolutely no notice before transferring you. It did not take him long to pack the total sum of his worldly goods; they fitted into one white plastic carrier bag: one small towel, a bottle of shampoo, two or three pairs of underpants and socks, and two cotton shirts. Most of these had been acquired through British Embassy personnel coming into the hotel, and Derek was wearing everything else he owned. He was delighted, therefore, when he discovered that I had managed to squash shirts, socks, pants, slacks and a sweater into our bag for him.

During breakfast, we found out that two of the newly-reunited families had already been moved out of the hotel, though, as usual, no one knew where they had gone. This news put a cloud over everything again, though I think everybody had been expecting something of the sort, and soon after we returned to our room, a few more couples were told to be ready to move. Stuart was a little grizzly this morning, so Derek said it would be sensible to get him and the rest of us checked by the doctor while we still had one available. Stuart was actually well, but we were given some diarrhoea tablets for him in case he went down with anything in the future. Craig, who had gone to the doctor only with some reluctance, provided us with a surprise because he was diagnosed as having a throat infection.

When we returned to our room an hour later, we found that another five or six couples were being added to the departure list, and they included my pregnant friend, Nikki, and her husband, Kev. Nikki and I had been through everything together almost from the start of the nightmare, and we both had a good cry at the prospect of being parted. We agreed that if we did not see each other again in Iraq, we would meet up at Heathrow Airport, though this was really only bravado because at that stage we could see no real hope of getting back to England in the near future, if at all. By this time there were only about half a dozen families remaining out of our original group of around thirty, and it was not long before two of these also left, so we began to wonder when, where and even if we ourselves would be moved. Our floor was fast taking on the appearance of a ghost town.

An Iraqi Ministry official, who was usually quite polite to Derek, was hanging about in the area where the guards sat, so Derek approached him and asked what would be happening to us. He replied that we could go there and then if our things were ready, and indicated that the place he had in mind for us was good and that there were children around the ages of our boys already staying there. We fetched our bags from our room and stood in the foyer for a few minutes until the official said it was time for us to leave. Derek asked if anybody else would be going with us because all the other families had been taken away in groups, but the official replied; 'No, it's just you, but don't worry – trust me.' Just as we were getting into the lift, a single man named Neil joined us and, after a hurried conversation among themselves in Arabic, the guards agreed that he could go with us. They asked if one of them could drive us there in our jeep while Neil and a second guard travelled with the official in his car. They said that after we had been dropped off at our new lodgings, the jeep would be brought back to the Mansour Melia where it would be parked and locked up, and that it would be returned to us in some way once the time came for us to return to Britain. We did not like to say they could not use it.

Our two-car convoy dodged in and out of the Baghdadian traffic jams as we travelled about twenty-five kilometres to the south-west of the city, and there seemed to be some confusion about where we were actually being taken. We stopped two or three times at what appeared to be different military bases of some importance before finally arriving in the huge industrial area called Central Refineries at what can only be described as some sort of converted single-storey office block. The whole of the perimeter fence was patrolled by armed guards. We got out of the jeep and were led into the building where we were greeted by a man who, we learned later, was employed as an interpreter and was called Jhallil. As we went through the door, we found to our left a reception area with a counter behind which were some easy chairs, a coffee table and a television set. The whole set-up seemed strange, but the welcome we received was even stranger because the first thing we were asked was whether we wanted some tea. It was just as if we were special guests arriving to inspect a factory and it was all so unreal.

The guard who had driven us there had to take some people from the installation back to the hotel with him. One of those returning with him was Alan, our last missing man who was going to be reunited with Theresa, and it came as some relief that everybody had now been accounted for. Also in the party were a couple called Bassem and Eleanor with their two children, one of whom was a baby boy who had been badly bitten by insects at the installation where they had been held previously. We were given the room that they vacated and, as the news quickly spread that someone new had arrived, a crowd started gathering in the reception area. Our arrival was apparently their big event of the day, but we did not seem to cheer them up very much; they were very low-spirited, though they all agreed that this installation was 100 per cent better than some terrible place in which they had been dumped two days previously. Bassem and Eleanor anxiously asked us questions about conditions in the hotel, and Derek was able to tell them much more than I because the Mansour Melia had deteriorated considerably between the time of his first arrival there and my own experience of it.

After they had gone, we settled into their room which we found kitted out rather like a family-sized bedsitter. At the far end were four beds with adequate bedding which all seemed fairly new. The other end had been turned into a living area with a three-piece suite, coffee table, fridge, television and small dining table. We were told that tea was readily available and were shown a kitchen where large flasks were kept lined up ready for use with milk and sugar nearby. It was all reasonably presentable and at the same time very odd because it was a bit like a self-catering holiday unit shut in the middle of a vast industrial complex. The plumbing facilities were abysmal: there were separate ladies' and gents' toilets which were just holes in the floor, and they each had a small hand-basin which also had to be used for washing up our plates and dishes. After a short while, Jhallil appeared with four cups, plates, dishes and sets of cutlery as well as a bowl of fruit. Perhaps we would be supplied with a few home comforts after all.

During the afternoon, we gradually met all the hostages being held at this particular installation; there were twenty-five of us in all. In a room near ours were a couple called Pat and Steve, and Craig was pleased to find they had three sons aged sixteen, fourteen and eleven. There was also a lad of about fifteen named Alan who, we were horrified to discover, was there by himself without anyone to look after him. He seemed to spend most of the day with Pat's three boys who had managed to bring with them from Kuwait a computer-game console which was like gold to the youngsters. Alan had been on his way home from boarding school to see his father and had been travelling alone on the British Airways jet that landed to refuel in the middle of the invasion. Both Craig and Stuart went next door straight away to team up with the four boys, and Pat and Steve came into our room so that we could swap stories about our various escapades and adventures. A lot of the other hostages here had also come off the BA flight; we were relieved that everyone seemed very nice and that the place we were in was reasonably comfortable.

We even managed to have a laugh while we were swapping stories with Pat and Steve. They told us that while being lodged in a hotel they had celebrated their wedding anniversary. The Iraqi guards at this place had been quite friendly and when they discovered that it was Pat and Steve's special occasion, they brought in a cake and a bottle of champagne for them. Unfortunately, their command of English was not that good and when they presented the gifts to them they said, 'We hope you live long enough to see your children grow up.' Pat nearly had a fit until she realized the guards were only wishing them a long and happy life together.

The guards at our new place were in plain clothes, and although I am sure they had guns, they never walked around with them. Jhallil the interpreter was very pleasant and helpful, and he kept turning up at our room during the afternoon with different bits and pieces for us. Yet although he and the guards all seemed harmless enough, we had very mixed feelings because we were looking over our shoulders all the time, and no matter where we were there was always somebody in an official position breathing down our necks. We were told by the other hostages that the meals were surprisingly good and were brought round to the rooms each evening. The most disturbing thing was that all our windows were boarded up.

We went for a wander round the building and noticed that the guards also had a lounge with two beds in it. One of the empty rooms we came across had a makeshift line strung up across it with one or two oddments of washing hanging there. During our travels we met a couple called Dale and Michelle who had a three-year-old daughter named Tamara and a little boy called Elliott who was a year older, and later in the afternoon they came round to our room to visit us. Stuart was pleased to meet a boy round about his age, and he and Elliott settled down together to draw pictures on some old paper that one of the guards had given them.

When evening arrived, we made the best use we could of the washing facilities, and having bathed Stuart and dressed him in his pyjamas, returned to our room and sat down to wait for our meal. At 8.45 p.m. the guards came to the door and handed us four containers of food and four canned drinks.

The food (usually something like chicken and rice) was passable but barely warm, though Craig and Stuart thought the cans were magic because they had not had a soft drink in days. After we had finished, we tidied up, washed our plates and cutlery, and left the empty food containers outside the door for 'room service' to collect.

Afterwards, the boys were very tired and went straight to bed, but Derek and I sat talking to Pat and Steve who were able to bring us up to date with news of the deteriorating crisis between Iraq and the West. The reason for this was that Steve had managed to smuggle a short-wave radio set into captivity with him. Each day, he conscientiously tuned into the BBC World Service, made notes and then wandered round every room occupied by the hostages passing on any relevant information. We went to bed at about midnight, but Derek was very fidgety and found it difficult to settle. He was obviously finishing the day as he had started it – by worrying.

Monday 20 August

After a very restless and troubled night, I awoke to find Derek up, dressed and sitting literally staring into space, and I lay in bed for a few minutes just watching him. He was obviously very worried and I felt so helpless because I could not take any of the responsibility from him. One of his biggest concerns was that the British Embassy in Baghdad had lost all contact with us because they had been forbidden access to us by the Iraqi authorities; no one knew where we were and we could have disappeared off the face of the earth without anyone being any the wiser. There was a lot of movement in the corridors this morning and the guards were talking together in Arabic, which in itself was unnerving because we had no real idea what it was all about.

I got up, dressed and, after talking to Derek for a few minutes about our problems, said I would wander round and try out the showers. What an experience that was! The whole washing, showering and toilet area was filthy and the smell was awful, though the cold shower did make me feel a lot better. Afterwards, I went back to our room and looked in vain for a plug to power my hair-drier. All the plugs in our room were out of action, so Derek went to have a word with the guards while I stood around with soaking wet hair. They promised they would get an electrician to have a look at the problem, and one of them found me a plug that worked in one of the spare rooms.

By the time I returned, both the boys had woken up and the guards had brought us breakfast, which was surprisingly good. The bread rolls were reasonably fresh and to go with them there were butter, jam, cheese and a hard-boiled egg each. It was not quite the Ritz, but much better than we had expected, and to my relief both boys ate quite well. Afterwards, Craig went off to have a shower and I took Stuart along to the bathroom to get him wahed. They were both eager to get this chore over and done with, because they were anxious to get round to Pat and Steve's room so they could join up with their new friends and have a go on the computer.

During the morning, a woman doctor called at each room to ask if anyone had any medical problems. She stayed with us for quite a few minutes and seemed fairly pleasant, and when she left she promised to return at approximately the same time next day. Not long after, Jhallil and another guard appeared and asked how everyone was, and they even brought a few toys for the younger children. Stuart thought it was his birthday and Christmas rolled into one when he saw the toy car, Lego-type bricks, colouring book and crayons they had for him. The guards asked if there was anything else we wanted and Derek, recovering some of his customary humour, asked for four airline tickets to London. They looked a little embarrassed at first, but then smiled when they realized it was just a light-hearted quip, and the incident passed without further comment. Jhallil even said that if we wrote down anything else we wanted, he would do his best to get it for us.

We noticed that there were a few uniformed guards with guns and dark-green tunics milling about in the reception area. They were in stark contrast to the more usual plain-clothes guards, one or two of whom were even wearing tracksuits, and we started worrying and nervously speculating about what they had come for. A couple of the uniformed men were very straight-faced and I would not have liked to have crossed them, but the majority seemed quite friendly and we began to relax a little since nothing seemed about to happen to us. Derek even screwed up his courage and asked one of them if the shutters could be taken down from the window and if we could be allotted some time outside the building for exercise. The man seemed doubtful that the officials in charge would allow it, but at least he said he would ask for us.

Lunchtime arrived and, once again, the food was plentiful and passable, but cold. Fruit such as grapes and dates were available in abundance, and we let the boys have two of the soft-drink cans we had saved from the night before and tried to treat the meal as a bit of a party. We had just finished when one of the guards arrived accompanied by two men in overalls who, after exchanging a few words with Derek in Arabic, started taking the boards off the windows. As daylight began flooding into the room, the transformation was amazing and really lifted our spirits, but it took one and a half hours to finish the work. We looked out of the window for the first time since our arrival and saw some grassed land, the inevitable wire perimeter fence and beyond that a road. When the workmen had finished, they moved on to the room next door which was then being used only for storage, and some more men came in and put up fly screens for us. They fixed them in place by drilling some holes and made a really professional job of them.

The removal of the boards was a shock enough in itself, but there was another surprise to come: we were told that we could go outside into the grounds and that within reason we could come and go as we pleased. We had made two requests for things that had seemed impossible and both had been granted in the same day – we could not believe it! News of our comparative freedom seemed to filter quickly through the hostage community and everyone wandered outside. Stuart met up with Elliott, and it was not long before they were happily playing together on some bits of old planks which they turned into bridges across some small ditches at the side of the building. The grounds around the complex were quite untidy, rather like wasteland in a redevelopment area, but we thought it was heaven to be out in the sunshine once more, and the guards even brought out one or two chairs for us to sit and sunbathe. Derek jokingly passed a comment that it would be nice to have a football for a kick around, but most of us were content just to sit and enjoy the fresh air and we stayed outside for a good hour. Derek went for a little wander round the outside of the building and no one seemed to object or tried to stop him, so more people gradually came out and did the same.

After we had gone back inside, Pat and Steve sought refuge in our room while the workmen – who were by now removing shutters all over the building – attended to their windows. We spent an hour playing cards, and when they had left, Derek told me some of the things he had seen during his wanderings outside. Right in front of us was some sort of recycling plant, while behind us there was a small power plant and some more building work in progress. To me the whole place seemed fairly innocuous and safe, and it was probably as well that I did not discover the truth until later or I would not have slept a wink at night.

At about 5.00 p.m. Stuart wanted to go outside again, so I went with him and we came across four men dressed in scruffy old dish-dashes who began working on the garden area and tidying it up. This was yet another peculiar happening in a very strange day; it was almost as if we were tourists staying in a new holiday complex that was just having the finishing touches put to it. The incident did make me wonder, however, exactly how long we were going to be kept there, because all these arrangements were beginning to look a little too permanent for my liking. It seemed as if our 'hosts' could not go to too much trouble for us, and this was underlined a few minutes later when one of the guards unexpectedly appeared with the football Derek had mentioned earlier in the day and gave it to Stuart. Immediately Derek and our two boys started having a kick around, and amazingly four of the guards came and joined in just as if they were holiday-camp activities leaders. The whole situation was getting stranger by the minute and I almost had to pinch myself to make sure I was not dreaming.

We went back inside at about 6.15 p.m. and a few of the other hostages gathered in our room to hear a summary of the World Service news bulletin Steve had listened to in the afternoon.

There was nothing new, just the usual comments and outrage of the Western powers, but at least it was reassuring to know that we had not been forgotten. Early evening was the worst part of the day because that was when time really dragged, and today was no exception despite all the extra activity and excitement. Dinner did not arrive at our room until nearly 9.00 p.m. and this was really too late for Stuart, but at least food was still getting through – even though there was progressively less of it day by day. Derek decided that something like a whist drive was needed to break the monotony, so he had a chat with the other families and, having found they all liked the idea, made plans for adults' and children's competitions the following day.

We were provided with a television, but the programmes were so awful that they might just as well not have bothered. The whole night was taken up by news broadcasts read in seven different languages, one after the other. That would not have been too bad if they had really had anything to say, but it was all absolute drivel and had no content at all. The newspapers were the same. It was hardly surprising, because people in Iraq were told only what the hierarchy wanted them to hear. There were lots of speeches by President Saddam Hussein and these did become quite important to us because, although we knew they would be dominated by propaganda against the West, we always hoped we might get some clue from them about what he was going to do with us. The most frustrating thing about them was the lies and deceit they contained which contrasted sharply with the real, factual news we were getting on the BBC World Service.

After dinner, we settled Stuart down to sleep and Craig announced he was going to see his friends for a game of chess and a go on the computer. We played another game of cards with Pat and Steve, then sat down with them to watch *Petrocelli,* a US detective series which was the highlight of every night's television viewing. After they had left us to return to their room, we all went to bed for the night, but it was impossible to sleep because we could hear the sound of drilling from the workmen who were still working on the window shutters around the building. After a while Derek got up and went to complain about it to the guards, who apologized and explained that the men were working on the last shutter and wanted to get the job finished that night. Silence came eventually and was quickly followed by sleep, though this was never a very pleasant experience.

Despite all the improvements we had won in our living conditions that day, we were still doing nothing other than existing, and mentally we were going through absolute torture. The moment you shut your eyes last thing at night was the time when all the thoughts and fears started rolling round inside your head. It was a most peculiar and frightening feeling to go to sleep not knowing whether you would still be alive to wake up in the morning.

Tuesday 21 August

The depressing reality of our detention hit me like a ton of bricks this morning when I woke up and opened my eyes, and I felt as if I just could not get out of bed and face another day. This was the first real sign that I was sinking lower, and I knew I had to make a conscious effort if I was to stop myself cracking up. Once more, Derek was out of bed and dressed, and sitting deep in thought. Eventually, I heaved myself out of bed and decided to pull myself together properly by taking a shower.

Before waking up completely, I had been aware of people moving about in the corridors with a kind of hammering noise going on in the background, and when I got outside the room I found myself in the middle of a lot of commotion with labourers rushing about the place. One of the guards smiled and wished me 'Good morning', so I asked him what was happening and he proudly replied that they were fitting a European toilet. Things were really looking up. I showered quickly and returned to our room to tell Derek the news.

Everything seemed very strange and there was a feeling of excitement and urgency in the air, so we knew that something special was happening. We had heard previously that the Red Cross was sending a delegation to Baghdad and had wondered if they were coming to visit us, and events throughout the morning only served to fuel such speculation. After breakfast, a small group of cleaners arrived at the building and we were told that they had come to clean the place up for us. They really only carried out a surface once-over, but it was certainly an improvement and a step in the right direction, and we were informed that they would in future be coming round at the same time every day. We had another call from the doctor and a visit by a group of army officials, including a general who really had all the guards running round in circles. I think he was the officer in overall charge, and he asked if all the 'guests' were all right and whether we needed anything. We told him we had handed in a list of our requirements the previous day and he spoke in Arabic to the guards. Derek told us later that he had ordered them to make sure we got everything we wanted.

After this final flurry of excitement, the rest of the morning passed without incident. We drifted up to Pat and Steve's room a bit later on and the men managed to tune in to the BBC World Service while the guards' backs were turned, but there was no news of much consequence to us. Several of the other occupants had taken to walking the corridors to get some exercise. Everyone was surprisingly calm and sensible about the whole situation and we had a number of long talks and discussions about it, though all our debating did not get us very far. Now that we were allowed to go outside, some people started getting their exercise by walking round and round the perimeter of the building, and a couple of them even started jogging.

After lunch had been served, a guard brought us an electric iron which was one of the items we had asked for the day before. Its arrival was very much appreciated because we were tired of wearing crumpled, unpressed clothes and it meant we could now keep ourselves looking semi-decent. A little later, the guards even brought us some badminton rackets and shuttlecocks, and said they were erecting a proper net so we could play outside. The whist drives also got under way and were a great success, and we agreed to hold the final stages of the competitions the next day.

Once we had packed the cards away, Craig decided to go and play on the computer with his friends while Derek and I went outside with Stuart, who wanted to play badminton. I sat and watched Derek and Stuart for a while and then one of the guards asked if I wanted a game, so we played for about forty-five minutes just knocking the shuttlecock backwards and forwards. By the end of that time the net had been put up, and all the teenagers came out of the building and played either badminton or football. All the guards ended up playing as well, and everybody – both gaolers and prisoners – seemed to be thoroughly enjoying themselves. Once again, the whole thing was totally bizarre. Another surprise awaiting us was that the garden had been tidied up and even chairs and tables put out for our use. We joked that it was a beer garden without any beer: although we had light-heartedly asked for drink, we did not really expect a traditional Muslim society to provide it for us, and it was one of the few things that failed to materialize.

By now, we were beginning to get a fairly accurate idea of the lay-out of the complex and of its daily routine. During the course of the day we had seen quite a few people walking around or away from the site, and they all appeared to be civilians. We gathered that many of them were outside workers who were brought in first thing in the morning and then returned home again at night. We also noticed that there was a medical centre right opposite our building on the other side of the road, and we presumed that this must be where the doctor came from every morning. On the surface, the whole place seemed fairly innocent and safe, yet there was always the presence on the gate of armed guards to remind us of the grim reality of our situation. We had to face the fact that the innocence could surely be only skin deep.

After dinner, everyone was very tired because of the long hours we had spent outside, so we sat down together to watch the nightly television news marathon, then settled the younger children in bed and had our customary game of cards, with the older boys joining in as well. The day on the whole had not been too bad, yet still hanging over us was this dark cloud which refused to go away. The fact remained that we were prisoners and that there seemed to be no end to our ordeal in sight. Pat was very, very worried and kept turning to me for reassurance that everything would be okay. Naturally, I gave it to her whenever I could because we had to think positively, but as the days passed I was steadily becoming more miserable and pessimistic myself, and words of reassurance would not always come readily to my lips.

The surroundings here were much more pleasant and relaxed than they had been at the hotel, the atmosphere was bearable now we had settled in, and the guards were very friendly and gave the impression that nothing we asked them to do for us was too much trouble. People who have never been in the situation in which we found ourselves and have only read about our experiences at second hand might feel that we had a leisurely life of fun and frivolity in something very much like a holiday camp. But we knew that we had been placed at a strategic location simply because the Iraqis hoped our presence would prevent it from being attacked by the forces of the Allied coalition, and from what we heard on the World Service it was a hope that was doomed from the start. We did not doubt that, in the event of war, our installation would be blown sky-high and we would go with it. Our captors went out of their way to give us everything we requested except for the one thing we really wanted – our freedom.

Wednesday 22 August

Breakfast was served a little earlier than usual and I had not yet awoken when it arrived. I think I must have been catching up on some lost sleep because I had not slept properly for more than three weeks, but getting up late did not matter anyway – there was absolutely nothing to rush out of bed for except a few little pastimes and long hours of boredom. Eventually I roused myself and went round to the bathroom, and when I got back the cleaners had just finished dusting down our room.

There seemed to be a lot of movement in the storeroom next door to us and we discovered that the guards were moving out all the stock. What were they up to this time? We discovered as the morning wore on that they were moving into the room themselves so they could vacate their old one and turn it into a communal lounge for us. Later on a video player and television were installed in it and the older children were delighted, as Pat and Steve had managed to bring some video tapes out of Kuwait with them and now had something on which they could be played. There had even been a dramatic improvement in the plumbing: the European toilet had now been finished and, although not fitted quite to Western specifications, it was heavenly comfort after the grotty hole in the floor.

Our meals, although still adequate, were gradually becoming smaller, so we were astounded after lunch when the guards suddenly brought round menus and invited us to choose what we wanted for dinner in the evening. It was just like an à la carte hotel menu with dishes such as chicken, steak, fries and lamb – really unbelievable. The main topic of conversation for the rest of the afternoon was what everybody had chosen and why we were being given this greatly improved diet, and for once we were all looking forward to dinner.

Our self-made fun and games resumed during the afternoon with the final of the whist drive, and Kim was declared the winner after a one-and-a-half-hour session. Everyone had very much enjoyed it and agreed that another should be organized, and a suggestion that a domino league should be set up was also received enthusiastically. Most of the older children had spent rather too long in the new video room while the card games had been going on, so we hauled them outside to get some fresh air. As the weather was still quite warm, we brought out some chairs and sat talking in the shade while the teenagers, guards and one or two of the men played football and badminton. A couple of people spent the time just strolling around as if they were on the sea front in an English holiday resort.

Stuart had by this time become very friendly with some of the guards and certainly seemed to have won their hearts. Naturally I was a bit apprehensive, but they all seemed very friendly and I reasoned that their necks would be on the block with their own superiors if anything happened to him.

Steve wandered out to join us after tuning into the World Service while everybody was occupied, and told us of the scorn and criticism that President Bush and Mrs Thatcher had heaped on Saddam Hussein for detaining us. We used to dread it when the bulletins were full of political sabre-rattling because we were living only for good news from home and it seemed as if we were being buried deeper and deeper in the crisis as the days went by. With hindsight, I understand that the British and American leaders were actually trying everything in their power to win our release, but at the time we clung to every pathetic little straw of optimism and were terrified for our safety whenever we heard our captors being censured. For there was no doubt at all that the Iraqis were stung and angry whenever they were berated, and their actions were very much influenced by what Mrs Thatcher and Mr Bush said. Our days were filled with hoping that something would happen to break the deadlock and that we would all soon be on our way home, and as a result our spirits always sank very low when the news was so negative.

We received a new shock at about 6.00 p.m., but this one was merely strange and even comic. A barber arrived on the scene from nowhere and insisted on cutting all the gentlemen's hair. Since we had been reunited, Stuart had barely left Derek's side because he was so frightened that his dad would disappear again, and he even used to follow him into the toilet and shower, so it came as no surprise that, when Derek went to have his hair cut, his little shadow went with him. Stuart had never seen a barber before – his hair had always been cut by a woman hairdresser – and as he watched Derek being shorn he suddenly asked if he could have his done as well. He was sitting quietly in the chair as good as gold while the barber snipped away when Steve, who was rather thin on top, walked into the room. Stuart said hello to him and then told the barber, 'I don't want my hair like his.' Everyone burst into roars of laughter and Stuart went very quiet because he did not know what was so funny about what he had said. As he had caused such amusement, however, he decided to try and do it again. When the barber had finished and had brushed the loose hair from round his neck and removed the cape, Stuart turned to Derek and said, 'I don't have to put that sheet on my head like an Arab, do I, Dad?' There was more laughter, a smile returned to Stuart's face and he walked out with an impish grin on his face.

We watched television as we waited with great anticipation for the arrival of our special evening meals selected from the new menu. When the food arrived, we almost ripped the foil covers off the containers in our impatience and found . . . the usual barely-warm rice, small portion of meat, grapes and dates. We could not believe it. We wondered whether it was just one more sick joke, but we hid our disappointment and did not say anything about it to the guards. If they were trying to pull tricks on us, we had no intention of playing into their hands.

Thursday 23 August
Today, my five-year-old son ceased to be a completely carefree little boy just like millions of others and was unwittingly catapulted into a nightmare of global limelight which will affect him for the rest of his life. Today, Stuart became the tiny 'British Bulldog' who apparently defied the most ruthless, murderous dictator of the 1990s and was witnessed doing so by television viewers all over the world. Because he was literally standing on the wrong spot at the wrong time, he has had to endure the sort of media pressure and hype that can make even toughened film stars crack under the strain. Only time will tell how he copes with it as we try to steer him through the trauma of adolescence and into the comparative safety of adulthood. I suspect he will still be 'the tiny British Bulldog' when he is an old man, and there are moments when I fear for him. We could not have realized as it happened that the consequences were to shatter the privacy of our once blissfully ordinary lives.

I awoke to the dull routine of a life in detention feeling at my lowest ebb yet. Derek had already embarked on his first brooding session of the day and the boys were still asleep. Every previous morning during my time in captivity I had taken a shower and washed my hair before breakfast, but this morning I just could not summon up the energy. It was a bad sign and probably my first real step on to a downward spiral. I merely had a quick wash and then got Stuart washed and dressed after he had woken up. Craig surfaced but, as usual, needed gentle persuasion before he would get moving, and he said he would have a shower after breakfast.

While we were still eating, a couple of the guards arrived and pinned up a picture of Saddam Hussein in our room. Lucky us! They went round the building doing the same in every other room, but we were only slightly surprised: we were becoming used to their erratic behaviour. They were followed by the cleaners, who went through our room even earlier and more swiftly than ever, and this, added to the extraordinary events of the past couple of days, made us sense a feeling of tension and expectation in the air. Shortly afterwards, one of the guards returned and asked Derek to go and look at the video machine, which did not seem to be working properly, and Derek wandered off with the shadow of Stuart by his side. With Craig away showering, I was left in our room alone, and I busied myself sorting out some washing and tidying up the beds.

As I passed the window, something caught my attention outside, and I looked out and saw fifty armed soldiers in the smart, dark-green uniforms of the Republican Guard scuttling around. They appeared to be running about in every direction imaginable, and a stranglehold of sheer terror clutched at my heart and stomach as the blinding fear that they had come to take us away surged into my brain. Suddenly, my shaking legs propelled me out of the room and I ran along the corridor to reach Derek and Stuart in the lounge, but when I arrived at the entrance foyer of the building, I froze on the spot in amazement. In the middle of this area was President Saddam Hussein himself, looking very regal in a smart designer suit and silk tie with a matching handkerchief in his top pocket, and he was surrounded by armed guards standing rigidly to attention. But it was something else that took my breath away and practically made my eyeballs leap from their sockets. Standing next to the Butcher of Baghdad was my precious Stuart – and the President was talking to him through an interpreter. I watched mesmerized as the ghastly tableau moved towards the lounge with Stuart still in the thick of the official party, then I backed round the corner until I was out of sight and turned and ran back to warn some of the other hostages.

By the time I reached them, my legs were like jelly and my heart was pounding so much that I thought it was going to burst. I had just started to spread the news when a guard arrived and told us all to go to the lounge, where the President wanted to talk to us. When we got there, we found that many people were already sitting down. Craig had arrived straight from his shower, Derek was sitting on the near side, and out at the front – next to the President – stood Stuart. The officer standing directly behind Saddam Hussein lifted up a chair and placed it next to Derek for me, and we settled down with our hearts hammering to hear what the man who had been responsible for all our troubles had to say and what he had planned for us. The atmosphere was electric, like the unbearable, suffocating pressure the minute before a violent thunderstorm breaks. The room was full of uniformed officers, and outside the windows wherever you looked you could see more soldiers with rifles covering every conceivable corner and every person in that room. A sudden move by any one of us towards the President would undoubtedly have attracted a bullet through the brain, and we sat not daring to move a muscle. There were officers with microphones, tape recorders and notebooks, and the lenses of photographers and a television crew were trained on us.

In a flash of clarity, I realized why we had been visited by the barber, cleaners and doctor during the last few days, and why we had been given that spoof dinner menu. It had all been part of an elaborate charade so that the President could be satisfied we were being given five-star treatment and could demonstrate that fact to the watching world in this publicity stunt. Looking round the room at all the other hostages, I could see that they were as shocked as I was, and even the Iraqi officers seemed a little tense. In fact, the only person completely at ease was the President, who was immaculate and the picture of perfection, and was in supreme command.

Stuart had been placed at Saddam Hussein's side, and several times the President tried to coax him even closer. At one point, it looked as if he wanted him to sit on his knee, but Stuart was having none of it and remained stiff and uncompromising. I nearly died when one of the officers tried to manoeuvre Stuart further towards the President in that gesture that became famous all over the world. My cold but sweaty hands grasped the side of my chair until my knuckles were white when I saw the way Stuart was reacting, because I had no idea what Saddam Hussein would do to him. But I need not have worried, because he seemed oblivious of the effect he was having on a normally lively, outgoing little boy. I could feel Derek become rigid beside me and I was frightened that he would try to intervene and would be shot, so I glared at him to make him stay put.

I could not decide why Stuart was behaving the way he was, for he had never acted in the same way to any other person. At the time, I could only speculate that his reaction was due to the unbearably tight atmosphere, the presence of so many uniformed soldiers and the fact that he must have recognized the President from his portraits which were plastered over absolutely every spot of vacant wall space.

Yet subsequent events have made me suspect that there was something more to Stuart's intractability, for Saddam Hussein tried his hardest to be pleasant and relaxed with him. Was it, for example, caused by coyness at meeting someone so important? Unlikely, because Stuart has since met Margaret Thatcher and members of the Royal Family, and has been totally at ease in their presence. Was it because Saddam Hussein was an Arab who could speak only his own native tongue? No, because Stuart had been brought up with Arabs who could not speak English. Someone has since told me that Stuart has the most beautiful and emotional eyes, and the clue to his behaviour can be seen in those eyes if you watch the video of his most famous moment. I believe they reveal that Stuart had a sixth sense which told him the President was an evil, dangerous man who had to be firmly but carefully rejected.

To my great relief, the President eventually let Stuart escape and began addressing us through an interpreter, and to be fair to Saddam Hussein I should record that the whole interview was conducted in a very orderly fashion. He started, inevitably, with the usual lecture on the history of Iraq and Kuwait, and claimed that Iraq had only taken back what was rightfully hers. Next he turned to the term 'human shield' which for some time now had been used by the Western media as a way of describing us and had become one of many clichés connected with the crisis in the Gulf. Although we have always believed he was lying, he tried to make out that the Arabic word for 'prevent' had been mistranslated by the West as 'shield'. For we were, he assured us, all ambassadors for peace who would help to 'prevent' a war from breaking out.

He added, 'Your presence here is to keep off the spectre of war, but we hope your stay will not be long. As an Iraqi, I appreciate your feelings and that you wish to be in Britain, but sometimes man is forced into a situation that is against his will. Please forgive us because we, too, have children like you.'

He apologized for holding us as 'guests' and hoped that one day, when this crisis was past, we could return to Iraq and see the country properly. I remember glancing at Derek at this point, and I just had to smile because he looked such a sight in the middle of so many smartly-dressed soldiers and officials. He had really been caught out, because he had not been wearing a shirt when he had been called away to examine the video, and he was now sitting there only half dressed. The President then invited us to ask him questions, and my heart leapt into my mouth again. Derek can sometimes be blunt, and I knew there was so much he wanted to say because he was furious at both our treatment and the way Stuart was blatantly being used, but I was afraid he would speak his mind and get into awful trouble, so I glared at him again and hissed at him through gritted teeth, 'Don't you dare say a word.'

One of the women, a doctor called Marla, spoke up straight away and, because she is very intelligent and bravely raised some penetrating points, she virtually became the spokesperson for the whole group. The rest of us deliberately kept our questions to a minimum because we could see she was getting the better of our adversary and we did not want to interrupt her flow. Her swift intervention may even have saved Derek from becoming embroiled in an argument that could have threatened his life. She carefully framed her questions in such a way that Saddam Hussein could not dive out of them with a long, drawn-out answer as was his normal style, and he was visibly shocked. The whole Arab world is a very male-dominated society, and I do not think he had ever before been spoken to in such a way by a woman – let alone by a foreigner.

Marla, who was with her two adult sons, had been travelling on the stranded British Airways flight, and she asked why the passengers had been taken off the aircraft as hostages when the jet had only stopped to refuel and technically they had not even set foot in Kuwait. The President clearly hesitated and we could see he had not been properly briefed by his aides on this particular incident. He asked them for writing materials, and that caused a flurry of activity amongst them and reduced the dignified meeting almost to the realms of comedy. All the generals and other senior officials leapt forward and offered their pens to the two colonels standing immediately beside him, and these two men were soon frantically sorting through a dozen or more pens to find the best, smartest and most expensive Croes or Mont Blanc on offer. At last one was selected and handed to the President, who started writing. We were sitting quite close to him, and Derek, who has a working knowledge of Arabic, was able to see that all he wrote was the flight number and the date and time the plane had landed in Kuwait. We will never know whether anything came of his subsequent enquiries and whether any Iraqi officials got into trouble, but it seemed to bother him that he had not been given all the relevant information about the affair. When we were able to discuss the matter rationally later on, we speculated that his advisers had filtered away a lot of the truth and had told him only what they thought he wanted to hear. He eventually escaped from his embarrassment by asking who had ordered the passengers off the plane and, having discovered that it had been a member of the flight crew, said he was sorry but there was nothing he could do about it.

However, Marla had not yet finished with the President, and she asked him how long we were to be detained because her two sons, like several of the other youngsters, were studying for important examinations and their schooling was vital to them. He replied very quickly that he did not know how long it would be necessary to keep us, but if it extended into term time, the best instructors in Iraq would be sent to us so that the teenagers' studies did not suffer. He even spoke to one of the officers who was taking notes to make sure a record was being taken of his exact instructions. He was then asked whether he feared that the rest of the world would see his actions as an attempt to hide behind women and children, but this time he just repeated his usual propaganda line about Kuwait belonging to Iraq and the threat of war being averted by our presence as 'guests'.

Emboldened by the fact that Marla had rattled him, Michelle complained that she had been turned out of her home in Kuwait with her husband and two small children, bundled into a bus and taken away to Baghdad leaving behind everything she owned. He apologized and, to our amazement, said that we would all be compensated for everything we had lost. This was the best promise we had received from any Iraqi so far, and it had come right from the top. Pat then pointed out that our families in England were very worried about us and she asked if we could get in touch with them by letter or telephone. The President replied that phone calls to England were not possible at that time, but of course we would be allowed to write home and he would also arrange for any recorded messages to be sent back to our families. In addition, he promised that we would be visited by representatives of Iraq's Women's Federation, who would make sure we were given anything we wanted.

The meeting lasted about two hours altogether but, despite the fact that the President was charming and gave us many assurances and promises, it was hardly satisfactory. We were no nearer to gaining our freedom and we had heard nothing that guaranteed our future safety. As this was a propaganda stunt for the benefit of the media, it was evident that the best parts of it from our point of view, when Hussein was ruffled and at a loss for his glib words, would be carefully edited out of the press and television reports. We had also felt inhibited about showing him what we really thought of him because of the ever-present threat of armed guards inside and outside the building. Always at the back of our minds had been the fear that if any of us said the slightest thing wrong, it could be curtains for everyone in the room – and that would certainly not have been shown on television. It was frustrating to have the architect of our misfortunes at arm's reach and not be able to try and throttle him. Derek, particularly, was champing at the bit in frustration and there were a number of occasions when he had had to bite his tongue.

At last, the President tried to bring the meeting to an end by saying that he would have liked to have lunch with us, but unfortunately had another appointment elsewhere. It was at this point that we made our greatest concrete achievement. Pat raised the question of Alan Barnett, the fifteen-year-old boy who was there by himself without his parents. The full circumstances were explained to the President together with a carefully-worded version of our views on the subject, and he immediately agreed that Alan should be released. He called Alan out to the front and asked him if he would like to go home, and the poor child practically broke down in tears of joy. We were all delighted for him. Saddam Hussein even gave him $500 as a leaving present. As a parting shot, the President asked if we would pose for a group photograph, and then wanted to shake everyone's hand before driving away with his entourage leaving the building feeling deserted.

After a brief silence, one or two of us started talking in whispered tones about this most incredible event of our imprisonment, and suddenly the whole installation was buzzing with excited conversation. The thing I was dying to know from Derek was how Stuart had been manoeuvred into the situation in which I had found him at the moment when I first saw our special visitor. It turned out that while Derek had been fixing the video recorder, he had sensed something behind his back and had turned round to see Saddam Hussein standing in the doorway actually holding Stuart by the hand. Stuart and the President had apparently met face to face in the doorway. Derek's first thought was to get Stuart safely away and he started moving forward to do so, but the President was already being led to a chair. Fortunately, Derek realized that if he strode up to Saddam Hussein and snatched our son away, there was a fair chance that a nervous guard would think the dictator was being attacked and would open fire. So as the official party walked past him, he unobtrusively caught hold of Stuart's arm and gently but firmly steered him to his side.

Derek then became conscious of the fact that he was not wearing a shirt, and told one of the President's most senior officers that he really thought he should take Stuart away and get them both properly dressed. This ruse to get Stuart safely back to our room did not work, however, because the man told him very politely, 'No, it's okay – please don't worry.' Derek was asked to sit down and then the President, whose attention had really been caught by Stuart presumably because he could see the propaganda potential of being pictured chatting to him, called our son over and asked him the question that was to become so famous: 'Are you getting your milk?' After a long pause, Stuart replied that he was and was also getting cornflakes to go with it, and the President said that even Iraqi children did not always get the cereal.

Our normal guards at the installation were delighted to have received a visit from their President, and they chattered excitedly about what had happened. I suppose that, for them, it was rather as if somebody on an ordinary English housing estate had answered their front door to find the Queen standing on the doorstep. In contrast, what the hostages were most pleased about was the impending repatriation of young Alan Barnett and hoped that it would not be delayed very long. It was disgraceful that he had been detained in the first place. One or two people were very sceptical about his being allowed to leave, but I felt that as the highest authority in the land had given his word on the matter in front of television cameras, the Iraqis now had no choice but to let him go. The only cloud on the horizon was that we did not know how long it would be before he was freed.

When we got back to our room, I told Derek that I was going to write a short note home to my sister, Judy, just to let her know how we were, and would ask Alan to post it when he reached the UK. I scribbled out a quick letter and then wandered down to Pat and Steve's room to ask Alan if he would take it back with him. Several other people had had the same idea, but Alan was still on cloud nine and said he did not mind taking them all. He was so deliriously happy that I think he would willingly have dealt with every envelope in London's

Mount Pleasant sorting office single-handed. Strangely, the atmosphere in the whole building had lightened considerably following the visit of the most feared man in the Middle East. Our normal guards were particularly elated. If our keepers were relaxed and jovial, it meant we could be as well because there was less of a threat to our safety.

We were still talking about the visit as we sat in our room after lunch, and Craig made us laugh when he told us about his part in the drama. He had still been in the shower when the party arrived, and he walked out right into the middle of it. His wet hair was unkempt because he had forgotten to take his hairbrush with him, and he had dropped his T-shirt on the floor of the shower room. When he saw what was happening, he dived back into the room and made himself as presentable as possible by putting on his wet T-shirt and smoothing his hair down with his hands as best he could. Craig added that, like Derek and me, he was very frightened and angry when he saw the President with Stuart and wanted to rush over to him and shout, 'Leave my brother alone.' Thank God he had had the sense not to; I went cold at the very thought.

A delegation of six women from the Women's Federation, accompanied by a few uniformed army officers, arrived at the installation at about 3.45 p.m. and found us outside. One of the men had come to take Alan on the first leg of his journey home, and the youngster excitedly started packing his 'luggage'. It did not take long, because like the rest of us he owned nothing but a few bits and pieces. He took much longer saying goodbye to everyone. We were all enormously pleased for him, though there were a lot of tears shed and it must have been very daunting for a lone English teenager to face such a long journey in a strange and hostile country. Before he left, the Iraqis asked if he would agree to be interviewed by one of their television crews and this was arranged for a little later in the afternoon.

All the women hostages were asked to go down to the communal lounge with the women from the Federation so that they could take down lists of all the things we needed. We agreed only reluctantly because no one really trusted them, but after talking with us for a few minutes they compiled a fairly comprehensive list of what we wanted. We asked for toiletries, various items of clothing and even some footwear, though we were by no means confident that we would get any of it.

Alan's interview began after our men had rejoined us, and the interviewer asked him the usual sort of stock questions about how he felt to be going home. When it was finished, the presenter asked if someone else would be interviewed but nobody seemed very keen on the idea. The presenter tried to persuade us by saying that the point was to film messages to be sent to our families in England, and eventually a couple of the older teenagers came forward. I was worried that Craig might end up on camera and I gave him a warning frown, but I need not have worried because his friends had already been interviewed and he was doubled up with laughter. He was obviously in no fit state to talk about anything and we were very pleased that he kept his head down and did not get involved.

The presenter then asked if a lady would go forward and speak, but none of us moved and all the Iraqis started getting a little cross. After a few seconds, I was 'volunteered', and the television crew asked me to take Stuart with me. I sat and answered a few questions, and then right at the end of the interview, the presenter leaned across to Stuart and asked him if there was anything he wanted. Right on cue he replied, 'I want to go to England to see my nannas.' For the second time in one day, bless him, he had ruined the Iraqis' attempts to make political capital out of an innocent child, and when we returned to our seats I noticed a lot of our women were crying. One of the television reporters asked me my name and I offered to write it out for him, but he insisted that he could cope with the English spelling himself.

The last interview was with a student called Bruce, who was eighteen but actually looked and acted far older. The questions fired at him were far more political than the earlier ones had been, and could have been quite dangerous if put to the wrong person. Bruce, however, handled the whole thing superbly and gave the Iraqis absolutely nothing that could be used in their favour, and eventually they gave up trying to put words in his mouth and abandoned the whole interview. We were then asked to go outside and pose for photographs which could be sent home to our families. Derek and a lot of the other men refused, so the women and children went just to keep the peace. One of the guards asked me where Derek had got to and why he would not have his photograph taken, and I explained it away by saying that he was camera-shy. The photographers and television crew finally toured our living quarters snapping away at everything they could find, including scenes of hostages watching television and the youngsters playing chess or on the computer.

In the meantime, the Federation women had been busy asking for the names, addresses and telephone numbers of our families in England so that messages could be sent to them. Again, none of us was very happy about parting with the information because we wondered exactly why the Iraqis wanted it and what pressure they might try to put on the British Government by stirring up our relatives. Derek and I managed to get out of it by saying that both our mums were very ill and that we were worried that any contact with Iraq might upset them too much, and fortunately our explanation was accepted. The women actually seemed very nice and pleasant, and when they left they promised to do their best to get everything we had asked them for.

At 8.00 p.m. we settled down to watch the evening news on television, and guess which story made the main headlines of the day? The whole bulletin was dominated by the President's visit to us and, although our interview with him had been carefully edited and what was shown was only a fraction of what had actually taken place, we sat glued to the screen. We returned to our room once it was over, but the item was repeated throughout the evening, and every time it reappeared one of the guards ran down the corridor to tell us.

Later on, Pat, Steve, Derek and I were just starting a game of cards and the children were about to watch a video, when a programme called *Guest News* came on the television. This was a compilation of all the clips and interviews recorded at our installation during the day, so we all gathered round the box again. I was dreading seeing mine, but when it came on everybody looked at my name spelt out on the screen and burst into fits of laughter. The so-called competent reporter, who had insisted on writing down my name himself, had managed to change Glenda Lockwood into Candelon Kut. I do not think anyone heard a word of my interview, owing to the fact that we were all crying because we were laughing so much; I felt as if my sides were splitting. Derek even rediscovered his natural humour and caused a second outburst of merriment when he told everybody; 'I'm glad we're not German because that would make me Herr Kut the German barber.' It became a standing joke for people to run up behind me in the corridor and shout 'Hi, Candy.'

What a strange day it had been. It had started with a bout of deep depression, had given me moments of terror and had ended in farce which had provided us with some much-needed entertainment. Ironically, our meeting with one of the most feared men in the world, who had caused us so much grief and anguish, had really been quite good for us. Previously he had been for us a bogeyman whose power had seemed so awesome because we did not know what he was like, and by appearing to us in the flesh he had actually stripped away much of the myth and potency with which our own imaginations had surrounded him. We were under no illusion that we were any safer or that he regarded us as anything other than an expendable commodity which might help him gain what he wanted. He was dangerous, but he was a man rather than a demon, and therefore he was not invincible. We had even seen a single, brave woman come close to humbling him just by the cleverness of her questioning.

All in all, I felt very much better when I returned to my bed that night than when I had left it in the morning. We were still being carefully watched by him as we settled down to sleep, however, for the face of His Excellency President Saddam Hussein continued to grimace at us from his portrait on our bedroom wall.

Friday 24 August

The wrath of the Western world was turned on Saddam Hussein today as his cynical attempt to use Stuart for propaganda purposes rebounded on him. The Iraqi video of us in captivity had apparently already been shown on British television, and the whole country was in absolute uproar. The President had intended that he would appear as a charming, smiling and kindly host – a type of international 'uncle' who was adored by children of every nationality. Instead, he had been seen as an overgrown bully who threatened women and children with armed guards and interned innocent civilians to protect military targets. He had been snubbed in front of millions of television viewers by a poor unknown British boy who, despite looking pale and tired, had stood up to him and had refused to be won over. Now the BBC World Service was buzzing with speculation about the identity of the little hero.

Derek and I were sitting outside in the sunshine watching the 'British Bulldog' at play when we first heard about the furore back home. We often whiled away the long, boring hours like this talking about the good times we had spent in Kuwait and dreaming of being repatriated to England where we would be free to go out or stay in as we pleased. This morning I was upset because I had just written letters home to both our families to let them know we were all right, and I broke down in tears at the thought that we might never see them again. Derek put his arm round me and kissed me on the cheek to try and cheer me up, but we found it difficult to talk to each other.

Eventually, we managed to strike up a conversation about the previous day's visit, and Derek told me how proud he was that Stuart had stood his ground and had not let Saddam Hussein force him to sit on his knee. Propaganda films, showing the President surrounded by happy, smiling children, appeared on Iraqi television every day and they always ended with a scene of a small child sitting on his lap. But Stuart had refused to allow himself to be used in such a way, for he had sensed that there was something about this man that was not very nice and that he should therefore be held at arm's length. I even managed to raise a smile when Derek told me how proud he was of both our sons and how glad he was that Stuart had been 'a bulldog and not a butterfly'.

Our moment of domestic peace was interrupted by Steve, who came outside to let us know about the controversy stirred up by the screening of the video in Britain. He was bursting to tell us that when he had tuned into the World Service on his illicit short-wave radio set, he had been amazed to hear his own mother speaking on the air. It seemed that when the video had been shown on television, an appeal had also been broadcast asking anyone who recognized any of the hostages to contact the television station. His mother had answered the appeal and had ended up being interviewed by a reporter. The sound of her voice had apparently made Pat realize how homesick she was and had really upset her, so I went in to comfort her and after a while she felt much better. We agreed that, no matter what the reaction was like back at home, we had achieved two things from the President's visit. First, Alan Barnett was – we hoped – well on his way back home, and secondly, our families now knew that for the time being we were all still alive. It was exactly a week since the British Embassy had been forbidden access to us, and to all intents and purposes we had disappeared off the face of the earth until the video had been shown.

We were also being given slightly deferential treatment by the Iraqi officials remaining at the installation. We had already received a visit from a special delegation who came to see if we needed anything and asked us if we had enjoyed the visit by their President. The party had been headed by the major who was obviously the local commanding officer, and he went out of his way to make a big fuss of Stuart when he saw him. A little later, we were also visited by the doctor again, and she asked a lot of interested questions about our meeting with Saddam Hussein.

Many of the hostages were still making the most of the amusement that the VIP visit had afforded us. A number of them, and particularly Val and Kim, kept the Candelon Kut joke going, and the older boys teased a couple of their friends who had been interviewed. One of Pat and Steve's sons was singled out for special treatment, because during his interview he had said that life in our installation was all right and the President 'seemed like a nice bloke'. His poor mum was so embarrassed, but the other lads just thought it was hilarious.

During the morning, the guards took delivery of a washing machine, which was then installed for our use right outside the men's shower room. We women were delighted, because we had to wash for so many men and teenagers who as their standard prison wear all seemed to have adopted jeans, which constantly needed cleaning. With the washing machine, iron and even a washing line, we could now provide an almost foolproof laundry service. (We had experienced a slight problem when the iron went missing and we were left without one for twenty-four hours. It was obvious that an Iraqi had taken it because none of us would have been able to go anywhere with it, and eventually a replacement was brought in by one of the guards.) As the boredom of the daily routine closed in on us again, doing the washing became the highlight of my day – a thing I would never have believed possible.

Boredom was actually becoming quite a serious problem, as it could easily lead to depression about when, or even if, we would ever be released. It was therefore very important for us all to try and keep busy, and different people achieved this in different ways. A couple called Alan and Barbara were always out running round the edge of the site, while Michelle and a man named Richard used to walk round the building for hour after hour. We were in a group who just used to enjoy the small freedom of going in and out of the building at our leisure, and we used to intersperse our wanderings with games of football, badminton and volleyball. Stuart spent much of his time charming the guards, and there was one man in particular whom he began to call his 'friend'.

Lunchtime came round again and we noticed that the portions of food were now really very much smaller than when we had first arrived at the installation. Pat and Steve were worried because their three boys were all big lads with big healthy appetites to match, and the rations were just not enough for them. True, we could always fill up with an abundant supply of grapes, but by now these were wilting a bit and looked as if they had passed their sell-by dates, so Steve went round collecting them from everyone and secretly started making some wine.

Everyone was still talking about Saddam Hussein's visit but

even this topic of conversation began to pall after a while, and the afternoon really started to drag. It was lucky that the guards came round with some unexpected delicacies for us – a handful of sweets and a couple of packets of crisps. Stuart was over the moon because he had almost forgotten what they tasted like, but the treat was very quickly finished. He nearly broke my heart when he went and asked his 'friend' if he could have some more and was told that they had all gone, but the man saw his disappointment and kindly promised to bring him new supplies the next day. Cigarettes, however, were being quite freely handed out and although I do not smoke, I always took my allowance for Derek, who was smoking rather a lot for some reason!

I think one reason time was passing so slowly was that it was Friday – the Muslims' holy day and the equivalent of our Sunday. At one stage, Pat asked Derek when he thought we would be allowed to go home, and he replied as he always did to that question, 'Saturday – maybe not tomorrow, but probably next week.'

Pat just smiled and turned to me and said, 'I love talking to your husband because he always cheers me up.'

Despite the way I used to see him worrying every morning, Derek managed to retain a lot of his humour. He was still joking with the guards, and whenever they came round to ask if we needed anything, he would always say, 'Just plane tickets to London and suitcases so we can pack all our old plastic bags.'

Yet even his brave joviality could not save us from a severe bout of depression that set in just before dinner. We sat down to watch television and heard for the first time of Saddam Hussein's ploy to try and unite the Arab world against the West by exchanging prisoners of war with Iran. We saw film of people getting on and off planes and buses and kissing the ground as they stepped back on to their native soil, and suddenly we wished so badly that it was us returning home. Although Hussein had told us that the likelihood of war lessened with every day that passed, we did not believe him and we felt as if our freedom were further away than ever. In addition, we felt oppressed by the Iraqi propaganda machine, which was pumping out the officially approved version of the 'truth' almost twenty-four hours a day, and our spirits hit rock bottom. We knew we had to think positively and we managed to do so when we were all together. The difficult moments were when Derek and I were on our own or when we settled down to sleep at night – that was when we had too much time to think and kept wondering how on earth we would ever get out of this mess.

Dinnertime arrived, and with a little persuasion we managed to get the boys to eat, despite their growing unhappiness and the appallingly boring diet. By this time they knew that if they did not eat what was put in front of them at meal times, they would go hungry because there was absolutely no alternative. We had our daily chat and game of cards and then went to bed, but sleep proved impossible at first because the guards were talking in their room next door. They still had their light on, and because all the walls between the rooms and the corridors had frosted glass panels, this also disturbed us. Derek stood it for so long and then went and asked them to turn off the light and keep their noise down because they were disturbing Stuart. They actually apologized and settled down to sleep, and eventually we did the same.

Saturday 25 August

We all heaved an enormous sigh of relief this morning because we heard on the BBC World Service that Alan Barnett had arrived safely back in England. His parents and the whole of Britain were delighted by his early return, but they could hardly have been happier than the rest of us who were still in captivity. We had been unofficial guardians to him while he had been with us, and we had taken the difficult decision to let him disappear from our protection with a group of complete strangers. If anything had happened to him we would never have forgiven ourselves, and news of his arrival home lifted a great burden of responsibility from our shoulders. We had thought that he might have completed his journey the day before because we believed that he was leaving Iraq via Jordan, but he had apparently been lodged overnight back in the Mansour Melia in Baghdad. This hotel, we discovered later, was being used as the headquarters for one of the secret police units and had become a central clearing house for hostages being moved about the country. It was near the notorious political prison where people disappeared for ever once they walked through its doors.

We also received news of a happy event involving two of the hostages at another installation, although we did not know them personally and had never met them. Debbie Hayes and her boyfriend got married, and we watched part of the event on television. The ceremony was conducted by Padre Jones who had travelled in our convoy from Kuwait, and the bride was even supplied with a wedding dress by the Iraqis.

Stuart's 'friend' kept his promise and appeared with some more sweets for him, and from this time on the same guard brought him some similar little treat every time he returned to the complex. The man looked as hard as nails and was one of the more senior members of the secret police stationed at our installation, but he seemed genuinely fond of Stuart and he must have had something good about him because my younger son had proved dramatically that he was a good judge of character. The 'friend' was very kind to him and often used to play bat and ball or football with him. Stuart got into the habit of wandering into the room next door and spending a lot of time with the guards in their lounge, and they all made a fuss of him. Their door was always kept open, and when Stuart was there we made sure ours was as well. We were not going to be too trusting even though I am convinced Stuart was perfectly safe the whole time he was there. Occasionally, he used to ask when we would be going home to England, and he seemed satisfied when we just told him 'soon'. It was amazing that he had taken all our strange and frightening experiences in his stride.

Craig had also coped tremendously and was very adult about the whole situation, and he was definitely helped by the fact that there was a group of teenagers round about his own age or a bit older. They played on Pat and Steve's computer, which was an absolute godsend and filled many tedious hours for them, and they were often joined by one or two of the guards. Derek began to get closer to Craig now that he no longer had work pressures to distract him. During our private moments together Derek told me, 'This should have happened earlier. He's a smashing kid and I will have to make more time for him in the future.'

By this stage there had been an even more pronounced deterioration in the standard of the meals that were being served to us. Previously the food had merely been bad, but now it was abysmal. The problem partly lay in the fact that it was cooked at a hotel outside the camp and was shipped in to us in containers. This in itself was bad enough, but for some reason the meals began arriving from another hotel even further away from the installation, so by the time they reached us they were stone cold. We complained to the guards and they supplied us with cooking pans so we could warm the food up in the kitchen, but this made it only slightly more palatable and probably increased the risk of food poisoning. Craig and Stuart now refused to touch it, and they kept body and soul together by eating the bread, jams and cheese with which we were supplied. Even this was pretty unappetizing, because the bread was becoming drier and staler by the day.

Just before lunch, we all received surprise gifts from our chief tormentor. The guards came round and handed out beautiful leather-bound photograph folders with pictures of ourselves inside. They were all inscribed on the front in embossed gold with the words, 'The gift of the President of the Republic of Iraq and General Officer Commanding and Chief of Staff of the Armed Forces, Saddam Hussein'.

Most of the hostages just received a copy of the group photograph, but our family was given special treatment: our folder also contained the pictures of Stuart with the President. One or two hostages who were by themselves without families did not get folders at all, and we think their mementoes – like the electric iron – had been pilfered by a couple of the guards. There is so little luxury in the life of the average Iraqi, and the temptation to keep something they would never normally be able to own was probably too great.

The guards claimed that the President would usually present such fine gifts only to important foreign dignitaries, and they were ecstatic about the outcome of his visit to their installation.

The courage of a five-year-old. Stuart refuses to respond to Saddam Hussein's propagandist show of friendliness, 23 August 1990.

The hostage group, 23 August 1990. Derek is holding Stuart at the back, Craig is crouching, front left, and I am standing on Saddam Hussein's right.

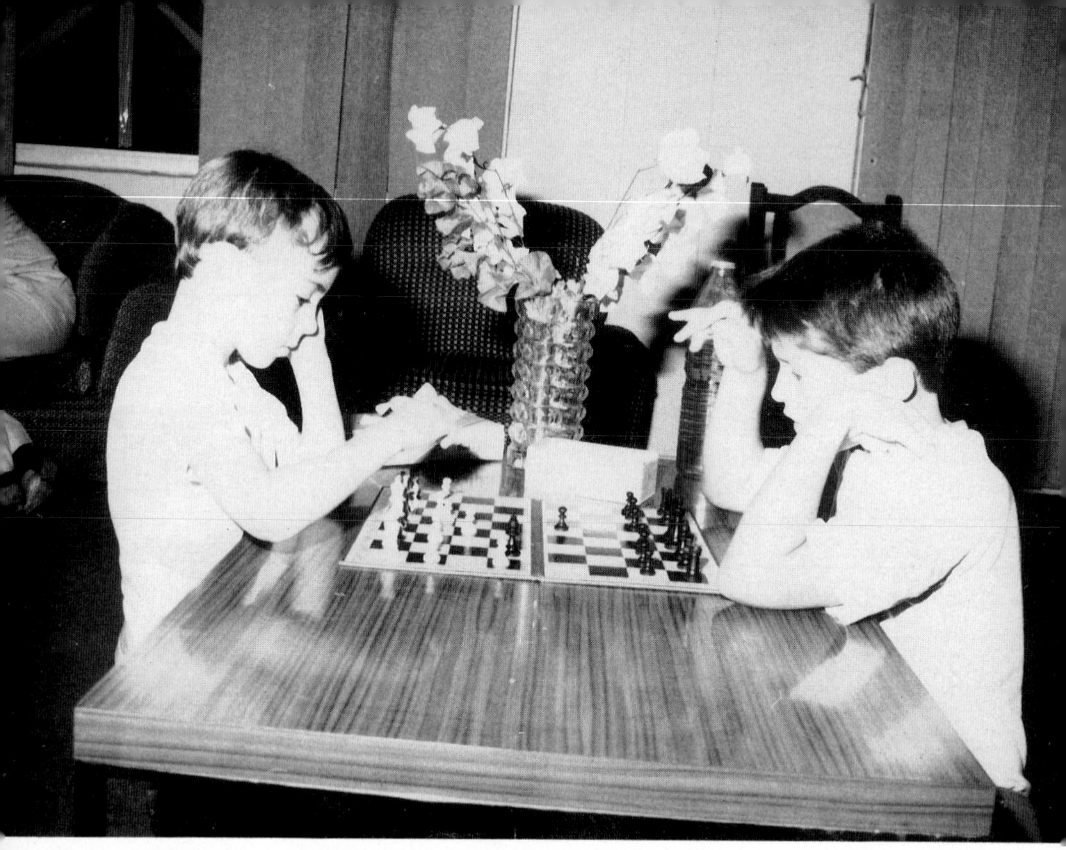

Stuart (left) and his young friend Ian playing chess to pass the time, 23 August 1990.

Derek (left), Craig (front) and some of the other men wait for the women and children to return from a session of photographs and interviews, 23 August 1990.

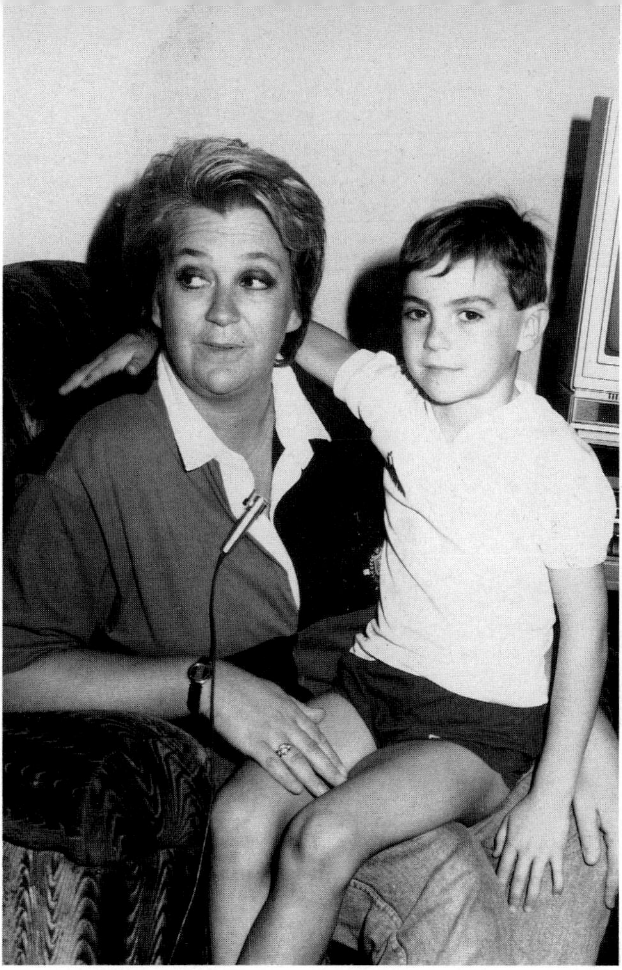

Stuart and me being interviewed by Iraqi officials for the television programme *Guest News*, 23 August 1990.

Pictures taken in our homes in Kuwait after the end of the war. Graffiti denounces the Emir, above, and our former house is shown to have been completely ransacked, below.

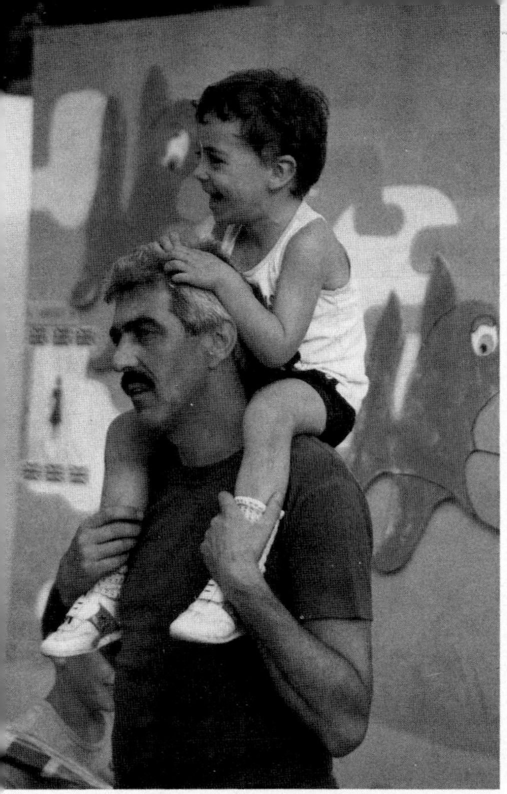

These family snaps were found strewn in the street in Kuwait City. Remarkably, they found their way to Derek in captivity.

Jesse Jackson carries Stuart through the crowds on our arrival in Britain, 2 September 1990.

Stuart, Craig and me, shortly after we had finally made it home.

The Duchess of York stands with Stuart as he waves to the crowds outside Westminster Abbey, after being presented with a Children of Courage Award, 19 December 1990.

Stuart after collecting a *Daily Star* award for bravery, 20 March 1991. With Margaret Thatcher, left, and with representatives of the RAF, the Navy and the Army, below.

Their euphoria, we discovered, was due not merely to the honour of the occasion, but also to the fact that we had saved their lives. One or two of them confessed to us that if we had displeased Saddam Hussein in any way, the whole incident could have been fatal to them. If we had tried to escape or to attack our important visitor, they would have been gunned down with us by the Republican Guard. No wonder they had seemed tense on the big day.

We were given a few extra photographs for which there was no space in our leather folder, and one of these showed Stuart and Saddam Hussein standing in the reception area with our chief interpreter, Jhallil, nearby. As soon as he saw it, Jhallil asked if he could have it to send home to his mother. It was not a very good photograph, and was even slightly out of focus, and we were only too happy to let him have it because he had been very kind to us and was a lovely man. He almost burst into tears and said, 'Thank you – my mother will be so proud of me.' He spent the rest of the day either thanking us again or showing the photograph to everybody in the installation. I hope so much that today, somewhere in Iraq, there is an elderly woman proudly displaying that photograph on her best cabinet and that she still has a fine, live son to go with it.

Sunday 26 August

The installation in which we were being held was not, we discovered, an innocuous office complex as we had thought, but one of Hussein's dreaded chemical plants. Guess who enabled us to make the discovery? Yes, the little 'British Bulldog' who had innocently become such a thorn in the side of Iraqi officialdom.

Stuart, whose confidence in the guards was growing all the time, had got into the habit of playing chess with them. When he went into their lounge for his customary game, before they could stop him he opened a locker to look for the chess board. As we watched through the open door, a box fell out of the locker and the lid came off revealing two gas masks. Immediately, the guards pounced on the box, replaced the lid and hurriedly stuffed it back into the locker while looking guiltily over their shoulders to see if anyone had noticed.

Derek feigned ignorance but the incident brought home to us the true nature of our complex. Clearly the gas masks were there for the use of the guards in the event of a failure in the manufacturing process. We did not really understand the implications of what we had seen, but anyway we agreed to keep the knowledge to ourselves because it would only have spread alarm and despondency among the other hostages if we had told them.

Some more photographs arrived for us during the morning showing me and the boys outside in the grounds. We were also given a new stock of pens, paper and envelopes for writing home to our families, as well as an address through which they could write to us. The address we were told to quote was PO Box 3990, Haifa Street, Baghdad, and this turned out to be the headquarters of the ruling Ba'ath Party next door to the Mansour Melia. I wrote a guarded, happy-sounding letter to both my mum and Derek's, and enclosed in each one of the latest photographs. I do not quite know how I managed it, because I did not feel the slightest bit happy. The improvement in our morale triggered by the excitement and fear of Saddam Hussein's visit had by now completely evaporated, and the long hours of boredom had again closed in on our shuttered minds. Despite the Arabian sunshine which beat down on us, I had the same feeling as that induced by a rainy Sunday afternoon in England at the end of November.

We had all been suffering from stomach upsets in varying degrees during our time in captivity, and when the doctor arrived for her daily check we asked for a new supply of diarrhoea tablets. She gave them to us, and as she did so she let slip the little snippet of information that everyone who had stayed in the Mansour Melia was being affected in the same way. She was convinced that the problem was the result of a bug in the hotel's water supply.

During lunch, one of my fillings dropped out. The reason lay in the food, which on this occasion was a huge carp-type fish which is caught in the River Tigris and is a typical Iraqi dish. The two boys would not touch it because it was very greasy and seemed to keep staring at us from its last resting place on the serving dish, but Derek and I decided to tuck in. A few moments later I wished I had not, because the thing was a mass of tough bones and it was one of these that cracked my filling. Michelle also had some dental problems, so after the meal we went to see Jhallil to ask if we could see a dentist. Straight away he made a telephone call and a short while later we were taken to the medical centre across the road. Here we were taken to a woman whom we recognized as someone who had sometimes accompanied the doctor during her tours of the installation. She put in a temporary filling and told me to go back and see her in a week's time. My heart sank like a stone – the only place where I wanted to be in a week's time was England.

Just before I climbed out of the chair, the dentist said how sorry she was that we were being held at the installation. The tone of her voice almost invited me to pour out my grievances to her and criticize the Iraqi hierarchy for imprisoning us, but somehow I sensed that I was walking into a trap so I kept quiet. It was lucky that I did, because she had obviously been setting me up so that she could shoot me down in flames with a carefully-prepared speech she had rehearsed beforehand. When I did not rise to the bait, she gave me a lecture anyhow and I had to listen to a five-minute tirade about how selfish and thoughtless we hostages were. She tried to make it sound as if the whole situation was our fault, and she seemed to enjoy painting for me a romanticized picture of the luxury we were living in compared with the lifestyle of the Iraqi people. She told me of sickness affecting the local children, and of her own mother who could not get any medical treatment despite the fact that she was a diabetic. In contrast, the hostages were receiving the best food and health care available.

I daresay that she was right in her assessment of the hard lot of the ordinary Iraqis, though I could have pointed out that we were being held in contravention of every known international law and that the local people would have been very welcome to our share of the resources if we had been allowed to go. I felt like telling her so, but managed to resist the temptation. It would have been futile and perhaps even dangerous to quarrel with her, and my continuing silence actually stopped her deriving the full enjoyment from her lecture.

In any case, it was not really her fault. She was only regurgitating the official Iraqi line about the crisis in the Gulf that was being fed to the people several hours a day on the state-controlled television. Saddam Hussein was always talking about the initiatives he was making for peace, and because of the way he dressed them up for his people, they could not be expected to know that he was telling them a pack of lies and that the proposals he was putting to the United Nations were both unjust and totally unacceptable.

Even we, with the benefit of understanding Western ways and with a daily dose of the BBC World Service, could not be certain exactly what was happening on the international stage. The average Iraqi must have wondered how we and our Government could be so unreasonable and unfair. Hussein, having directed his rhetoric solely against the Americans at the start, was now becoming more and more anti-British, and was attacking our nation for the way it had helped to redraw the boundaries in the Arab world. The man in the street was being urged to become extremely hostile to the British and this gave us a very uncomfortable feeling. We had somehow felt a bit safer when only the Americans had been the big bad ogres.

The cleaners who came to visit us every day were also clearly amazed at our attitude. They were actually Christians and were lovely women, and they spent every working day walking between five different installations on the complex to carry out their duties. While they worked their fingers to the bone, we seemed to them to have nothing to do except relax, and we were eating far better food than them while we were doing it. They could not understand how we could be depressed and want nothing more than to shun the special hospitality being extended to the foregin 'guests' by their country's leader. Unlike the angry dentist, these kindly souls were just very puzzled, and now that their country has been ruined, I am sad that they will probably never understand.

Monday 27 August

The clothing and toiletry parcels arrived from the Iraqi Women's Federation, and we all took part in a novelty fancy-dress competition. It was actually great fun and very amusing, because most of the supplies they had sent us were awful and would have been ideal if we had been going to a 'bad taste' party. The main problem seemed to be that hardly anything fitted anyone.

The stuff arrived in big boxes which were unpacked by the guards, who then delivered various items of clothing to the different rooms. Soon everyone was trying on something or other. The hostages began going round to visit one another and to try bartering something that did not fit them for something that did, and it was not long before the whole installation looked like one gigantic bring-and-buy sale. It was absolute chaos, as many of the things that had been ordered for the men had been provided in children's sizes. Craig had been equipped with a bright-red sun hat, but even that did not fit properly. For the ladies, there were bras and various pieces of underwear, and these were also in the wrong sizes.

Included in the delivery were three sets of extremely bright Bermuda shorts, each with a matching shirt, and for some reason the guards had given them all to us. There was one in green, one in yellow and one in orange, and they had palm trees and setting suns plastered all over them. Derek tried them on but they were far too small, so he gave them to Craig, who tried them on and found they were far too big. In any case, I think Craig would sooner have walked around naked than wear them, and I attemped to give them to the other hostages who graciously declined the offer. We were stuck with the damn things, though we did find that they really brightened up our rooms if we left them draped over the chairs.

Once the dust had settled and we had passed a very amusing hour dressing up, we discovered that the Lockwood family appeared to have been luckier than anyone else. Stuart had a new T-shirt and Derek ended up with some jeans and running shoes, which fitted so well that he eventually brought them out of captivity with him and is still wearing them today. Craig and the other teenage boys even started their own fashion craze by grabbing all the men's vests that had been sent, drawing cartoon characters on the front and wearing them over the top of their T-shirts.

Other goodies in the parcels included hairspray, nail files, nail varnish and lipstick, though the colour of the latter was deep red. All the women tried it on anyway, and suddenly the place was full of people who looked rather like Bette Davis in the 1940s. Val caused an enormous laugh when she said, 'Let's have a girls' night out. Come on – throw your handbags in the middle of the floor and we'll dance round them.'

We all appreciated, however, the amount of trouble to which the members of the Women's Federation had gone in order to find us things that to them were the height of luxury and were in very short supply. In addition, they had used a lot of kind thought for they had also sent us packets of biscuits and sweets for the children.

Earlier, Stuart became the proud owner of a new pet. He and his 'friend' went out foraging in the grounds of the installation and returned triumphantly with a little chitchat lizard. Stuart put it in a cardboard box, and because I would not let him keep it in our room he moved it into the guards' lounge. All was well until his small friend, Elliott, saw it, made a grab for it and pulled off part of its tail. Stuart cried and cried, but fortunately the lizard survived and Stuart spent most of the day nursing it and making sure it recovered. When our clothing parcels arrived, we found we had been given a little pair of nail clippers, and Stuart hid these in his pocket and took them outside to use for cutting some grass for the chitchat. It was pretty hard work and he would have found it much easier to pull the grass up with his hands, but he felt so important with a special implement for the job and it kept him happily occupied.

Under his watchful eye, the chitchat made a full recovery during the day, and immediately before our evening meal we persuaded Stuart to take it out into the grounds and let it go. He had just returned from doing so when Elliott appeared with another chitchat which he had captured and some peculiar-looking bugs he had picked up. Poor Stuart. He had only wanted a pet as something to care for and to take the place of his parrot, Peter, which we had been forced to leave behind in Kuwait. The sight of Elliott's chitchat set him off crying again, but we eventually managed to pacify him. We convinced him that wild animals are happier in their natural environment and that he had done the right thing by setting his own lizard free to return to its mummy and daddy.

Meanwhile, we had discovered that one of Pat and Steve's sons, who was also called Craig, was due to have his fourteenth birthday the following day, and we started making plans to help him celebrate as normally as possible. Derek, Steve and one or two of the other men even tried to hoodwink the guards that it was an essential tradition in England for a boy to drink beer on the day he reached the age of fourteen. I am not convinced that their motives were entirely selfless, and neither were the Iraqis, because not even this could persuade them to supply a drink that is banned by their religion. Birthday cards were available, however, and Jhallil kindly went to the trouble to get some for us.

There was a pleasant surprise awaiting us at dinnertime because it was pizza on the menu, and for once the boys managed to eat a squarish meal. Stuart remembered seeing on Kuwaiti television an advertisement for a company called Pizza Italiana which showed a waiter wheeling round a trolley serving slices of the dish, and suddenly he wanted to be a real-life Pizza Italiana man. He begged the guards to let him help with the serving of the meal, and suddenly there was a new and very small waiter dispensing the nightly rations to all the hostages. Each evening we were also given canned drinks imported from Jordan, and these were considered the big treat of the day. Derek and I used to go without ours so that the boys could have two each. Stuart was now handing out these drinks which had come to mean so much to him during a drab existence, and there was a very proud smirk on his face as he did so. He left everyone with the impression that the drinks were on him and he was giving them away himself out of sheer generosity.

He disappeared for quite a long time after serving our pizzas and I was worried that his was going to get cold. However, when we went to search for him we discovered that he was sitting with the guards in their lounge and was already tucking into a meal with them. This left a spare portion of food in our room, and since everyone seemed to have overlooked the fact, Craig surreptitiously devoured it. Unfortunately it had gone cold by this time and was not as tasty as his first piece had been, but it was very welcome and filled a gaping hole in a ravenous teenage appetite.

Tuesday 28 August

We smelt the first scent of freedom today, but it was a bitter, unhappy experience because it led to our being parted from Derek for three months and nearly losing him for ever.

The day had started happily, however, as we all made plans for the birthday of Pat and Steve's son. Craig was for once awake and already active by the time Derek and I came round. He was lying on his bed making a birthday card for his friend and, considering the meagre materials he had to work with, he was making a pretty good job of it. After breakfast, we wandered down to Pat and Steve's room to give our cards to the birthday boy. Everybody seemed to have either managed to buy a card or taken the trouble to make one, and he was delighted. His mother had been a little upset and thoughtful during the few days leading up to his birthday, but this morning she was more cheerful – although I have no idea whether it was all a front for her son's sake or whether she genuinely felt better. Steve managed to catch the news on the BBC World Service while we were there, but apart from the continuing outrage and condemnation of our television show by the authorities back home, there was nothing of any real interest.

The rest of the morning passed quite quickly, and I think this was because of the hustle and bustle of the birthday and the planning of a surprise party for the evening. Even the guards got caught up in the excitement. They told Pat they had ordered a cake, which would be delivered later, and said that the get-together could take place in the lounge. Stuart was in his element at lunchtime because the guards let him help with the serving of the meals again and he took it very seriously. Afterwards we sat and read until the worst of the midday heat had passed before going out to enjoy a spot of sunshine. The weather was still very warm and in the middle of the day it was too hot for the children to play outside. Fortunately the building was air-conditioned, otherwise we would have been very uncomfortable.

Later in the afternoon, Derek organized another whist drive which everybody enjoyed, and suddenly it was evening and time to start getting ready for the party. Pat and Val said that in honour of the occasion they were planning to put on their new make-up, and we all had a good laugh because the colours were extremely bold.

While we were all gathered together, we had a more serious discussion about what would happen to our children's education if we were to be kept in captivity for any length of time. As nearly six days had passed since Saddam Hussein had assured us that this would be taken care of, we decided to write to him personally to remind him of his promise, and we even got as far as drafting a letter. In the end, there was no need to send it.

There was a flurry of excitement shortly after 7.00 p.m. when Val came rushing into our room to tell us that a recording was about to be shown on television of a meeting between Saddam Hussein and a second group of hostages. We switched on the television and immediately recognized a number of the detainees. This meeting seemed to be taking place in some sort of palace, with the President sitting on a very regal-looking, throne-like chair at the end of the room and his 'guests' sitting in rows in front of him with a central gangway through the middle of them. The ever-present minders were very conspicious, but that did not stop the detainees asking lots of questions.

Jackie, who was sitting with her little boy Daniel, bravely told the President how unfair it was that he should hide behind women and children and that it was particularly hard on the youngsters, who did not understand what was going on. He fobbed her off with the same answer he had given us – that he felt our continued presence in Iraq would help to 'divert' a war. He was then asked rather sarcastically in what order the hostages would be allowed into the air-raid shelters in the event of an attack, and he seemed to find that a little amusing. He replied that women and children would be first followed by foreign males and finally the Iraqis, but we all thought he was talking rubbish.

The meeting was attended by representatives of all the major nationalities being held hostage – British, American, French and

Japanese – and it was almost as if Saddam Hussein wanted to demonstrate to the world that they were all involved and that all his main adversaries would lose some of their citizens if they attacked Iraq. One of the Americans made a very clever suggestion to try and get the women and children released. He said that if they were repatriated, the President would have shown the world that he really wanted peace and that his intentions were for a peaceful solution.

There was a spot of added drama right at the end of the meeting, involving another of our friends who was also called Jackie. She was being held with her two children, Colin and Rachael, and when the President learned that it was Rachael's birthday, he said the whole family could be released as a birthday gift. We were all very envious of them and at the same time delighted for them, but we felt so sorry for poor Pat. She was quite upset. She could hardly help thinking that in view of the fact that it was her son's birthday, she and her family might also have been on their way home if she had been at this second meeting or if the President's visit to us had been just five days later. It was pointless fretting over what might have been, however, and after talking with her for a few minutes we managed to cheer her up and persuade her that the best thing was for us all to throw all our energies into her son's birthday party.

We had dinner and then went round to the lounge, where we found the birthday cake sitting there waiting to be cut. Someone had decorated the room with a few balloons they had managed to get hold of, and we even had music to dance to, thanks to some forward planning by Steve. His radio set, which had kept us in touch with the news via the World Service, doubled up as a cassette player, and he had spent ages earlier in the day scrubbing the short-wave radio symbol off it with toothpaste so that he could use it at the party without exciting the guards' attention.

Pat got the function off to a merry start by carrying out her threat to wear her new make-up, and the teenagers and the guards produced a motley collection of tapes, but, just like at any social event back home in England, everyone seemed too shy to dance. So to break the ice, Pat and her younger son started dancing, and Derek and Stuart joined them while everyone else began clapping. Derek then did a little Arabian dance with one of the guards and that had everybody howling with laughter, and with the party now in full swing, the cake was cut and slices were handed out to all the revellers. We had just finished devouring it when one of the balloons accidentally popped and Derek had the whole room in uproar again by diving on to the floor and shouting, 'Where's the shelter?' A couple of the guards could not stop laughing, and with tears in their eyes they explained the joke in Arabic to their colleagues whose English was not good enough for them understand it. The party was really warming up by this time and we were all enjoying ourselves – but it was about to end in tears.

At about 11.00 p.m., Dale suddenly came in from the television room and said it had just been announced on the news that the women and children would soon be free to leave. Then one of the guards came into the room and whispered something to his superior officer, who stood up and walked out. The fizz was now draining rapidly out of this wonderful party, which had been our most relaxed and enjoyable time since our arrival in Iraq. All the confused hostages began milling around talking anxiously to one another in subdued tones. We asked the guards if what Dale had heard was true, and they replied that they understood it was, but that we would have to wait for confirmation of it until 10.00 a.m. the next day when they were due to receive further orders.

I suppose I should have been elated by the news, but I was not. In fact, I was very upset and I went straight back to my room where I sat down and wept. I think I had known before that this was a possibility – particularly in view of the fact that the American hostage had raised it with Saddam Hussein personally – but now that it had materialized, we were left with a terrible dilemma as to how we should react. Already, my mind was turning over with the two stark choices that lay before us. Either I had to abandon Derek to a most dangerous and uncertain future when all I wanted to do was stay with him, or Derek and I had to risk our sons' young lives so that we could find solace in each other's company. They were two lousy choices and I wanted no part of either of them.

Craig walked into the room in the middle of my turbulent thoughts and anxiously demanded to know what was happening. I had not hidden anything from him since the moment Derek had been kidnapped in Kuwait and I felt that this was no time to start, so I told him. Craig was as upset as I was and he refused point-blank to leave his dad ever again, and when Derek came to join us a few minutes later, Craig told him so. Derek said that if the women and children were being freed, Craig, Stuart and I would have no choice but to go. He added, however, that he felt everything was getting out of control, the whole thing could well be a hoax and we must wait until we were sure of the outcome before taking any decisions. Craig's reply was short and to the point: 'If it is true, I'm not going.' Then he flung himself into bed. Stuart could hardly help but sense that something was badly wrong, but he was worn out and fell asleep very quickly.

I also went to bed, but I could not sleep and lay awake crying for what seemed liked hours. Derek sat up for a time, deep in thought over the heartbreaking decision that now threatened to break up our family once more. He was a different man from the comic Arab dancer who had so amused us less than two hours earlier. He came to bed eventually, but he was very restless all night as his troubled mind churned with the distasteful duty that lay before him.

Wednesday 29 August

As soon as I opened my eyes, I knew that today our lives were going to change completely. I had a splitting headache because of a chronic shortage of sleep, but this did not stop me seeing through the scepticism with which some people had greeted the momentous announcement of the night before. To me there was no doubt that today the women and children would be told they were free to leave. I was convinced that once such an announcement had been made so positively and publicly by the Iraqi leader, it would definitely be put into practice. I was also certain of something else – I would be staying with Derek no matter what he said to the contrary.

I was in tears again almost as soon as I stepped out of bed, and I went straight round to the shower room to try and knock myself into some sort of shape for the ordeal ahead. The first person I met was Barbara, and I asked her what she would be doing. She replied that she would be staying behind with Alan, and she seemed very calm and collected and had obviously thought it all out very thoroughly. She added, however, that she had based her decision on the fact that they had no children and that she might well have taken a different view if they had. We were soon joined by Michelle, who, despite the fact that she had two small children, was also planning to stay with her husband, Dale. Her reasoning was that she would cause her youngsters more damage by separating them from their father than by letting them remain with her as hostages, though she was by no means certain she was right.

As I returned to our room, I was more determined than ever that I would be staying, but I ran into the brick wall of Derek's obstinacy as soon as I stepped through the door. I burst out crying as he told me that I had no option but to leave him and get the boys safely back to England, and I understood that all the tears in the world would not get him to change his mind. Pat was also in tears when she came down to see us because Steve had told her exactly the same, and Val had received a similar response from her husband, Kim. A black cloud seemed to hang over the whole installation. Among so much despondency, there was just one happy family: Marla and her two sons were delighted to be returning to her husband who was waiting for them in London. One person's meat is always another's poison.

Meanwhile Craig was still broken-heartedly protesting that he had no intention of leaving, so Derek sat and chatted to him for a long time. He explained that although he did not want us to go, he would feel much happier to know that we were out of this horrendous danger and safe back at home in England. Derek also said that it would be less of a burden for him to have only himself to worry about, and if there were ever any chance of escape it would be much easier for him to make a break for it on his own. Yet his words fell on deaf ears: Craig burst into tears and flounced out of the room still defiantly announcing that he would not leave.

The daily routine of prison life continued throughout the morning, but there was a very subdued air about it. The cleaners arrived and were followed by the doctor, but there was only a heavy silence between us and them in place of the usual pleasantries. They obviously sensed the atmosphere of desperation engulfing us and quietly carried out their duties before leaving as swiftly and quietly as possible.

The nightmare became grim reality just before lunchtime when three of the guards came into our room armed with a notebook and pen. They asked, 'Are you and your family going back?' and we immediately thought there had been a change of heart and that Derek was being allowed to leave with us. But as soon as we asked them if this was the case, we knew the answer even before they said 'No'. The wry smirk and light laugh that greeted our enquiry were like a spike being driven into a gaping emotional wound; it seemed as if some of the Iraqis were incapable of understanding or experiencing any real feeling whatsoever. Derek immediately said that I would be leaving, I said I would not, then I burst into floods of tears while the guard lowered his eyes to the floor and practically hopped from one foot to the other in embarrassment. He said that we must talk it over and that he would return later for our final answer, then he went into Alan and Barbara's room opposite.

A few minutes later, I heard Barbara weeping in the corridor and venting a stream of impotent anger on one of the guards as she told him how unfair it was that we had been put in this heart-rending situation. I truly believe that those guards were completely taken by surprise at our reaction. They really thought that they were going to make everyone happy by allowing the women and children to leave, and simply could not comprehend the deep hurt that was being caused by the division of so many families.

Derek sat down beside me, lovingly put his arm round me and told me that although he desperately wanted us to stay, there was absolutely no doubt in his mind that we had to seize this opportunity and go. He said that any man faced with the chance of getting three out of four people safely away from such a volatile situation should take it without question. Craig came back in and stood listening as Derek talked, and this time he did not interrupt.

The guard had obviously been experiencing similar problems with some of the other families; he was very quiet and sheepish when he returned for our final answer, and left as quickly as possible after receiving it. Derek's words tore at my soul like a death sentence as he told the guard that we would be leaving. He asked when we would have to go, and the guard said he thought it would not be until the following day. I was still very upset but I felt a bit better when I heard we had a little more time together.

Lunch was brought to our room as usual and was taken away again virtually untouched. Shortly afterwards, one of the guards returned to tell us to start packing because we would be leaving in fifteen minutes. I felt as if the bottom had been kicked out of my world, as yet again my hopes and expectations were dashed to pieces by another cruel Iraqi trick, and I burst into floods of tears for the umpteenth time of the day. Craig, who suddenly realized that he must be more adult than ever because I needed his support now that we were losing his father again, silently started sorting our things and packing them into the plastic carrier bags that had become such a part of our lives. As a final touching gesture, he said he would leave behind his precious Walkman and cassettes for his dad to use; we also gave Derek the first-aid things and all the toiletries.

Derek was very quiet, but he went round to the reception area to try and discover where we were being taken. Would we go straight to Jordan by road or go to the airport to wait for a flight or stop off overnight at a hotel? Nobody seemed to know, or, if they did, they were definitely not saying. Yet again, the terrifying thought flashed through our suspicious minds that none of us was going home and that the whole thing was merely a ruse to split us up.

Our next visitor was a man called Mike who came to ask me if I would take home a letter to post to his girlfriend, Sheila. She lives very near my home in Worcester in England, so he also gave me her telephone number and asked me to call her when I got back and tell her how much he loved her. He started crying – which set me off as well – and I promised to do as he had requested.

By this time, everybody was gathering in reception in readiness for the departure, so we collected our bits and pieces together and went to join the crowd. Everyone was in tears, and one of the more kindly guards started walking round amongst us trying to cheer us up. He kept saying, 'Don't be upset – our President is sending you all home so your children can continue with their schooling, and it will not be long before your husbands will be leaving also.' Then one of the senior officers standing in the reception area went over and spoke to him quietly, and he said very little after that. He had obviously been censured.

I would have thought that by this time everyone would have bled themselves dry of tears, but amazingly we still had some left to shed when we were given the order to leave and said our final goodbyes. Stuart was weeping inconsolably, and his tough-looking 'friend' came over, picked him up and kissed him. For once, Stuart did not want to be with him, and he struggled free and ran into his daddy's arms. Craig's fragile hold on his stiff-lipped resolve fractured completely, and he again pleaded with me to stay and kept on pleading until I was in absolute turmoil. I do not remember how we got on the waiting bus; I seemed to be moving in a daze.

At last, we were settled in our seats and Derek and Steve were standing outside the vehicle on the pavement. Two of the guards came to check that we were all there, and when they saw how distressed the boys and I were, they even started crying themselves. They returned to Derek and told him to come and give us a last cuddle because they could not bear to see us leave in such a state. He climbed on to the bus and walked up to our seats, and again assured me that we were doing the right thing. Then he was asked to leave, and the vehicle slowly reversed out of the slip road in front of the installation and drove off. Despite the dangers we had faced in both Iraq and Kuwait, this was my worst single moment of the whole ghastly experience during the Gulf emergency, and I felt as if my heart had been ripped from my body. What I then feared might be my last ever sight of Derek was seen through eyes blinded with tears. I can still see him standing there all alone waving, and I am crying again now as I think and write about it.

We had no idea where we were going, so when I had recovered some of my composure I asked the guard who was accompanying us on the journey. It came as something of a shock when he replied that he thought we would stop off at a hotel for the night before being taken out of Iraq through Jordan. He believed we might stay at the Al Rasheed, but when we arrived in Baghdad we drove past the turning for it and, to our amazement, ended up at our old friend the Mansour Melia. Here we were ushered to our quarters in one of the upper storeys, where Craig, Stuart and I managed to get a room next to Pat and her three boys. The place seemed very empty, and we started worrying about what was to become of us and how long we would have to stay there.

By this time, Craig was at the end of his tether and he flung himself on his bed and cried and cried. When he at last managed to stop, he begged me to ask if we could go back to his dad. Just at that moment one of the guards, whom we had got to know during our first stay at the hotel and who was a very nice man, arrived to fill in our registration forms. He was very distressed to see Craig in such a state and told me he would personally take us back to Derek if I wished it. Craig redoubled his efforts to try and persuade me, and the offer was really very tempting, but I had to turn it down. I knew that if we did return to the installation, Derek would insist on our going away again and we would have to go through all the trauma of being parted once more. In the end, the guard saw that we were in no fit state to give him the information he needed, and said he would return later.

Stuart had been abnormally quiet and withdrawn throughout all this, and I was beginning to get very anxious about him. But his silence gave me the chance to talk to Craig and explain why Derek had wanted us to leave him and how much safer it would be for both us and him in the long run. It took a long time to make Craig fully understand, but we got there in the end.

When the guard returned to fill in the forms, I asked him how long we would be held in the hotel and he said he thought about twenty-four hours. This was a real blow, and my face must have shown how disappointed I was not to be going home sooner, because this kind man stayed and talked to us for a long time. He said that when the freeing of the women and children had been announced, the general feeling among the guards at the hotel had been that only about half would take up the offer, and they had been surprised when so many decided to leave. He told us that he had seen us on television, and finally spoke of his family and of his three-year-old daughter whom he very rarely saw because owing to the present emergency virtually all his home leave had been stopped. I think he was trying to say that the Iraqis were also experiencing hardship and being separated from their loved ones, so he knew how we felt at this moment.

When he had gone, Pat dropped in to see us with the news that some people she had met previously in detention had just arrived at the hotel, so we got our five boys organized and went up to the floor above to see if there was anyone else we knew. To my surprise and delight, most of the women from Fahaheel were already there, and our reunion was remarkably happy considering the circumstances in which it took place. There were only five who were missing because they had decided to stay with their husbands; most of the men had taken the same decision as Derek – that their families must leave while they had the chance. Everyone was disheartened by the news that we would be at the Mansour Melia for another twenty-four hours because we would all rather have stayed with our husbands just that bit longer. One of the main topics of conversation was Stuart's starring television role opposite Saddam Hussein, which all the women seemed to have watched. He was also recognized by the other guards throughout the hotel, and they made quite a fuss of him.

We returned to our room about an hour later. Craig was now very quiet, but he seemed a little better and our reunion with old friends had obviously done him good. Our friendly guard returned to see us just before dinner and was very relieved to find Craig in better spirits, and I took the opportunity to explain to him how cruelly we felt we had been treated. 'First you took my sons' daddy away from them in Kuwait,' I said, 'then you reunited us and said we would not be parted again, and now you tell us that we can leave but their daddy has to stay. Do you see?'

That kindly man did indeed see, and he apologized and quickly left us alone with our sorrow.

We were all completely drained, and the boys went straight to bed when we had finished dinner. I stayed up and wrote a letter to Derek, and felt a lot better when I had done so. It somehow seemed to bring him closer to me, and our nice guard had promised to post it for me the next day. I hoped Derek would hear that we were staying at the Mansour Melia, though I doubted that such information would get through to him. Of one thing I was certain – he would not rest until he heard on the World Service that we had touched down safely on British soil. My thoughts were still with him as my tired eyes and brain drifted into the sleep that brought an end to the unhappiest day of my life.

Thursday 30 August

The one good thing about the Mansour Melia was that it was somehow a lot more relaxed than it had been the first time we stayed there. Although we were restricted in much the same way as we had been before, our movement between floors seemed less closely watched, there were fewer guards on duty at the ends of the corridors and they were all anxious to please us. The children were allowed a session in the swimming pool at 10.30 a.m., and Craig and Pat's three sons were down there on the dot to take advantage of every second.

Pat, Stuart and I were following them a few minutes later when we were stopped by one of the head guards who was walking in the opposite direction with two men in plain clothes. It transpired that these two were members of a television crew and they wanted us to take part in yet another interview. Neither Pat nor I was very keen but they were persistent, and while we were gently arguing with them, Stuart wandered off to join his brother at the pool. We tried to say that we had to go and look after him, but the guard said he would make sure that Stuart had got there safely and that Craig was looking after him. With our last excuse for not taking part now gone, we were led back to the hotel foyer.

There we found that television cameras had been set up and the whole area had been turned into an impromptu little studio with a number of official-looking men in smart suits standing about the place. Pat and I made a final attempt to get out of the interview by saying that we were worried about leaving the boys on their own at the pool, and the men reluctantly let us go once we had promised to be back there at 12.15 p.m. While we were at the pool, we asked the other women in our group if they had been approached to take part in an interview and most of them knew nothing about it. This made us even more unwilling to get involved.

The foyer was very busy when we returned from swimming because the television crews were recording a number of *Guest News*-type interviews in which the hostages were being asked what they felt about going home. We went back upstairs to get everybody changed, and when midday came we debated between ourselves whether anyone would notice if we conveniently forgot to turn up. In the end, we decided that we had better go, because we did not want to get into any bother at this late stage and jeopardize our chances of going home.

There was a furious quarrel going on when we reached the ground floor, and it was happening in the middle of the foyer in front of the television cameras. It had blown up because a woman called Maggie had started getting very angry while being interviewed. She told the interviewer that the Iraqis had better watch their step because the Americans would be flying over very soon and they would flatten the whole country. The poor man did not know where to put himself. We certainly admired her bottle: we ourselves would not have dared to speak out like that. The trouble was that the Iraqis had almost brainwashed us and had got us into a state of being afraid to say anything in case it endangered the husbands we were leaving behind. We were not prepared, however, to be the puppets they wanted us to be and to say how great the Iraqi nation was. We were very grateful to Maggie because, with all the furore she caused, the officials in charge of the television crew forgot all about us and we were able to escape discreetly back upstairs without anybody noticing.

As we were finishing our lunch in the dining room some time later, I was approached by our friendly guard who confessed that we would not now be going home that day. I was very upset and disappointed, and strangely the guard was as well. He was one of the more senior officers there and the information he gave us was always far more reliable than anything we heard from any other Iraqi source. As we got to know him better, he revealed that he did not like parting with information unless he was certain it was correct, and the fact that he had misinformed us on this occasion over such an important matter had obviously made him feel very guilty. I had written a second letter to Derek, which I asked the guard to get delivered for me, and he was only too happy to try and make amends in any way he could.

This latest delay to our repatriation hit Pat very hard and she started worrying until I became concerned that she would make herself ill. She was very mixed up and was seriously beginning to doubt whether we would ever get home. I think her trouble was that she tended to dwell on things too much. Maybe I was being hopelessly optimistic, but you had to think positively, and in any case, I still believed that when Saddam Hussein made a big public announcement that something would happen, it usually did. Yet every woman then being held in the Mansour Melia was becoming increasingly bitter about the delay, because we all saw it as a waste of precious time that could have been spent with our husbands.

The signs were looking good for us, though, because the hotel was gradually becoming more and more crowded with hostages of all nationalities. All the time I kept recognizing familiar faces I had not seen since before the invasion of Kuwait, and it was wonderful to know these people had come safely through such a terrible experience. A Frenchman introduced himself to me as a friend of a girl called Karen I had known well in Kuwait. They had both seen Stuart on television and we all laughed when the man told us that Karen had said something must have been wrong during the interview because Stuart was not normally quiet like that.

By now we were comparing notes with some of the other groups of women about the installations in which they had been held, and I was amazed at the vast range of different treatment we had all received. The guards at some places had been helpful and friendly, as several of them had been at ours, while the guards at others had been rough, unpleasant and threatening. Some hostages had even been supplied with . . . ALCOHOL. It was typical of Derek's luck that we had ended up in a temperance chemical-weapons factory!

One of the most frightening experiences I heard about involved the hostages who had taken part in the second televised interview with Saddam Hussein a couple of days after ours. Guards had arrived at one installation at 1.00 a.m. and wanted to take the women and children away by themselves without saying where they were going. Some of the men had bravely stood up to them and had refused point-blank to agree to it. The hostages were taken to a hotel and were transferred some time later to another building. After that, they were taken to Saddam Hussein's palace, but they had no idea where they were going because the curtains on the buses were kept drawn all the time. Clearly, the Iraqis had only been trying, in their customary ham-fisted way, to confuse everyone in an effort to ensure the total security of their leader, but it could not have seemed like it at the time. The hostages must have thought that a concentration camp or a firing squad awaited them rather than a television camera.

Throughout the late afternoon and early evening, we were kept busy having our photographs taken and giving brief details of ourselves to various officials so that we could be issued with the temporary passports to get us back to Britain. We were also interviewed by staff from the British Embassy about the location and nature of the installations where we had been held. They took down as much information as possible, and it was doubtless put to good use during the dark months that lay ahead. I have to say that the British Embassy in Iraq was as helpful and efficient as the Embassy in Kuwait had been lax.

The weirdest happening of the day was that Stuart was offered the chance to see the sights of Baghdad. He had been delighted to meet up once more with Thomas and James, his special little friends from our days in Kuwait. By and large, however, he was never on his best behaviour when we were in the Mansour Melia because he hated the place. Unlike the International Hotel in Kuwait City, the Mansour provided no puzzles or toys for the little ones who quickly got very bored, and he became so fractious that even our friendly guard noticed. When I explained to the man what was wrong, he offered to take Stuart out into the city for a picnic. It was a lovely thought and I am sure he meant only to be helpful, but it was a risk I dared not take and I very politely declined the invitation.

Friday 31 August

I had my first brush with the international press today and it was not a very pleasant experience. In a final attempt to show that we were being well cared for, the Iraqis had allowed Western journalists into Baghdad, and had run them to our hotel and told us we were free to meet them and say whatever we liked to them. After nearly a month of largely fabricated, propaganda-laden Iraqi news bulletins, we could not believe the sudden openness to which we were being treated. Following the latest batch of *Guest News* interviews the day before, however, most of us had had more than enough of talking to the media and I for one had no intention of tangling with them.

We were walking across the hotel lobby when Stuart started grizzling and insisted on being picked up. I caught him up in my arms, turned round and suddenly found a whole pack of reporters bearing down on me. I think the action of picking up Stuart had helped them to identify us, and I felt as if I were the target of a rogue elephant charge.

Poor Pat was almost sent flying and I was very angry with the man responsible and pushed him back. Microphones were being shoved at me from all directions and one man made me jump when he shouted over my shoulder and asked me if I thought our men would be treated any differently now that we were no longer with them. I was furious with him, but I hid the fact and politely replied that they would not be treated differently at all. The man was only trying to do his job but he had touched a raw nerve by suggesting exactly what we all did fear, although we did not dare say so.

While all this was going on, Craig was enjoying his moment of glory. He had been buttonholed by a reporter from the *Daily Telegraph* and had started recounting his experiences beginning with day one of the invasion more than a month earlier. The reporter was dutifully taking notes, though it must have crossed his mind that he probably did not have either the time or a big enough notebook to record everything he was being told. Eventually, the press gang realized that I was not prepared to say anything of real substance, and they let me rescue Craig and flee to the sanctuary of our room.

By this stage, we were getting very fed up with being strung along and not receiving any concrete proof that we would soon be going home. Some of the women had given lengthy interviews to the British press on this subject as well as on a number of others. Tempers were becoming quite frayed, and a couple of the women even suggested going to the dining room and staging a sit-in as a protest.

At lunchtime, I was approached by a lady who had been on the British Airways flight stranded in Kuwait and she told me that she had been billeted by the Iraqis in our house at Fahaheel. She had recognized me from our appearance on television and could see that she was in our home because of the family photographs we had left behind. She confessed that, as she had lost her own luggage, she had been forced to help herself from the things we had left behind, though she added that the house had already been ransacked by the invaders before she arrived there. It would have been unreasonable to be offended, because she had been in exactly the same difficulty as me, and anyway I would never have known if she had not told me herself.

Moreover, she generously invited me to her room to pick the clothing over and take a few things I wanted. It was a peculiar feeling to be offered a gift of clothing that had once belonged to me. It would have been rude to grab too much and leave her with very little, so in the end, I compromised by choosing just a couple of Benetton cotton shirts and two pairs of trousers for Derek and parcelling them up for the friendly guard to send off to the installation. I thanked her and she said she hoped I did not mind, and we parted on good terms.

The irony was that while we were carrying our few things about in an old bag, she was using my best suitcase and Craig's own case inscribed with his initials. I had to laugh about it, and I was to enjoy a moment of even greater amusement the following day. While we were waiting at the airport to leave Iraq, Craig happened to be standing right next to his suitcase which the lady had left standing on the floor of the airport terminal.

'That's just like the one I used to have,' he told me.

I did not dare to tell him the truth in case he did not understand and tried to grab it back.

Meanwhile an unofficial coffee shop had been set up in a bedroom. Violet was one of the slightly luckier wives who had been held in Kuwait and had been allowed to bring her husband, Dick, with her to Baghdad to see her off. She had also managed to bring with her tea, cake and coffee, and we took it in turns to drop in at her hotel room and sample these long-forgotten treats. She even had some chocolate for the children.

During the evening meal, the nice guard smiled at me a number of times to attract my attention and eventually came over to my table. 'You will be going home tomorrow, God willing,' he told me.

'You said that yesterday but we are still here,' I replied suspiciously.

'I know,' he said, 'but this time I am almost certain.'

The food in the restaurant had shown a marked improvement during the day. Things like butter and jam, which had previously been given out only reluctantly when we asked for it, were now freely available and drinks such as Coke had come back on to the menu. We were worried that the newly-arrived hostages, who had come from Kuwait, would think we had been living like this the whole time and would be jealous. It was as if the Iraqis were trying to give us a right royal send-off by creating a party atmosphere. A jaundiced person could have been excused for thinking that the arrival of the world's press might have had something to do with the sudden display of generosity.

Saturday 1 September

I always missed Derek at meal times. After being with him at the installation where one of the big events of the day had been the serving of food, I could visualize him whenever it was time to eat. I could see him sitting there with his plate in front of him, and I worried about what he was being given and if there was enough for him. I was also very concerned that he might be moved again and about what his new place of detention would be like, although I always tried to push this to the back of my mind.

I was lost in the middle of such thoughts as we walked back to our room after breakfast, but I was brought back to the present by our friendly guard who was talking to his colleagues at the junction of the two corridors on our floor. He said he wanted to talk to me, and he followed us into our room and closed the door. He did not have much to say but what he did say was certainly worth listening to. It appeared that a flight of hostages was almost certainly leaving Iraq that day, and although he did not yet have a list of the people who would be travelling on it, he would let me know as soon as he did.

The news put our usual humdrum morning into total disarray. The swimming pool was again thrown open to us, but we were afraid to use it in case the list of names came through while we were there and we missed it. I was starting to become anxious in case we were cheated of freedom at the last minute, but I managed to stay calm because of my relationship with Pat. We had got on well since the word go, our boys had a lot in common and, because our predicament was identical, we were creatures together in adversity and gave each other great strength. Pat was constantly seeking reassurance from me that everything would be all right, and somehow I always managed to give it her.

The hotel was by this time bulging at the seams with hostages, and at lunchtime the crowded dining room was buzzing with speculation about whether we would at last be leaving. The air was rife with rumour and some people started spreading despondency by suggesting that some of us might be left behind, but nobody really knew any hard facts. We sat at the table for as long as possible to put off the dreaded return to the four walls of our rooms, but eventually we had to stand up and make our way to the lifts.

The friendly guard joined us in the lift, but it was crowded and he could not talk to us properly. When we stepped out at our floor, however, he asked if he could have a word with me in his room which was virtually opposite ours. Pat promised to look after the children while I went, and I took with me yet another letter for Derek in the hope that the guard woud post it for me.

This time, the news was positive and better than I had dared hope. Our names were on the embarkation list and our flight was due to leave Baghdad International Airport at about 6.00 p.m. It seemed that there would be two flights – one going via Jordan and the other flying direct to London – but the guard did not know which one we would be on.

He talked a little about England then, and he was obviously intrigued by the country. I asked him if he had ever been there, and he said he had not but would very much like to one day. He seemed to be a very pleasant, kindly man, and he had certainly taken a lot of trouble, and possibly risk, to be helpful to us. But one of the saddest things about Iraq is that, although it is a country with many decent ordinary people, you cannot afford to trust anyone, and so a certain awkward reserve still remained between us. He even told me how much he would miss us, though in the circumstances I found it impossible to return the compliment.

We were given the order to move at 2.45 p.m. We were told to pick up our bags and make our way down to the dining room where we had to sit at the tables. About half a dozen guards were standing round a table on which there was a pile of passports, and they kept shouting out the names of different travellers who had to pick up their bags and travel documents, leave the hotel and climb aboard one of the buses waiting outside. We were fairly relaxed because we knew we had been selected for one of the flights, but we were surrounded by people with strained, anxious faces who sat on the edges of their seats almost willing the guards to call out their names. We were actually in one of the last batches to be dealt with because we were having to use emergency passports which were valid for only seven days.

When we walked out of the hotel, we found that the travel arrangements for the first stage of our journey home were an absolute shambles. People were just being piled on to the buses without any proper method or order, and at one stage it looked as if there might not be enough room for everybody, but with a little bit of reorganization and a doubling up on the seats, we all managed to get settled. I noticed that even a few of the women who had believed they would not be on the flights now appeared to be travelling with us, and it was great that everyone seemed to be going home together.

My thoughts were again with Derek as we moved off because we seemed to be driving towards our installation, and I could not help wondering yet again what lay ahead for us both. When we arrived at the airport we were told to remain in our seats because it appeared they wanted to unload one bus at a time, and this was a really sticky experience. The weather was still very hot, the air conditioning on the vehicles was non-existent and after a few minutes the sweat was pouring off everyone.

Eventually we were allowed to squeeze out of the packed bus and we stepped thankfully into the comparative coolness of the airport terminal. We were confronted by a British Embassy official who asked if we were being met by anyone at the other end. I replied that I did not know, but I thought we probably would be if our families were notified of our return. After this, we joined the first of several queues so that we could be processed through a system which was weighed down with Iraqi bureaucracy and which took ages to complete. While we waited, a few of the airport officials recognized Stuart from his television appearance and started calling his name and waving to him.

The slowly-moving queue turned out to be for a baggage check, though I have no idea why it took so long when most of us had so little to declare. By this time, television cameras and reporters had started coming out of the woodwork and the boys and I were very much in demand, but the crews seemed to be very understanding when we did not want to say anything. I was then approached by an ITN crew who had been looking for us and who told us that Judy and Phil, my sister and brother-in-law, would be meeting us at Heathrow. I was so delighted that I agreed to give them a quick interview on how we felt to be going home, and after a few minutes they set us free to tackle the next hurdle.

This proved to be the usual marathon form-filling session, after which we had to queue again to hand the blessed things in. We then had to join yet another queue for a body search, but we were rescued from this when two guards recognized Stuart and said we could go straight through to the departure lounge. When we got there, I bought the children some sweets and drinks for the flight, then Pat and I sat talking while the boys wandered off to look in the airport shops.

Craig's mood was very quiet and he was obviously troubled and confused. I knew how he felt because our departure left us with an awful mixture of emotions. It was devastating to want to go home so much yet be leaving behind a loved one to a dangerous, uncertain future.

By now, most people had negotiated the seemingly endless string of formalities, and the departure lounge was quickly filling up. We had even been joined by the guards from the hotel, so we knew several of the uniformed figures who milled around amongst us, breathing down our necks and watching our every move. We also had a surprise travelling companion: our friendly guard suddenly appeared in front of us and I noticed a yellow boarding card in his top pocket. I asked him why he had got it, and he replied that he had been told he would be joining us and would be staying in London for a whole week. He seemed very pleased that he was about to achieve his ambition – particularly as it was something that could never normally be experienced by the average Iraqi – and I was pleased for him. Once again he had some reliable information for us: we learned that we were to fly direct to London instead of calling in at Jordan. We will never know whether the order he received to accompany us was a coincidence or whether he had engineered it, but I saw him on the flight afterwards and he was smiling.

After waiting for ages, we were told to walk to another lounge and we thought that at last we would be going out to the aircraft, but there was no such luck because we were just asked to find a seat and wait even longer. By this time it was nearly 6.00 p.m. – the hour at which we had been scheduled to take off – but there was still no sign that we were about to leave, and as hour after hour passed, everyone started getting fidgety. Surely there could not have been a last-minute hitch to prevent us from going? Surely the whole thing could not be a final, cruel hoax? We did not think so, and yet once again the atmosphere became tense as we sat in the lounge waiting to get on the plane and it sat on the tarmac waiting for us.

A Ministry official came round handing out PO box numbers so that all the women would have an address where they could write to their husbands, and at last a rumour started buzzing among the crowd about the reason for the hold-up. We were apparently waiting for Senator Jesse Jackson's flight to arrive from Kuwait, although we had had no idea that he was even in the Middle East and we could not see, in any case, what he had to do with us. It was not until later that we heard how he had involved himself in trying to free some of the hostages and had flown to Kuwait personally to rescue people who were in danger of being left behind.

By now the children were beginning to get uncomfortable and quite distressed because none of us had eaten or drunk anything since lunchtime. After continually complaining to the guards, we were actually served with an in-flight airline meal. It was hardly very special but it was very welcome.

At midnight, after we had been sitting in the airport terminal for something like eight hours, the guards began calling out the names of people who could start embarking. They worked through their lists by dealing with one nationality at a time and, naturally, the Americans and British were last to be called.

It took ages for everyone to filter through the system, and by now Pat's eldest son, Gary, was becoming very ill and looked really poorly. We got him on to the plane and settled him down wrapped up in a blanket, and we could only hope that he would be okay until we got to England.

At the last minute, when we were strapped into our seats, Jesse Jackson himself got on to the plane and walked up the aisle with his bodyguards in tow waving to everybody. He and his entourage went upstairs to take their seats in the first-class section, and the plane taxied on to the runway and stood shuddering for a few moments with its engines roaring. The pilot let off the brakes, the huge jumbo jet leapt forward and accelerated along the runway, and as it lifted off the ground an enormous, relieved cheer broke out along the length of the fuselage and everyone started clapping.

I sat glued to my seat with my children sitting beside me and tears streaming down my face. Craig was also very upset and Stuart, who was completely worn out, just stared out of the window. My mind flitted back over the four very happy years we had spent in Kuwait. They had been one of the best periods of my life: I had seen one of my sons grow from a boy to a young adult and the other from a baby to a boy with a wonderful, idyllic, opulent lifestyle in which we were surrounded with friends. I could hardly believe that it should all end like this with us returning home almost as paupers and the dearest, most important member of our family missing.

At that moment, the pain in my soul became almost unendurable and something died inside me. I knew that it would not live again until Derek was returned to us safe and sound, and in my heart of hearts I feared that this might never happen.

FREEDOM

Sunday 2 September

The moment when we flew over English soil for the first time in the Iraqi jumbo jet bringing us home from Baghdad was lost in the dark obscurity of a chilly autumn morning. The south coast slid past unseen nearly 30,000 feet beneath us, but the captain announced over the tannoy that we were back and the passengers broke into cheers as the tension at last drained from the aircraft. I suppose I should have been elated as well, but the symbolic event, for which we had waited so long, only produced in me a peculiar mixture of relief, anticlimax and extreme sadness. I was relieved to have my sons safely back in their native country and I knew I was doing the right thing for them, but my heart was back in captivity with Derek as what I most wanted was to be with him. The family had been split right down the middle and tears welled up in my eyes once more as the reality of this hit home.

The five-hour flight had been largely uneventful and Craig and Stuart had managed to sleep through much of it, though my turbulent emotions had made it impossible for me to settle. All around me, families had been exchanging excited pieces of gossip, and it was from this source that I heard of the ordeal of an American woman who had hidden in the International Hotel in Kuwait when the rest of us were taken from it, and had escaped being taken to Baghdad. Shortly afterwards, 200 Iraqi soldiers were billeted in the building, but she had lain low in her room and managed to survive on food smuggled to her by the ever-faithful hotel staff. She was in a very difficult position when the women and children were released because the Iraqis had no record of her, but Senator Jesse Jackson fought to win her freedom and succeeded.

About half an hour before we had flown over Paris, one of the Iraqi cabin stewards had asked if I and the boys would go to the front of the aircraft to meet Senator Jackson. We did so and it was at this point that we at last learned of the impact that Stuart's television appearance with Saddam Hussein had had throughout the world. The Senator's bodyguards told us how Stuart had unwittingly taken America by storm, had caught the popular imagination from coast to coast and was the biggest thing to hit the States since the Beatles. This was clearly why the official American party wanted to meet him. Senator Jackson was absolutely charming and invited us to sit with him in the first-class area, but we wanted to stay with our friends and fellow hostages in the main part of the aircraft. We had been through so much with them and we were going to stick with them right through to the end.

So Senator Jackson asked if instead I would allow him to talk to Stuart while his aides videotaped the interview, and, against my better judgement, I agreed. He sat Stuart on his knee and kept asking him questions about his interview with Saddam Hussein which were way over Stuart's head because he was too young to understand. Stuart seemed to like him, however, and started prattling to him about some of the things we had done while in the Kuwait International Hotel. He made the whole thing sound like a holiday camp and Senator Jackson, who thought Stuart was talking about the hotel in Baghdad, was clearly confused. We returned to our seats thinking that was the last we would see of the Senator, but we had not reckoned with his natural politician's ability for using the media and extracting every last ounce of publicity from an opportune moment.

What struck us most when we landed at Heathrow were the piercing flashes of light from the cameras of a complete bank of press photographers, who stood herded together on the tarmac taking dozens of pictures of the aircraft as we looked out of the windows. We queued up to get off the plane and, as we got halfway down the steps, we saw that Senator Jackson was waiting for us. Even then I did not foresee what was about to happen, but when we reached him, Senator Jackson picked up Stuart and took me by the arm and began steering us towards the photographers, who had obviously been primed beforehand by his press assistants. Instead of stepping back on to English soil, I was virtually bundled on to it, and I kept reaching behind me for Craig because I was afraid I would lose him in the crush. Already, the media circus was conveniently ignoring his existence just as it would on many other occasions during the months ahead.

There, on the tarmac, Senator Jackson gave an impromptu press conference while the photographers fired off shot after shot of us and kept shouting instructions to Stuart: 'Smile, Stuart!' 'Stuart, look over here!'

We were mesmerized and I was also embarrassed about the whole incident. I just wished that it was not happening but, as I had found in Kuwait and Iraq, I was caught up in a nightmarish event that there was nothing I could do to stop. I was also getting very concerned about the fact that our friends had reached the airport bus laid on to take us to the terminal, and I felt that, after all they had been through, it was wrong they should be kept waiting a moment longer when all they wanted to do was be reunited with their relatives. Eventually, to my great relief, Senator Jackson saw us to the bus and, as a parting shot, asked for our address so he could send us a copy of the video recorded on the plane. Without thinking, I gave it to him – and I was very angry with myself afterwards – but we have never heard from him since.

Senator Jackson has been heavily criticized for what he did by the same newspapers he tried to use, and I have thought long and hard about what I feel about him. Yes, he did try to squeeze every last bit of publicity from our homecoming, he put us through a last-minute ordeal we could have done without and he used my little son for propaganda purposes exactly as Saddam Hussein had done. I can forgive him, however, because I believe that his part in trying to secure our release was performed for basically honest reasons and that, simply because he is a powerful politician, he was unable to stop himself taking advantage of a publicity gimmick when the opportunity arose. He was the first politician to intervene personally in the hostage crisis, he may well have risked his political career by doing so, he took the trouble to fly to Kuwait from Baghdad to rescue some sick hostages when it would have been easier to forget them, and he fought for the release of the American woman who hid in the International Hotel. No matter how much criticism is levelled at him, he took a lot of trouble to get people out of Iraq and I shall always respect him for that.

At last, we reached the terminal and burst anxiously into the airport lounge for a traumatic reunion with our relatives. Wherever you looked, groups of people were hugging one another frantically and bursting into tears. The ITN film-crew in Baghdad had told me that my sister, Judy, and her husband, Phil, would be waiting for us, and as soon as we saw each other, we flew into each other's arms. Jude was sobbing and kept saying, 'I thought I'd never see you again,' and Phil, who normally has quite a lot to say for himself, was for once speechless. I had never seen him like it before, and they were both weeping buckets. To relieve the tension, one of them – I cannot remember which – suddenly produced snacks and drinks they had obtained from the airport cafeteria in case we were hungry. In a moment of heady elation, they seemed to have grabbed nearly every scrap of food in the place. It was bizarre, and also rather comic. There we were in the middle of almost more emotion than I had previously experienced in a single moment, hugging each other and weeping, while at the same time we were being surrounded by mounds of sandwiches.

I was exhausted from over-emotion and lack of sleep, but I now had to do something I had been dreading throughout the journey home – I had to ask how my mother was. She was elderly and had suffered from heart trouble for ten years, and I had been very worried that the shock of learning what had been happening to us might have done her irreparable damage. If I am honest, I had been subconsciously preparing myself for the possibility that she was dead. Happily, she was still very much alive, though I now discovered that she was ill and had been in hospital for ages.

While I was coping with this piece of news, the uproar caused by the identical crying and excited chattering of the other hostages and their families continued unabated all round us. My good friend Pat was nearby and she grabbed hold of me, introduced me to her mother and told her, 'This is Glenda – I would never have got through it all without her.' Poor Pat. She was so generous with her praise and her friendship, yet there had been many times when I had relied on her support, and at present she had far more to worry about than I did. Her son, Gary, had been violently ill on the plane with dysentery and was at this very moment probably being taken straight to hospital.

Yet difficult as our homecoming had been, the staff at Heathrow Airport handled it superbly and went out of their way to welcome us. Food and drink were laid on in case we needed it, the necessary immigration procedures were completed as quickly and efficiently as possible, and all the younger children received lovely gifts to take their minds off the precious belongings they had had to leave behind in Kuwait. Stuart was given a Harry Heathrow teddy bear and a bag with loads of colouring books and pencils in it. The press were also kept well away from us while we were reunited with our families. There was one spot of awkwardness, though, which nobody could do anything about and of which we only now became aware. Suddenly, in the few bits of clothing we possessed, we felt incredibly scruffy, and this feeling was accentuated by the presence of so many smartly-dressed or uniformed officials, immigration officers and airline staff. It was a bit like a family on holiday leaving the beach in their T-shirts and swimming costumes, returning to their hotel and walking into the middle of a wedding reception with all the guests wearing top hats and morning suits.

At last it was time to leave for the last leg of the journey home, and the airport staff helped to minimize our exposure to the waiting reporters and photographers by laying on another bus to take us to where our relatives' cars had been left in a parking area. As we walked from the coach, the photographers recognized Stuart and called to him, and he turned towards them, smiled and waved. He was really posing for them and the next day his picture was on the front page of every newspaper in the country. Someone asked me if I realized how popular Stuart had become in Britain and how much trouble I would have with the press in future. I had no idea at that point, but during the weeks that lay ahead I was to find out.

*

Eventually, we were all safely in Phil and Judy's car and the boys settled down to sleep as we began the final stage of our long journey with a 100-mile drive to their home in Worcester, which is not far from our own. Alone with them at last, I was able to ask for the full story behind the television broadcasting of the video of Stuart with Saddam Hussein. As they talked, I came to understand fully the enormity of my son's popular appeal. On the night the video was first shown in Britain, Judy and Phil had just returned from their summer holiday in the Canary Isles and, tuning in to the television news, had been flabbergasted to see their nephew apparently snub the Iraqi President. The world in general had no idea of the identity of this brave little 'English bulldog', but he was recognized by my next-door neighbour in Worcester who contacted the local BBC radio station the next morning. As the BBC has a computerized system that enables all its broadcasting stations in whatever country to plug into one another's news schedules, Stuart's name had become a household word all over the world within little more than an hour.

Judy and Phil then asked me how Derek was, but every time I tried to speak about him, I burst into tears and they both joined me. The three of us just howled as the car bowled along the country roads and motorways to the Midlands, and it was a wonder that the boys slept through all the noise. Jude and Phil are both very fond of Derek and gave me 100 per cent support during the whole time I was without him. They also prepared me for the fact that the press would be camped on my doorstep for the foreseeable future and, sure enough, when we arrived at their house, a small party was waiting to welcome me. They were polite and so was I, and after I had promised to talk to them a bit later on, we all managed to escape into the house.

There I found my niece Hayley, who had stayed with us in Kuwait earlier in the year, and Phil and Judy's two younger children, waiting for us. Also there was my mother who had been released from hospital just for the day. It was her seventy-third birthday so there was another emotional reunion, but it was a bit muted because Mum did not fully understand what a dangerous situation we had just escaped from. Because of her delicate health, Judy had underplayed the severity of the situation in Kuwait, and Mum even believed that Derek had stayed behind out of choice.

I could not settle until some time later after I had had a shower and washed my hair, and although Craig was completely exhausted, Stuart came to life a little when he met up once more with his cousin Grant, who is the same age. I telephoned Derek's mother at her home in Huddersfield and discovered she was also having problems with the press, though goodness knows how they got hold of her address. The reporters waited there for two days, but eventually she outwitted them by sneaking out of the back and round to her next-door neighbour's so that they were waiting outside the wrong house.

The telephone never stopped ringing with calls from either relatives and well-wishers or the dreaded newspapers. During one telephone conversation with Derek's younger brother, Kevin, I broke down completely, and from then on Phil handled all the calls for me. He also dealt with reporters outside his house and he was absolutely marvellous. To tell the truth, I think he quite enjoyed the drama of the situation as it helped to take his mind away from Derek's plight. The group on the doorstep was growing all the time as other reporters arrived from the national papers. Phil made us all laugh when he said he would have left the van of his roofing firm outside if he had known there would be so many photographers, because then he could have got some free advertising. Eventually, I was persuaded that the reporters might leave if I gave them an interview, and I stood on the doorstep with Craig, Stuart and a thumping headache as they gathered round and fired cameras and questions at us. They wanted to know more or less everything from what I thought of Saddam Hussein using Stuart in the television video to how we were celebrating our return and what we were going to have for lunch. I was very guarded in everything I said about what had happened in Iraq – I was very conscious of the fact that my smallest remark might be monitored in Baghdad and Derek's safety could depend on what I was quoted as saying.

The interview only lasted about five minutes, and the reporters seemed fairly happy when I ended it. They all left, although some of them returned later in the afternoon.

It was a pattern that was to be repeated time after time, and we were under siege for nearly three days. I had swapped the house arrest of a dictatorship for the house arrest of a democracy, and there were some alarming similarities. Every time I went to the window they were there, and some of the photographers even sneaked up a track at the side of Judy and Phil's property to try and snatch pictures of Stuart and Grant playing in the back garden. I know they were only trying to do their job and I have always tried to be fair and to co-operate with them, but there are limits to one's patience.

I went to bed early to try and get some much-needed sleep, but I ended up crying again and Jude came in to me. She sat on the bed and we had a long heart-to-heart chat about everything that had happened and everything that might happen. In the midst of so much uncertainty, however, there was one thing of which I was sure – we would never again return to the relaxed anonymity of family life that we had taken for granted. Because of a three-minute videotape, Stuart was now an international celebrity and he would have to live with that for ever.

Tuesday 4 September

Today was the first day of real freedom because, at last, I managed to shake off the press. A few reporters were still outside Judy and Phil's house in the morning, but when the deadline for the day's evening papers passed without our appearing to give another interview, they all decamped and left. Mum had gone back into hospital for another month's treatment, so the boys and I moved to her house about three miles away while the coast was clear. Our own home, which is only a mile from Jude's, had been let throughout the time we had spent in Kuwait and we could not live there because the tenancy contract still had nearly two months to run.

Little of note had happened the day before except that we had turned down an invitation to appear as a family on the Terry Wogan chat show. As it turned out, however, Craig was in the end quite disappointed not to have taken part. When he tuned in to the show on the television, he saw that the other personality appearing on it was the England footballer Paul Gascoigne, and he would have loved to meet him even though he did not relish the idea of an interview about our experiences as hostages. It was interesting to see Craig and Stuart's reaction to British television after what they had become accustomed to watching in captivity. The programmes in Iraq were extremely biased, and the sight of two hours of film of children dancing in the street while chanting slogans of support for Saddam Hussein and the Iraqi cause had become the norm for my boys. They were astounded by the variety of programmes available to them in Britain, while I had to keep reminding myself that the news broadcasts I was now watching were something in which I could actually believe because what they said was very close to the truth.

Yet now we had this freedom, we felt strangely guilty because we could not get used to it. We would go out of the house, walk down the street and somehow feel we should not be doing it. We almost kept looking over our shoulders, half expecting to see someone in authority bearing down on us to haul us away to face the reckoning for daring to step out of line. Just to go out of doors and sniff the fresh air was a luxury in itself, and yet we felt we should not even be doing that. It was a peculiar sensation – almost as if we were not ourselves but were outside our own bodies looking at these three cowed strangers coming to terms with real life again. If this is akin to what is experienced by ordinary men, women and children who have to live in the world's totalitarian states, I pity them from the bottom of my heart.

Once we had got ourselves settled in at Mum's house, we went downtown to go to the bank and sort out the family finances and to start building up our clothing stocks once more. It was wonderful merely to have money in our pockets and to be able to go into any shop and buy anything we wanted. It is impossible to explain to someone who has not been through our type of ordeal what a thrill it can be to watch your children buying sweets, crisps and soft drinks. Stuart could hardly believe that we could all drink lemonade again, though Craig was much more laid back. Certainly, he shared my own childlike joy in the rediscovery of these simple pleasures, but he had behaved like an adult from the moment

Derek and the other men had been taken from us back on our housing complex in Kuwait exactly a month earlier, and he was going to continue behaving like one now when I still needed a man to help me keep our family unit intact.

Our first, and most important, call was at the bank so that we could make sure we had some money and could get our account working again. I was still emotionally unstable, but the staff were superb and bent over backwards to make everything as easy as possible for me. Then we started wandering around the town centre and at one point, when we went into a newsagent's shop, Stuart was amazed to see pictures of himself in all the newspapers on sale. They were still carrying that photograph of him waving and smiling at Heathrow, and we bought virtually every paper displayed on the shelves.

We started shopping for new clothes and here I found myself being extremely careful about what I spent. It would have been very easy to go mad and buy everything that we needed, and more, but we did not do that. Our month of deprivation had left me with a feeling that I must save something for the future and that our priority must be to acquire just a few essential things that we had been missing. As a result, I bought both the boys socks, underwear and a couple of outfits, and decided to leave any further shopping to another day.

In any case a new problem had arisen, because by now we were being recognized by ordinary passers-by. Total strangers would pat Stuart on the head and say 'Bless him' or they would stop us, wish us good luck and express the hope that Derek and the other hostages would soon be home. It was very thoughtful of them and it was nice to know how much everybody cared for us in our predicament, but being reminded all the time of Derek's detention in Baghdad began to upset me, and I decided to cut short our expedition and return home. I had escaped from the media only to run straight into the kindness of the British public. We did one more thing before fleeing to the sanctuary of my mum's house. The boys had been longing for good old-fashioned fish and chips, and we stopped to buy some as we drove home. Stuart's only previous experience of them had been during holidays spent in Cyprus and England.

After Stuart had gone to bed, Craig was very quiet. The loss of his dad had hit him very hard and so I sat up talking to him. He kept looking at his watch, working out the three hours' time difference between Britain and Iraq, and imagining what the hostages would be doing at that time of day. It somehow seemed to bring Derek a bit closer. I was trying to reassure Craig that everything would be all right. It was the first of many such evenings that I spent not only lying to him, but also lying to myself. The only way I could keep going was to convince myself that Derek was going to survive and would eventually be home, but, thinking about it honestly now that my family is safely together, I have to admit his eventual release and repatriation were little short of a miracle. To this day I can not work out why Saddam Hussein finally decided to free all the male hostages, and when the dust of this sad destruction in the Gulf has finally settled and historians analyse the conflict in years to come, I think they will find that it was his biggest mistake.

Wednesday 5 September

This was another important day in Stuart's life because I took him to enrol at his first British school. The brave hero who had stood up to the world's current most infamous dictator was suddenly just one more little boy who was apprehensive about what the future held for him in a strange new environment. He was quiet and shy as he contemplated the greatest and loneliest ordeal that all children have to face – his first day in a school ringing with the confident boisterousness of older youngsters who have got their feet under the table and are very much at home. The headmistress, Miss Probert, had seen many other children in the same situation and was aware of the extraordinary experiences Stuart had just been through, and she knew just how to put him at his ease. She gave us details of the uniform he would need and said he could start when he wanted, then she took him along to meet his class teacher, Mrs Gough, who was also very nice to him.

Next we went on to the secondary school where Craig was

hoping to start, but here we ran into problems. My mother's house, where we were staying, is not actually in the school's catchment area, and the head had doubts about whether they would be able to take him. However, he began to change his mind when I explained that we would eventually be moving nearer the school into our own home, when the tenant had vacated it. Even so, he had to telephone the education authority so that the officials there could sanction Craig's being taken on to the school roll.

Craig was still far from happy, however, as the educational system he had been under in Kuwait was slightly different and he was not sure how he would fit into English school life. He was very apprehensive because he did not know what he was going into and, except for his cousin Hayley, who would be in the year above him, he did not know anybody at the new school. The final blow came when the head mentioned that games lessons would include rugby. Craig's face really fell because he had never played that sport before and was afraid he would look foolish. By this time I was starting to get on edge as well, because I could see his unhappiness. I had not foreseen these problems; the school was actually the one I had attended as a teenager and I had thought it would suit Craig. Just as things were getting uncomfortable, a face from my past came to the rescue. During my schooldays I had been in the school swimming team and, when we went to meet the head of Craig's year, we discovered it was my former swimming coach. That really broke the ice and my elder son left the school that morning a lot happier than when he had first arrived there. We have never had any serious problems since: he now plays rugby without a second thought and has his own special friends.

The two boys and I went straight down into town to purchase the uniforms they would need, but a new and upsetting surprise was waiting for us at the school shop. As we walked in, we were really taken aback because the assistant took one look at us and burst into tears. We did not know her and had never met her before in our lives, but she recognized us from our pictures on the television news. It transpired that her niece's husband was among the hostages being held in

Baghdad, and the unexpected sight of us in the flesh had been just too much for her. She and I spoke together for quite a long time, and she told me how upset she and her niece were. She asked me anxious questions about what life was like for the hostages and sought my 'expert' views about what might be the eventual outcome, hoping against hope that I would say the men would all be home soon. She was yet another friend I had found in adversity, though I must have provided her with little comfort because really I was incapable of giving her the support she needed. I was in desperate need of reassurance myself, and I was quite depressed again by the time we left the shop.

To cheer ourselves up a bit, we decided to have lunch in town and we made it an event to remember: Stuart's first burger in a McDonald's. Even this was not without some confusion, however, because Stuart mistook it for an American fast-food chain that had had a branch in Kuwait. As a result, he kept calling it 'Hardee's' and nobody knew what he was talking about. Before returning home, we called in at the hospital to visit Mum and discovered that she was in good spirits and making satisfactory progress. When we got back to the house, we settled in front of the television for the evening. The boys, who were by now recovering from the worst of their tiredness, were still amazed by the large choice of programmes and could not take their eyes off the screen.

Meanwhile, Jude was still having a hard time with the ladies and gentlemen of the press who had by now discovered that the birds had flown the coop. I do not think I could have coped without her. She did not give away the address of our new bolt-hole or the telephone number, though she must have been sorely tempted because her own phone had barely stopped ringing with calls from newspaper and broadcasting people asking all sorts of silly little things. It becomes rather trying when you have to spend half the day answering questions about whether Stuart always has cornflakes for breakfast.

Monday 10 September

For the first time, both my sons were at school today and I felt completely lost – alone and pining for Derek. Stuart had started school the previous Thursday: although the teachers had given him special dispensation to put off his attendance until he felt ready, he was anxious to take his place in the classroom and I was only too happy for him to do so. It was, after all, one of the main reasons he had been brought back to England and I knew that he would suffer far less damage if he settled into a normal routine as quickly as possible. A reporter from the local evening newspaper, who had met us at Heathrow on our arrival back in Britain, asked if he could take a photograph of the occasion, and I reluctantly agreed because he had been kind to us. A picture of me standing outside the school with Stuart, who was clutching his little lunch-box, was plastered across the front page the same night. I hardly recognized the haunted face of the pale, nervous woman who stared out of the newspaper at me.

Between then and today, my days had been filled with haring around Worcester getting our act back together after nearly four years away. During one of our home leaves more than two years earlier, Derek had bought me an elderly red and rust Ford Escort which was stored in the garage of our home, and that had to be fetched out of mothballs and given an MOT. I still had our finances to sort out and I had to start making arrangements for moving back into our own home when our tenant's lease ran out in October. Craig also needed to be provided with the rest of his school uniform we had not been able to buy already and with kit for rugby and the other sports he would be expected to do – and any mother who has gone through this task knows that it is almost a full-time job in itself.

Now both Craig and Stuart were at school and, apart from spending part of my mornings racing round to the hospital to see Mum, I found time weighing very heavily on my hands. It was not boredom, it was a strange, empty feeling of helplessness and frustration, and I have since discovered that Derek felt the same in the various installations where he was being held back in Iraq. It was a case of existing from day to day in a nightmarish state of semi-trance – hoping for some glorious tomorrow which never came. Even worse was the dreadful suspicion that it could never come because, like the mythical pot of gold at the end of the rainbow, it did not exist. This was the first admission I made to myself that Derek might not ever be coming home, and it was something from which I shied away to save myself from cracking up completely.

What we were feeling were the first pangs of something we were to experience with growing desperation over the next three months. It seemed as if the men still in mortal danger in detention had been conveniently forgotten by British officialdom now that the women and children were safely home. Those now back home were receiving loads of support and sympathy but seeing no action, and we ached for some kind of political initiative that would bring our men back.

With the benefit of hindsight, I now understand that the Government probably could not have done anything other than what it did. The satisfactory conclusion to the emergency, with all the hostages being saved and the Gulf War being won so swiftly with such light Allied casualties, has to be seen as a vindication of its policies. But at the time, I – and most of the other women who were beginning to set up hostage support groups round the country – could not believe the apparent indifference with which the safety of the remaining hostages was being treated. It almost seemed as if the Government was prepared to let Derek and the other men be completely blown away rather than enter into any negotiation with Saddam Hussein about them.

As the crisis in the Middle East deepened and the Allied task force began massing in Saudi Arabia, the television news became compulsive viewing. Even Stuart showed an avid interest when anything about Iraq came on the screen, though he was far too young to understand the implications. Just as the BBC World Service had been to us in captivity, the international news now became a drug which I could not give up no matter how bad it was.

I tuned in each evening in the vain hope that Margaret Thatcher, who was then still Prime Minister, would make some conciliatory gesture about the hostages. Every evening I was disappointed because she was forever sabre-rattling and the British view was becoming steadily more entrenched. It was just as bad, I later discovered, for Derek, because every time she made such a speech, it led to a cut in his already meagre food rations and to a withdrawal of the few privileges that did exist. His food eventually reached the stage where it was nothing but rice and a bit of goat flesh with the hair still attached, and it literally moved on the plate because of the weevils in it. Even the guards refused to eat it, but the hostages had to: starvation was the only alternative.

There is no doubt that the Iraqis hated and feared Mrs Thatcher more than any other world leader, and it could be argued that she knew what she was doing and that her firm line may well have resulted in the hostages' eventual release. It was impossible for me to see this argument at the time when I had Derek's very life as a powerful vested interest in peace-mongering. I take some pride, now, in the fact that my only public statement on the matter was one of muted support for the official government line.

In the absence of obvious help from the Prime Minister, I turned to the only higher authority. I have never been a regular church-goer or committed Christian, but each night I prayed for a successful end to this living hell that was tearing my soul apart. Craig also prayed regularly, and in school assembly Stuart and his little friends asked God to release all the daddies. It was his first experience of praying to a Christian God because he had only been to an Arab playgroup before. In Iraq, Derek was also praying.

Thursday 20 September

The boys wrote their first letters to Derek. Craig told him how I had been dragging him round 20,000,000 clothes shops, which was a slight exaggeration, and gave him news of some of the major football results involving Manchester United and Liverpool. Both boys had been bought pet guinea-pigs – because I could not cope with a dog, which was what they really wanted – and Stuart drew Derek a picture of the two animals with their hutch and wrote underneath, 'Dad I want you back home to see my guinea-pigs, Love Stuart.'

They were delivered to Derek a month later and he pinned the picture up over his bed. The Iraqi censor could apparently see nothing seditious about a drawing of two guinea-pigs, though the letters may well have been allowed through only as emotional ploy to try and break Derek's resolve.

I felt very sorry for Craig because his first attempt at writing had to be torn up. He had already written his letter and I asked him if he had included any reference to my mother being ill, which might have lowered Derek's morale, or had mentioned things that could have been dangerous for Derek when read by the Iraqi censor. Craig's face fell; it was obvious that the letter was full of such banned subjects, and he tore the already sealed envelope in half.

Derek and I were writing to each other every day. The majority of his letters reached me; I received more than ninety throughout the time we were parted. Derek's mailbag was not so full because he received only twenty of my letters. He was comparatively fortunate, however: some hostages received nothing the whole time they were away. It became a common thing for grown men to weep like babies – some because they had received a letter from home and some because they had not.

The previous weekend had been a real red-letter time for both of us. Derek received the shirts and trousers I had posted to him from the Mansour Melia Hotel two weeks earlier, while four of his letters to me arrived on the same morning. In one of them, he managed to reveal that he had been moved to a new installation, but it was not until after his return that I learned of the cruel way this was done. Whenever he was due to be transferred – and this happened several times – the guards would arrive at his room without warning in the early hours, kick the door open and tell him that he had to leave immediately. He would then be taken out into the night not knowing whether he was actually being taken to another installation or whether he was about to be put before a firing squad.

His four letters also said that, despite the fact he was missing us, he believed we had made the right decision and I must not question it for a moment. In addition he noted, 'There is some kind of bond between us all here – no matter what our different nationalities – because we are all hostages together. It really hurts being cut off from the world. There is so much time in which to think, and I am getting to know my strengths and weaknesses which is something I have never done before.'

One of his letters even gave me a rare laugh. He mentioned that a man newly arrived at his installation from Kuwait had seen us landing at Heathrow on television and had told Derek how Senator Jackson had carried a little boy called Stuart off the plane. Derek concluded his letter, 'Is that who I think it is?'

The BBC World Service was wonderful to us throughout this time because it had established its *Gulf Link* programme through which the hostages' families could send personal messages to their loved ones in captivity. Every night at 7.00 p.m., the men would tune into the right frequency on their short-wave radio sets and hear the latest news from home. It was far more reliable than the post because the censor could not intercept it, and it also became their life-line to sanity. During a time when they were bombarded for many hours every day with the lies of Iraqi propaganda, it was the single voice of freedom and truth on which they knew they could rely.

I tried several times to record a message for Derek, but on every occasion I broke down completely. In the end, I had to write out my message and one of the World Service girls read it out for me. Derek did hear one voice he recognized, however, because Jude recorded something for him.

Sunday 30 September

The end of our first month back home and my spirits hit rock bottom once more. For by now I had expected Derek would be reunited with us or that, at the very least, we should have received some indication of when he might be returning. Instead, we had heard nothing and the world was accelerating inevitably towards war and taking with it everything for which we had worked together.

I was so low that Judy came round and dragged me and the children off to the park with her. It was very thoughtful of her, because since our earliest times together Derek and I had always enjoyed strolling in the local park and feeding the ducks. Now she and I threw nearly half a bakery to our feathered friends until we were covered with crumbs, while Stuart and his cousin Grant quickly got bored and ran off to explore.

Judy even sent a letter to Derek to tell him all about our little outing and explained that crumbs were getting everywhere. Being able to share it with him made him seem closer somehow. As she wrote, I discovered that all the messages she had sent him had included details of Mum's illness. My self-imposed censorship had obviously been in vain!

Judy's letter, which Derek still keeps among all the communications that reached him while he was in Iraq, also revealed how Craig was continuing to be an adult. She told Derek, 'Glen has her good and bad days, but Craig has really been good to her and is standing in for you until you return.'

A couple of days earlier, the boys had written to Derek again. Stuart drew him a picture of a jumbo jet on which he could fly back to Britain and wrote underneath, 'Dad, I love you'. Aircraft seemed to be on Stuart's mind a lot probably because he realized Derek would have to catch one to get back to us. I was walking along a street in Worcester with him one day when he suddenly picked up the receiver in a public telephone kiosk and started chattering away.

'Who are you talking to?' I asked him.

'I'm talking to Daddy,' he replied. 'Oh look, he's hung up now. He's up in the aeroplane.'

These little fantasies of Stuart's gradually became part of his life because they helped him cope with grim reality. He once told his teacher that he was being picked up from school by his grandfather, yet both his grandfathers have been dead for several years. He has always wanted a granddad, and just at that moment he needed a man in his life.

Stuart was becoming something of a regular letter-writer around this time because he also sent one to Saddam Hussein asking him to free all the daddies he was holding. We thought it might help to melt the tyrant's stone heart and it certainly made Stuart feel better. In all honesty, however, Stuart found a letter of any length rather difficult to cope with, and so the historic note was written for him by Craig, who held the pen in his left hand so that the writing looked more childlike.

With each day hanging more heavily on my hands, I decided that it was time I went out and got myself a job. Not only would it help me to take my mind off things, but also I needed the money because of Derek's continuing absence. I applied for a post in the telephone room of a local mail-order company, was given an aptitude test and then offered an interview. I heard a couple of weeks later that they were prepared to take me on and it was a godsend. They are very pleasant people and have been extremely good to me at a time when I have really needed every bit of support I could get.

Towards the end of the month, I wrote to Mrs Thatcher gently asking for a change in government policy and suggesting that the hostages might be saved if she took a softer line with the Iraqis over them. The reply that came back from her private secretary was very courteous, but there was no doubting its message – my ideas did not find favour with the Iron Lady. My first positive attempt to win Derek's release had failed.

Tuesday 2 October

A new month was under way, but it made little difference to the state of aching loneliness and fear in which I found myself. The main event of the first week was that Mum's health improved sufficiently for her to be released from hospital, and we were soon settling her back into her home where we had taken up lodging. Naturally this entailed a lot of extra work and worry, but it was actually good for me because it gave me something positive to do.

It was probably just as well that I did not discover until much later that Derek and the other hostages were really up against it throughout this period. Whenever the international news turned bad for the Iraqis, the mood of the Iraqi captors changed with it and they would take their frustrations out on the prisoners. October was an appalling month for them because the trade sanctions were beginning to cripple the Iraqi economy, the main build-up of Allied forces in Saudi Arabia began in real earnest and the contemptuous international outpourings led by Mrs Thatcher and President George Bush continued unabated.

To a regime that would not normally tolerate the slightest hint of criticism, this was more than flesh and blood could stand, and their exasperation was made worse a little later in the month when twenty-two Palestinians were shot dead in Jerusalem by the Israeli police. As a result, all medical cover was withdrawn from the hostages for more than a week and the food deteriorated so much that one man, an American called Alan, took a stand against the harsh treatment and went on hunger strike. He did not eat for five days and was responsible for the Iraqis' introducing fruit back on to the menu for a day.

By now, Steve and Derek had been parted, and Steve understandably took his short-wave radio set with him. As they had nothing on which to listen to the World Service's *Gulf Link*, the hostages had the brass neck to complain to their captors and were astonished when the guards supplied them with a replacement set.

A new face by the name of George now arrived on the scene. He had almost escaped from his previous installation by unscrewing the window and bars of his room with a Swiss Army penknife, putting on an Arab dish-dash he had smuggled into captivity with him and making a run for it. Unfortunately, he was quickly recaptured and was so roughly treated by the guards that he was sent to the Mansour Melia to recuperate for a few days. While he was there, he met the singer Cat Stevens who had made his first abortive journey to Baghdad to try and win the release of some of the hostages.

George eventually arrived at Derek's installation with a cutting from the *Daily Telegraph* of Debbie Hayes's wedding, which we had seen on television while still in captivity, and a fund of anti-Iraqi jokes which were a real boost to morale.

Question: How do you get fifty Iraqis in a telephone box? Answer: Tell them it belongs to somebody else.

Question: What is yellow and looks good on Saddam Hussein? Answer: A JCB.

Another new arrival was a Scot called Alec who refused to

shake hands with the guards because, he told them, he did not do that sort of things with liars.

Not to be outdone, Derek decided to stop the Iraqis from just bursting into his room by hanging on the door a sign that said, in English, 'People in civilized countries knock on the door before entering a room.' A short while later, there was a knock at the door and an interpreter, who had been one of the worst offenders, popped his head in to tell Derek that he had read the sign and had translated it into Arabic for his colleagues.

Sunday 7 October

Today I made my second positive attempt to bring about Derek's release. The former Prime Minister Ted Heath was talking about intervening personally in the hostage crisis by going to Iraq and trying to fetch home some of the sick detainees, so I wrote to him and explained Derek's circumstances.

Most people do not know that by this time, Derek's health was giving everybody quite a lot of cause for concern. I never mentioned it publicly during the emergency because I did not want it thought that I was playing to the gallery for sympathy, but he had been suffering from a skin allergy and an eye complaint for some time, and they had both been getting worse throughout his period of detention. He was also losing weight at an alarming rate and was now in quite a serious condition, so although it was more than I dared hope, I thought there might be a chance of his being included in any party that Mr Heath was able to bring out with him. Mr Heath evidently thought so too because he replied to my letter and promised he would do his utmost to take up Derek's case. He also undertook to act as an unofficial postman by agreeing to deliver a letter to Derek for me.

Mr Heath was heavily criticized by many sectors of public opinion for the stance he took on this issue; but those of us with a husband or father in detention were solidly behind him. At a time when we felt abandoned and ignored by the Government, he was prepared to face up to personal risk abroad and ridicule at home because he saw a possibility of rescuing hostages with honour and keeping open the lines of communication with Saddam Hussein. He was just about our only hope and we turned to him because there was nobody else to help us. We clung to every straw that was floating in the wind and there were few other straws available.

Mr Heath was due to leave for Iraq five days later and I could hardly contain my excitement as the moment for his departure drew nearer. Yet again, however, my hopes were dashed to pieces because his trip was postponed at the last minute, and I crawled miserably back into my protective shell of merely existing from one day to the next.

In common with the families of the other hostages, I was always looking for the slightest crumb of comfort. Whenever I tuned in to the news, I would be cheered by the smallest hint of optimism and think it was the first sign of light at the end of the tunnel, but on every occasion I was left nursing a bruised and bitter disappointment.

Only the day before I wrote to Mr Heath, we had been very hopeful about the outcome of a visit to Iraq by the Soviet special envoy, Yevgeny Primakov. This was just about the only thing we had in common with the Iraqis: they were also apparently very hopeful that he would wave a magic wand and bring an end to the emergency; but his visit ended in the same old stalemate.

One piece of good news was that the job with the mail-order company was working out well. It was hard work, but it brought some much-needed money into the house and meant that, for four blessed hours every day, I was too busy to waste time just uselessly fretting.

In Iraq, the object of all my worry was being examined by an eye specialist who, by coincidence, had worked in Derek's home town of Huddersfield for eight years. To enhance Derek's chances of being repatriated, this kind and brave man jeopardized his own safety by reporting that he could not treat the condition himself, though even this did not mean the patient would necessarily end up on the sick list. The reason was that Derek was accompanied to the medical examination by one of the ordinary guards as well as a member of the secret police, and they had to make separate official reports on what the doctor had said. The two reports were then compared at the headquarters of the presidential police, who would look deliberately for inconsistencies between them and if there were any would want to know the reason why.

Throughout the examination, Derek and the doctor chatted together about the way the trade embargo had affected even the post from England and may have contributed to the hostages' shortage of letters. The doctor complained that he usually bought the *Lancet* on subscription, but had recently received only one communication from the publishing company – the bill for the copies of the magazine that had not reached him.

At least one person had something to smile about, however, because on the day I wrote to Mr Heath, Kim became the first hostage in Derek's installation to receive a letter from Britain. After reading it, he lodged it in his hat and walked round displaying it as a reminder that the detainees had not been forgotten by everyone.

Thursday 18 October

At last, we moved into our own house and shut our front door on the uncertainty and danger of the outside world. The tenant's lease had expired the day before and, although we had been told that it would have been possible for her to vacate it earlier, it had suited us well enough for her to remain there because it had meant that we could look after Mum's house while she was in hospital.

Derek and I had bought our house just before we first went to Kuwait and we had intended that it should be an investment while we were doing our globe-trotting. It was just as well we had because that nest-egg now became the only roof we could have over our heads if we were not to be forever relying on the kindness of friends and relatives. In addition, we had never lived in it and therefore it did not hold any memories for me of Derek. I could live there peaceably without forever imagining him coming downstairs, standing in the kitchen to make a cup of coffee or walking round the garden.

Craig particularly was much happier after we moved in. By this time he had settled down at his new school and had made a number of friends, several of whom lived in and around the immediate area of our home. This meant that he could just nip out of doors and stroll round to a friend's house without my having to get out the car and run him there as I had had to up until now, and it increased his confidence and feeling of independence. In addition, our house is just down the road from Judy and Phil's, and this also helped us all to settle.

I gained from the move because the extra work it entailed gave me another outlet for my restless energy and provided me with something else to keep me occupied. It seemed easier to ignore the danger in which Derek was living and to assume that he would after all be coming back, and to set about the task of making our home as pleasant and comfortable as possible for his return.

It is useful to have a man about when you are moving house, and once again Craig did his best to substitute for his absent father. He changed lightbulbs and plugs, and did all sorts of small domestic jobs that he had never tackled before. I decided to cheer us up a bit and put our own stamp on the house by buying a new central light for the dining area, and it was not until we were driving home that I remembered we had no one who knew how to fit it.

The following day, I got home to find that Craig had taken apart the rose in the middle of the ceiling and was doing his best to put in our new purchase. In the end it beat him, because it is more complicated than a plug and is something that is rarely tackled by amateurs, even grown men. The job was finally completed for me by the husband of a friend of mine, and Craig helped him and learned how to do it properly.

From a local DIY store we bought several new pieces of furniture you had to assemble yourself, and my cousin Beryl and her husband, Alan, were invaluable in helping us to get things straight. Alan assembled the furniture for us, but there were a couple of items he did not have to touch. Again I got home and found that Craig had forestalled everybody and was standing proudly behind his new desk, which he had put together himself in his bedroom. Once more, my elder son had proved that he was truly a man and my heart swelled with admiration for him.

After we had settled in, news came through that the wife of one hostage had travelled to Iraq on her own initiative to try and win her husband's freedom. Gilly's trip ended in failure because she could not get a meeting with any Iraqi official of any importance, but her action stirred the first feeling that maybe we could do something ourselves to bring our husbands home. We had acted together during our time in detention and it had worked, so why should it not now?

I was still pinning my hopes as far as Derek was concerned on Ted Heath's visit which had been rescheduled for the following Tuesday. Yet I was by no means convinced that my caution was right and kept changing my mind about whether to apply for a visa so I could return to Baghdad. One day I would be determined to make the journey, but by the next day I would have allowed my anxious relatives to talk me out of it.

The newspapers did not help my state of uncertainty, either, because every time Gilly or one of the other wives took some sort of private action, reporters would ring me up and ask me what I was going to do and my reasons for my decision. I have no idea how some of them got the telephone number because it was supposed to be ex-directory. Thinking logically about it all now, I believe that only one thing stopped me from going. I feared that if I were reunited with Derek but then failed to bring him home with me, I would not be able to cope with being parted from him for a second time.

Tuesday 23 October

Ted Heath arrived in Baghdad and within a very short time came the announcement that he had been successful in winning the release of thirty-three sick British hostages. I hoped so much that Derek would be among them, and my spirits sank to their lowest ebb yet when I discovered that he was not. Apparently, the 'sick list' had been growing daily as one by one the hostages became ill and weak because of the conditions in which they were living, and there were over 200 names on it by the time Mr Heath got there. The Iraqis were prepared to let him take only the most serious cases back to Britain, and I had to content myself with the thought that at least Derek did not fall into this category.

Once more, I had to try and shrug aside the burden of bitter disappointment and bend myself to the task of living without Derek, but each time this type of thing happened, the going became steeper and tougher. Something that made my heartache even worse was an incident involving a member of the press which was the most disgraceful single act that anyone from the media perpetrated against me. It concerned a suggestion from Richard Branson's Virgin Airways that it might fly out to Iraq with the relatives of hostages who were freed by Mr Heath so that the families could be reunited at Baghdad Airport.

I was sitting at home in the evening waiting to hear any news of Mr Heath's visit when the telephone rang and set my pent-up nerves jangling. Thinking that this was the call for which I had been waiting, I dived hurriedly for the receiver, but was disappointed to find that it was only a woman reporter claiming to be from a very popular daily newspaper. She told me that Derek was on a list of sick hostages that the Foreign Office was believed to have compiled, and she asked if I intended taking up the offer from Virgin Airways. When I said I was not sure, she asked if her newspaper could use our seats instead.

I could not believe that anybody could be so callous just to try and get an exclusive story, and I was absolutely furious with her. After I had shouted that she certainly could not have my seats, I slammed the receiver down and burst into tears. I was absolutely devastated, and, when I had pulled myself together, I telephoned the Foreign Office to complain. The Foreign Office was very sympathetic but explained it sadly could do nothing to censure the newspaper.

Although Derek always displayed a brave front and tried never to say anything to worry me, he was also sinking lower. He was desperately unhappy that no mail was getting through to him, and I seethed with impotent fury at the thought that all my letters of encouragement to him were gathering dust in the corner of some Iraqi sorting office.

Derek's continued absence was made harder for me by the fact that other hostages were going home. After holding a four-hour debate about whether all the French should be freed, the Iraqi Parliament voted in favour. The debate had seemed to be going badly for the French throughout and they had become very dispirited, but right at the end, the delegates were told that Saddam Hussein favoured their repatriation and they dutifully rubber-stamped his edict. The French got back to Paris a week later. Meanwhile fourteen seriously-ill Americans were also sent home.

The Friday after Mr Heath's success, I was watching the television news when, to my astonishment, I saw Pat and Steve being interviewed together in the comfort of their own home in South Shields. Steve had been among the thirty-three freed detainees. I was amazed because he had been in perfect health the last time we had seen him, but unknown to us he had suffered three heart attacks while in captivity. My mind and emotions were in a complete whirl as I looked at the screen. I was delighted for him and Pat, yet at the same time green with envy, and I felt more desolate than ever at that moment when I thought how such a happy reunion might have been mine.

Pat and I had remained in regular touch since our return, so I quickly telephoned her to congratulate them both. I also had an ulterior motive: I was dying to speak to someone who had seen Derek more recently than I had, and Steve kindly spent ages talking to me.

He gave me a lot of information and assured me that, although the situation was daily getting worse, the guards at Derek's installation were quite approachable and conditions there were not too bad. Throughout the month, the Iraqis had tried to persuade the men that it would be nice to send further video messages home to their families, but our husbands saw this as a cheap propaganda trick designed to cause further heartache as well as put pressure on the British Government, and they refused to have anything to do with it. I told Steve that I was thinking of going out to Baghdad, and he left me in no doubt at all that this was the last thing Derek would want.

At almost the very moment I was speaking to Steve, Derek was hearing some news that made his heart drop like a stone. For a change he had tuned into Dubai Radio, and he heard an announcement that the hostages would definitely be 'abused' in the event of an attack on Iraq. As reports had also been coming in recently that Kuwaiti citizens had been subjected to such tortures as having their fingers drilled and their eyes gouged out with spoons, his imagination raced overtime with thoughts of what this latest information might mean.

He quickly tuned in to the World Service and then to Voice of America, which was broadcast by the United States, and found the item was not being carried on either, but he still felt that there might be some substance in it. He told Alec about it and, after some discussion, they decided to keep the hideous knowledge to themselves so as to avoid the risk of lowering morale.

Amazingly, Derek had managed to retain some of his humour, and hardly a day went past when he did not ask the guards for a plane ticket to London, a suitcase for him to travel with and a plate of chips to keep him going in the meantime. Even the guards started entering into the joke and, to Derek's surprise, they granted one of the requests three days after my conversation with Steve. Plates of steak and chips appeared for dinner and the men tucked into them voraciously.

Derek would actually sooner have had the plane ticket, but he did not say so. In any case, he had his own secret plan for winning his freedom. He sent a letter to BBC Television's *Jim'll Fix It* asking if Jimmy Savile could reunite him with his family.

Wednesday 31 October

While a major drama was being played out on the international stage, a rather more important event was happening in Stuart's world back in Worcester. I had to go along to my first parents' afternoon at his school to hear a progress report about him. It was a lonely business for me: it highlighted the loss caused by Derek's detention. I looked round at all the other parents and, when I saw that many of them were there as couples, it was all I could do to stop myself breaking down. This was a vital day in Stuart's life, and his father had missed it.

Stuart's teacher told me that he was settling down and that under the circumstances he was doing remarkably well. She was a little worried about his tendency to romanticize and there had been a few problems in his playground relationships. Yet she did not expect him to be entirely problem-free after the experiences he had been through, and I could also take comfort from the fact that he was developing a deep friendship with his cousin Grant. All things being considered, I was pretty pleased with the headway he was making.

If only things had looked as promising on Derek's horizon. The Iraqis were still pursuing their policy of making everyone feel insecure and, to this end, were continually moving people about from one installation to another. A favourite trick was to select an installation where there were, for example, two Japanese, and move one of them to another site so there would be one man left by himself unable even to speak the language of his fellow prisoners. Derek has since spoken of how all the hostages managed to band together into a truly international community and of how he developed friendships of convenience with men who could not understand what he was saying and who could not make themselves understood to him.

Derek himself was moved in the early hours one night as October ended – and in the meanest and most frightening manner possible. The door of his room was suddenly opened and he was taken away to be driven to another installation. This one was adjoining a foundry, and sleep became virtually impossible here because of the roar of the machines surrounding him.

From my point of view, another month was drawing to its close and the prospect of Derek's being freed seemed further away than when it had begun. As a fine, beautiful English autumn gradually died and faded into the dark and wet of winter, my morale started to die with it. The words of encouragement I had heard back in Baghdad from that Iraqi guard, who had assured us our husbands would be joining us soon, now returned in my mind to haunt and mock me.

Fate and the Iraqis still had one more trick up their sleeves. We hoped and hoped that the men would be home for Christmas, but those loathsome *Guest News* television programmes suggested that the wives might like to fly to Baghdad for a seasonal reunion. At a stroke, our tormentors again stirred up all the terrible regrets and indecision caused by our original parting exactly a month earlier. It was probably the cruellest thing that Saddam Hussein ever did to us, and in his black, evil, twisted heart he must have known it.

Saturday 3 November
A minor miracle happened today, but we did not feel the benefit of it. The Iraqis suddenly allowed the hostages to telephone their families although there were stringent conditions. The men had to try and persuade their wives to join them in Baghdad for Christmas and there were guards and interpreters breathing down their necks the whole time to make sure they obeyed orders.

Derek tried to ring me at my mum's house because he thought we were still living there, and he did not even know his own home telephone number because he had never lived at our home. In any case, Mum was out at the time and he went back to his room nearly in tears. His disappointment was made worse by the fact that almost everybody else had managed to get through, and they sat up half the night talking about their calls which had lasted exactly five minutes before being cut off in mid-sentence.

Not all the hostages' news was good and, in one case, it was tragic. An American called Keith discovered that his wife had been murdered six weeks earlier near the farm they owned in Thailand. He found out nearly three weeks later through the Red Cross that the American authorities had telexed Baghdad immediately after her death, but the Iraqis had deliberately withheld the knowledge from him. The excuse they used was that he already had enough to worry about.

At the time Derek was trying to telephone us, we were at a Guy Fawkes bonfire party at the company where Judy works. It was the first time that Stuart had been to such an event or seen fireworks, and I was a little worried that the bangs and flashes might bring back to him horrors about the war in Kuwait. He was certainly mesmerized by the fireworks but that was as far as it went and I think the fact that Grant was not in the least concerned helped Stuart to take it all in his stride.

Even without the blow of not getting through to us on the phone, the month had started badly for Derek. News filtered through to him of a bereavement involving some friends we had known in Kuwait. The family's two student sons were being repatriated and were being driven to the airport to catch their plane when they were involved in a car crash. One of them was killed and the other was seriously injured. For a time we almost forgot our own worries and our hearts really went out to these people because we felt their loss.

The Iraqis began increasing the pressure on the hostages to persuade their wives to join them for Christmas and the men were always talking about it. On 2 November they had been very upset by a terrible programme on the World Service about how some of the wives were coping. It became obvious that the ordeal was proving difficult for the women because they started crying while being interviewed, and Derek and the other men nearly cracked up at the thought that their own wives might be in the same state.

The timing of the programme could not have been better for the Iraqis, but even this did not make our men waver in their determination that they would try everything to stop us from flying back to them. It was ironic that the World Service, which had helped us so much and had provided us with a link to the hostages when we most needed it, should now play straight into the enemy's hands and aid the Iraqis' emotional blackmail of the hostages.

The day after his first abortive telephone call, Derek managed to get through to his mother in Huddersfield and she gave him our number. He telephoned us straight away and I picked up the receiver in our living room and heard the wonderful sound of his voice on the other end. It was a sound I had feared I might never hear; I burst into tears and he could get very little sense out of me. I did manage to tell him that I had received all the letters he had written up to 4 October, and that made him feel a bit better.

The men had agreed that when speaking to us of the proposed Christmas trip which the Iraqis wanted so much, they would use some sort of slang code to try and discourage us. Derek set about this task by saying he had already told his 'hosts' that I would not be able to go because both our mothers had medical problems.

'What problems?' I asked.

'You know – the way they've been so ill – it really is difficult for you,' he replied, and eventually I got the message.

Alec, the Scot, had a more forthright way of dealing with the problem. He told his wife that he would give her a 'Glaswegian kiss' if she went to see him, and the listening Iraqi censors mistook it for a term of endearment, not knowing it was Scottish slang for a head butt.

Stuart now grabbed the receiver from me and started spilling out all his news to Derek about the two guinea-pigs. 'Dad-we've-got-two-guinea-pigs-and-mine's-all-right-but-Craig's-has-died,' he gabbled without pausing to draw breath.

Craig was not too pleased because he thought it made him sound careless.

When the call was unexpectedly cut off, Derek returned to his room and found his first piece of mail, which the guards had left on his bed in his absence. It was not one of my letters but a 'Miss You' card I had sent him, and the sight of it so soon after he had spoken to us nearly ripped him apart. The Iraqi blackmail machine was working overtime.

Monday 5 November

The fragile patience of the hostages in Iraq and their families in England exploded with fury simultaneously. The cause of the furore was not Saddam Hussein, but the Conservative MP Sir John Stokes, who had chosen bonfire night to launch the most amazing, cowardly and unprovoked attack on us. Having heard various wives being interviewed by the media, he said we should keep a stiff upper lip and stop 'mewling and puking'.

His outpourings were roundly condemned by all shades of public opinion, but the damage had already been done. We felt we had been brave and strong above the call of duty at the time when it mattered, and we had every right to express our anguish and protest at the way we had been caught up in one of the cruellest examples of political manipulation in history.

The unwarranted criticism came at a particularly bad time for Derek who was feeling very low about missing Stuart's first bonfire night. He felt it was one of those golden moments that can be shared by a father and son only once in a lifetime, and they had both missed it. Derek had to make do with sitting in his room at the installation trying to imagine the smile of wonder on Stuart's face as he looked at the fireworks.

He was due for something of a surprise, though, because the Iraqis chose this day suddenly to kit all the men out with new suits. Derek and his friends half hoped that they had been supplied with the outfits in readiness for their return home, but the real reason was that they had recently been complaining about being cold after a change in the weather and their captors did not have any other warmer clothing to give them.

The suits were grey in colour and, despite the fact that they were double-breasted, were actually very smart. They even caused something of a laugh when Alec told everyone, 'We'll all be able to walk off the plane looking like the Blues Brothers.'

Life improved still further for the hostages at Derek's installation the following day because they were allowed to take exercise properly in the open air for the first time. They were turned loose into a little compound where they met with a second group of hostages who had been separated from them and put in another part of the same complex.

Derek was able to telephone us again later in the day, though I broke down in tears once more. He actually got more sense and information about what was happening at home by talking to Craig who reported that I was managing to cope. Our elder son had a real man-to-man chat with his father, and told him that he was hoping to get into the school football team and promised to look after me until Derek returned.

Stuart then went on the line, but he had had eight teeth out earlier and Derek could not understand what he was saying. Stuart did not think very much of his first visit to a British dentist.

Wednesday 7 November

At last I discovered what Derek really wanted to say to me without the restriction of the ever-watchful Iraqis. When the mail dropped on my doormat this morning, I found it included a letter from him which had escaped the censor. He had smuggled it out of detention with one of the homeward-bound French people who had posted it for him. The news in it was already two weeks old, but at least it helped me to build up a more accurate picture of what was happening to him.

Yet as I read it, I realized that parts of it were almost like a final goodbye, for Derek had accepted that the worst might happen to him. He was not scared of dying, but he was upset that he would in effect be losing us. He said he was glad he had met me, thanked me for all the good times we had had together and described me as a smashing mum who had given him two lovely boys.

'At least I have had a full life through meeting you and, without you, my life would have been empty because you are simply the best,' he concluded.

My eyes swam with tears as I read the letter sitting in my house at the end of a quiet, safe suburban cul-de-sac, and it was not just the terms of endearment that made me so upset. Derek had faced up to something that I had dared not admit even to myself. It was like hearing a condemned man pass his own death sentence.

Throughout this period, I had become increasingly shirty with anyone who dared to suggest that the hostages might not be saved, and a number of people had caught the furious lash of my tongue through making some innocent remark. One such person was a man who had recently visited us to remove some old furniture from our garage. He recognized me from my various appearances in the media, and he asked after Derek and began making polite conversation. I started talking about what I was planning to do when Derek came home, and he said, 'You think they will be coming back then?' The poor man barely knew what hit him.

Derek's note of realism galvanized me into action now. Just as I had written to Ted Heath to ask him to plead Derek's case during his visit to Baghdad, I wrote to everybody I could think of who might be able to help. I wrote to Mrs Thatcher, asking again for a change in her stance on the hostages, and throughout these dark weeks I sent off literally hundreds of other letters. I also became involved in the work of the hostage support groups and even agreed to the odd press photograph of Stuart in a desperate attempt to ensure that the hostages remained in the public eye.

Throughout all this, I continued to receive the support of family and friends, and particularly of Judy. I grew closer to my sister than probably I had ever been before, and she also became involved in the hostage work. Like myself, she developed friendships with the families of other hostages and an information network naturally established itself all over the country. All the families pooled the information they had received in their telephone calls and letters from abroad, and I was able to find out extra things about Derek by comparing my own discoveries with those of some of the other women.

Another thing that helped to save my sanity was my developing friendship with Sue who lived near me and whose husband, Nigel, was also a detainee. By giving strength to each other, we found extra reserves of strength for ourselves, and we talked more and more about the ever-present dilemma of whether or not to go out to Baghdad to try and fetch our husbands home.

Nigel took the same view as Derek – that we should stay safely in England – and the Foreign Office also advised that a trip to Iraq would be foolish. Increasingly, however, we were beginning to wonder if this was true, and hardly a day would go by without us talking about it on the telephone. One day Sue would ring me up and say she was definitely going, and then next day she would ring again to say she had changed her mind. Later the same week, I would be doing the same to her, and we kept each other in a dither of indecision. We were like two novice bathers who kept teetering on the brink of diving into the deep end without actually doing so. My confused state was not helped by the fact that one member of the family even said my departure for Baghdad would be selfish and could rob Stuart and Craig of both parents instead of just one. I also felt Sue might have more inside information than me as she received calls from Nigel every day, since the guards at his installation were far more relaxed than those at Derek's. It seemed that the further away our men were from Baghdad, the better things were for them.

The television and radio news continued to be a drug to which I was addicted and I used to spend the whole evening channel-hopping to catch every available bulletin. I seized on the slightest optimistic sign in the Middle East and made of it a crumb of comfort which often did not exist. At Mum's house we had had to rely on the normal scheduled television programmes, but now we were in a home of our own we had a set with the Teletext facility, and I was forever clicking the remote control to tune in to it. I do not think the poor boys watched one of their programmes the whole way through without me interrupting them.

Meanwhile in Iraq, Derek was up to his ears in mail. He received seventeen of my letters in a single batch and spent all day and half the night reading them and almost crying over them. He also got the chance to smuggle another letter out to me with a German hostage called Pete who was released and took the precious note with him.

Two days later, Derek received another seven letters, including three that Judy had written to him. They were the last to be delivered and at the same time he lost his telephone link with us. The World Service reported that the Americans were sending more troops to Saudi Arabia and the Iraqis retaliated by suspending all the hostages' calls until further notice.

Thursday 15 November

This evening, I had to endure again the misery and utter loneliness of going to a parents' evening by myself – this time at Craig's school. As usual, everybody was extremely kind to me and went out of their way to try and put me at my ease, but ridiculously this made me feel worse. I could sense the waves of pity reaching out to me. The news of Craig's progress was mixed and, no matter how the teachers tried to dress it up, there were problems which had to be overcome. Nobody needed to tell me what a fine young man Craig was becoming – I had seen ample evidence of that myself over the past three and a half months. The difficulties lay with his schoolwork which was obviously suffering because of worry over his father. We could all only hope that Derek would be back with us soon and Craig's problems would right themselves. Some hope, I told myself bitterly.

Having started badly, November was steadily deteriorating and, when I look back at it now from the safe refuge of my happy, rebuilt life, I see that it was the worst month of the whole wretched emergency. Winter was closing in with its short dark days and miserable weather, and it seemed to mirror the decline in my luck and my spirits. The situation in the Gulf was getting daily more unstable and dangerous, and Derek's absence, which I had once naïvely imagined would be measured in terms of weeks, was beginning to look permanent. Just like the parents' evenings and bonfire night, everything in which I became involved seemed merely to underline the fact that he was not there to share it with me.

The previous weekend, I had taken the boys up to see their grandma in Huddersfield for the first time since our repatriation. We had been going to see Derek's mother and visit his old haunts up there for so many years as a couple, and of course it was just not the same doing it without him. The trip was not helped by the fact that it took place during the Remembrance Day weekend which is never a light-hearted festival.

Had I but known it, Derek was at that time taking part in one of the strangest ever Remembrance Day parades. The hostages organized it themselves, and at 11.00 a.m. they all stood stiffly to attention to remember the dead of two world wars. What made this occasion so unusual was the fact that all nationalities took part and that Britons and Germans stood side by side to pay homage to the men who died while their two countries had been fighting each other. The Iraqi guards must have wondered what the heck was going on.

One thing that made life a bit more comfortable for the British hostages was the arrival of the first 'comfort packs' from our Embassy in Baghdad. Several of the other nationalities had received little luxuries from their governments from quite early on, and, although we could not possibly prove it, we wondered if the late arrival of the British supplies had been caused by the Iraqis' deliberately withholding them to vent their spleen on our men in retaliation for Mrs Thatcher's firm line over the hostage crisis. Certainly, the Embassy had been trying to get them delivered for ages.

Six British 'comfort packs' now arrived at Derek's installation and, to his great delight, one of them contained my letter which Ted Heath had taken out to Iraq with him more than three weeks earlier. The men found the delivery included a number of bottles of whisky for 'medicinal' purposes and some cans of beer. There were also some packets of dry soup which, with the addition of potatoes supplied by the Iraqis, were made into a gigantic, comparatively nourishing stew. The bottles of whisky were shared round among the hostages, and all the men had a party. From that day onwards, the food supplied by the guards gradually began to improve.

Derek was now continually complaining to the guards about his worsening health and they said he must write personally to Saddam Hussein. Derek refused to do so, but his two sons wrote instead. Stuart, aided and abetted by Craig's left hand, sent the tyrant another letter asking him to release all the daddies.

Three days after Craig's parents' evening, it was announced on Iraqi television that the foreign 'guests' could be released in a slow trickle between Christmas Day and 14 March. Naturally, there was a proviso – the repatriation programme would halt immediately in the event of an attack by the Allied task force.

Although in some ways a hopeful development, this was also a double blow to our hopes for the men's safe return as it not only spread their detention a long way into the new year, which was something we had not contemplated before, but also insisted on conditions that would enable Iraq to keep Kuwait. The whole thing was yet another cruel Iraqi charade which had been suggested for just one purpose. Saddam Hussein knew that the Western powers would have to reject it and he hoped the hostages' families would become outraged and put pressure on our governments.

Thursday 22 November

This was the day when a historic era in British and world politics came sadly to an end. Mrs Thatcher announced that she was stepping down as Prime Minister, and she went to Buckingham Palace the following Wednesday to tender her resignation to the Queen. After the way I had disagreed with her policy about the hostages and had written to her asking in vain for a change in her stance, it might be supposed that I was glad to see her go. Yet nothing could have been further from the truth for I admired what she had achieved and the way she had taken a strong positive line on the Gulf question, even though I did not necessarily agree with it.

In any case, my views about Mrs Thatcher and how her policies affected us were beginning to change. The reason was that Derek's uncensored letters made it plain that many of the hostages solidly supported her views because they realized how much in awe of her the Iraqis were. The guards used to ask whether she was in charge of Britain's armed services and whether she had any sway with the Queen, and were plainly amazed that the answer was yes. Because they were so accustomed to the ways of a male-dominated society, they could not understand how a woman could wield such power.

As I have said earlier, we had felt ignored and conveniently forgotten by British officialdom when our only concern was to protect the hostages by keeping the Gulf situation as stable as possible. I now freely admit that my attitude was probably wrong and that Mrs Thatcher's refusal even to discuss the hostages – never mind take a soft line over them – may very well have led to their being saved. At a time when I needed fighting spirit and backbone, her example gave them to me and I shall always be grateful to her.

There cannot be many people who have met both Mrs Thatcher and Saddam Hussein, and as I have done so, I would like to take this opportunity to compare them. The Iraqi President certainly had an aura of importance and power, but he achieved this only by a reign of terror and he was a pale shadow of Britain's first woman premier.

Derek and I met Mrs Thatcher together the following March when Stuart received a *Daily Star* award from her. Even though it was four months after her resignation, she still dominated the crowded occasion by the sheer force of her presence and positively glowed with power. To have met her earlier, while she was still at the pinnacle of her political career, would obviously have been a formidable experience.

Another reason the hostages supported her was that they felt an Allied air raid might give them a chance of escape. Derek and his friends had even worked out what they would do if they managed to get out of their installation in the confusion. As they had no compass to guide them, they planned to get to the nearest railway line or river and just follow it at night; they realized that, no matter what direction it went in, it would eventually lead to one of Iraq's borders with Jordan, Iran, Syria or Turkey. Whenever Derek was taken from the installation to be examined by a doctor at the nearby hospital, he always took the opportunity to observe the lie of the land in the immediate area.

During this week of Mrs Thatcher's resignation, a lot was happening in Derek's world. Two days earlier, the Dutch and the remaining Germans had been freed, and the very day before, Kim, who suffered heart trouble, was given just thirty minutes' notice before he was repatriated on humanitarian grounds. He and Derek had become the firmest of friends, and Kim was only too pleased to smuggle out another uncensored letter for me.

November 22 was American Thanksgiving Day, and the Iraqis had for several days been trying to put pressure on the families of United States hostages to join their men for the great occasion. They got short shrift, however, from Keith whose wife had been murdered in Thailand. He told them not to make any special arrangements for his relatives because his son would soon be flying over Iraq anyhow – as the pilot of a B52 bomber!

Kim arrived home only a couple of days later and posted Derek's letter to me straight away. Once more, I sat in my lounge weeping as Derek opened his heart to me and told me how much he loved me and the boys. Like me, he feared that if I flew out to Baghdad to try and bring him home but failed, the pain of parting again would be unendurable.

He added, 'I love you and the boys far too much to take the chance and it has brought home to me how much in love I really am. If love can hurt as much as the partings we have already experienced, it just shows what power love has. The sight of you and the boys so broken-hearted at our last parting is something I never want to see again.'

As soon as I could compose myself, I telephoned Kim who spent some time answering my anxious questions about the deteriorating state of Derek's health. Kim said that he was becoming very concerned about him, and he assured me he would now start fighting to bring about Derek's repatriation as a matter of urgency. Derek's weight had apparently fallen below eleven stone for the first time, which does not leave much surplus flesh on a man well over six feet tall. Even the Iraqis were becoming worried and had let Derek contact the British Embassy in Baghdad to ask for his medical records.

In desperation, I started making regular telephone calls to the Foreign Office and tried to insist that they took up Derek's case. Although the individual civil servants who dealt with my enquiries did their utmost to cut through the red tape, the Foreign Office as a whole would never give me a straight answer or firm commitment, and I ended up seething with frustration, anger and a terrible feeling of dread.

My emotional turmoil was total on 24 November when it was announced that about a dozen British women had travelled to Iraq and had been rewarded with their husbands' freedom. Naturally, I was delighted for them, but Sue and I were left with the growing conviction that we were doing the wrong thing by not travelling to Baghdad. The fact that both our husbands were against the idea had been a major factor in persuading us to stay in England, but we were fast reaching the stage where even that was not enough to stop us. If the worst happened and the men eventually died, we would at least feel that we had tried everything possible to bring them home.

Because all European and American airlines had by now stopped flying to Iraq, it was no easy matter to get there. The only way was to fly to Jordan and then do the last leg of the journey by land or air. This meant having to obtain visas for both Iraq and Jordan, but even this was not going to put us off any longer and I sent off for the necessary visa application forms for both of us.

Sunday 25 November

Craig went away to Wales with a party from his school for an adventure week, and his departure cast a new gloom and despondency over our home. We went to see him off, and Stuart burst into tears as the coach pulled out of the school drive. He continued weeping as if his heart would break throughout the journey back to our house and he was moody and upset for the rest of the day.

At last the scales fell from my eyes and I understood why he was so distraught. Stuart had not made many coach journeys during his short life, and the last one had led to the heartbreak of parting from his father. My younger son was terrified that he would never see his brother again, and when he had calmed down he confirmed my suspicions. He kept asking for assurances that Craig would be coming back and would not have to stay away like Daddy.

It was all I could do to stop bursting into tears of anger and misery myself when he first asked me. To think that a five-year-old boy could not innocently see his elder brother off on a school trip without feeling such crippling insecurity. At that moment, I hated the tyrant of Baghdad for the hideous and insidious blight he had quite deliberately put on all our lives. The next seven days were to be miserable for me as well because I had come to rely on Craig so much as my man about the house. Yet, at the same time, I felt the most enormous admiration for him because he had become the first member of the family to be brave enough to make a long trip away from the safety of our home.

I was decorating the boys' bedrooms later that day when the telephone rang and I heard the blessed sound of Derek's voice on the other end. Neither of us could say what we really wanted to because of the listening Iraqis, but it was better than nothing. I had not heard from Derek recently because, following the announcement that Britain was to send extra troops to the Gulf, all telephone calls (and cigarettes) had immediately been withdrawn from the hostages. I explained to Derek that I was decorating, and with that touch of humour which helped to keep him sane throughout those dark days, he said he only wished he could be back at home so he could watch me.

During the month, I had become friendly with Sheila, the girlfriend of Mike who had been in detention with us in Iraq.

Upon my return, I had delivered a little personal message to Sheila for him because their home was near mine. They were not actually married, but had lived together for some years and had a small child.

Like Sue and me, Sheila was also toying with the idea of travelling to Baghdad to try and win Mike's freedom, but when she took the final decision to do so, she came up against a most unexpected and heartbreaking stumbling block. When she applied for a visa, it quickly became apparent that she was the only hostage's partner who was unwelcome in Iraq. The hypocritical explanation was that not only did she have no claim to Mike, but also under Islamic law she was committing a mortal sin by living with him.

Wednesday 28 November

By this stage of the month, the high streets of Britain were gearing up for Christmas. Council workmen had been erecting the usual coloured lights to make Worcester look festive during the weeks ahead, a number of Father Christmases were opening their grottoes for business in the city centre and shop windows were bursting with everything from tinsel to computer toys. The merrier the city looked, however, the more my misery deepened as I contemplated the end of Derek's third month without us in captivity. There was one last initiative on which I was pinning all my hopes for his safe return in time for Christmas.

Like a number of other politicians before him, the Labour MP Tony Benn landed in Baghdad today to plead for the release of further hostages. I had written to him some time earlier asking him to take up Derek's case and I waited to see whether he would succeed in freeing him.

Mr Benn had a meeting with Saddam Hussein who was by this time freeing hostages in small groups of two or three, and then went on to address a gathering of 300 hostages who had been brought specially from Kuwait. The detainees really thought they were going home, but as soon as the MP had finished speaking, they were taken back to their installations. They felt bitter and cheated, while all Mr Benn could do was return to Britain with a small group of people who had been working in Iraq and had already been promised they could leave.

Only one good thing happened to us on this day. An American woman had been to our housing estate back in Kuwait after we had been removed to Baghdad, and had picked up personal family photographs from a number of houses which had been scattered all over the road outside by the looting invaders. A handful of our photographs, which showed Craig and Stuart at a young age and were therefore irreplaceable, were somehow passed down fragile links of communication until they came into Derek's hands. They provided him with precious, happy memories at a time when he badly needed them, and today they form a valued part of our family album. We can never be grateful enough to the woman who took the trouble to salvage them and pass them on.

I now reconciled myself to the fact that Derek would not be home for the festivities, and a number of kind friends and relatives invited us to spend Christmas with them. After discussing the invitations, Craig and I agreed to turn them all down because we would not celebrate again until Derek was reunited with us. We planned just to exchange simple presents and spend the holiday alone at home.

In an attempt to keep the plight of the hostages in the public consciousness, I and four other women with relatives in the Gulf agreed to take part in a radio interview about our plans for Christmas. The whole thing became too much for us, we all started crying and the girl who was carrying out the interview joined us too.

Stuart was now well into rehearsals for his part in his first school Nativity play, and the local radio station went along to his school to talk to him. I wish I had realized what the news item would sound like by the time the editors had finished with it; as it was, when I heard it I completely broke down. Against a background of children's voices singing carols, I could hear Stuart asking Saddam Hussein to give him back his daddy for Christmas. I managed to get hold of a cassette of the recording and intended to include it in a Christmas parcel for Derek, but at the last moment I decided not to send it. If it had had that sort of effect on me, it might be enough to make Derek crack up altogether.

Throughout this period, the men in Baghdad had been put under the most enormous pressure to persuade us to fly out to join them for Christmas. Just as they had done with the American hostages at Thanksgiving time, the Iraqis were trying to persuade the British that they wanted a real seasonal knees-up complete with a Christmas tree. They had special plans for the Lockwood family because they particularly wanted me to go out there with Stuart. That would have been a real propaganda coup for them. The whole thing was designed yet again to make the hostages feel homesick and to encourage their families to stir up political trouble for the British Government.

For those of us dithering over the decision as to whether to try and bring our husbands out through personal intervention, it presented an added, cruel dilemma. The feeling of aching isolation experienced by the hostages and their families was never more acute than in those last few terrible weeks before Christmas.

I have tried many times to find the exact words with which to describe this feeling, but nothing I can say matches those of Brian Keenan, the Irish journalist who was held in Beirut for four years and four months. After his release on 30 August 1990 – two days before my own repatriation from Baghdad – he was quoted as saying, 'Hostage is a crucifying aloneness. It is a silent, screaming slide into the bowels of ultimate despair. Hostage is a man hanging by his fingernails over the edge of chaos, feeling his fingers slowly straightening.'

It is the perfect description of how Derek and I felt as the wretched month of November drew to a close.

Sunday 2 December

A 'Yellow Ribbon' day was being planned in London today to try and make sure the rest of Britain did not forget the plight of the hostages. Because of a breakdown in communications between the various Gulf groups, we had not heard about it until only three or four days previously, and it was Derek who told us about it from his prison in Iraq. He heard about it on the

World Service's *Gulf Link* and mentioned it to me during one of our telephone conversations. There were also to be prayer vigils all over Britain.

The day before the big event, we decided that we would hold a little ceremony of our own in Worcester. Judy and I, the children and a few other local people including Sue and Sheila went to the Cathedral at 8.30 a.m. With the permission of the Bishop of Worcester, we tied a yellow ribbon round the War Memorial and said a little prayer while the local press took photographs of us. The ceremony lasted only about thirty minutes, but the ribbon stayed there for months afterwards. This seemed so appropriate because we wanted the safe return not only of our hostages, but also of all the young servicemen who would shortly be fighting in the Gulf.

On the Sunday, Sheila, Sue, Stuart and I travelled down to London in Sheila's Ford Sierra with me driving. Craig had decided not to join us because he had just returned home from his trip to Wales and was worn out. We wondered exactly what would be waiting for us, but we were willing to try anything that might persuade the tyrant to free our men before yet another month passed. We got there in plenty of time for the start of the ceremony in Piccadilly Circus.

At 11.00 a.m., people began tying yellow ribbons round poles which had been specially erected for the occasion and then Glenys Kinnock, the wife of the leader of the Opposition, made a statement to Saddam Hussein calling on him to release the hostages in time for them to spend Christmas with their families. A number of the media people recognized Stuart and he was suddenly in great demand for photographs. He was pictured with Mrs Kinnock tying a yellow ribbon for his daddy, and the photograph was carried on television the same night and in many of the Sunday papers the following day. For once I did not mind the attention he received because I thought it might help achieve the thing we most wanted.

Next came the big event for which everyone, and particularly the television cameras, had been waiting. A huge tarpaulin cover was pulled aside and 1,400 yellow gas-filled balloons –

one for every British hostage still in Iraq – flew into the air in a huge cloud which darkened the sky for a few seconds. Stuart stared in disbelief as the balloons rose into the air and started drifting away. I had told him that they were flying to Iraq to remind Saddam Hussein that we wanted all the daddies back, but I think he may have got confused and imagined one of the balloons landing in Derek's lap.

As the balloons dispersed, we all felt much better for our big symbolic gesture. It did not matter that most of them would probably sink to earth again and burst on trees and bushes before they even reached the coast. For as they disappeared into the sky, they seemed to carry our prayers with them and to lift a huge burden off our shoulders. At last we had done something more positive than sit weeping alone at home. We had reduced our worries by sharing them and we were really pleased to have taken part in such an unusual spectacle.

Also in Piccadilly Circus were thirty-five exiled Kuwaitis and their supporters who had chosen the same day to march through London carrying 'Free Kuwait' placards. Many of the demonstrators saw Stuart and remembered him from his television appearances, and they all wanted to have their photographs taken with him.

Afterwards we started wandering through the city centre looking at the sights until we reached Trafalgar Square where the Kuwaitis' march was scheduled to end. Yet again, Stuart had taken the most unusual circumstances in his stride and a special little treat was now awaiting him. I stood proudly watching him as the pigeons swooped down from Nelson's Column and fluttered round him to be fed.

In Iraq, the British hostages were still being pressured by their hosts to celebrate Christmas in some way and the guards continually asked them whether they wanted a turkey dinner at their installations or in a hotel in the city. They became quite angry when the prisoners said that they wanted neither and indicated that if they could not return to their families in England, they would prefer not to celebrate the festive season at all.

Derek put into operation his own plans to try and help us celebrate the occasion, and he enlisted our elder son to help him. He wrote to Craig enclosing a letter authorizing the bank to transfer £100 from his account so that Craig could buy presents for Stuart and me on his behalf, and so that the two boys would have enough money to buy me a present from themselves.

Thursday 6 December

The news for which we and the whole Western world had been waiting broke today. On the 126th day of Derek's detention in Iraq, we heard that all the hostages were to be set free. It was announced shortly before lunch in Britain and around mid-afternoon in Baghdad – and the Brits being held at Derek's installation nearly missed it!

Derek was lying on his bed when he heard one of his friends whooping, cheering and running about. 'JJ' had been the only person bothering to tune into the radio when, out of the blue, Saddam Hussein issued a statement on Radio Baghdad that he had decided to let his 'guests' return home in time for Christmas. 'JJ' poked his head round Derek's door to tell him the glad tidings, but Derek did not believe him and rather sarcastically told him so. 'JJ' continued spreading the word round the installation, however, and, as more and more men started shouting and jumping for joy, Derek began to think that he was missing something and joined in the euphoria. Within half an hour, the news had been picked up by various monitoring agencies and was being beamed round the earth by the World Service.

Judy was the first member of our family to hear, and I was at work when she rang to tell me. The girls in my office stopped dead in their tracks when she got through to me. I think they could tell by my face that I had received tremendous news, and they were hugely excited when I came off the phone and told them what had happened.

I was elated and yet I did not really dare to believe it. I was expecting another kick in the teeth because I could not think that the Iraqis would let the men go so easily. There just had to be a catch, and when I telephoned Jude back for a longer chat during my lunch break, I thought I had found what it was. The measure had to be officially agreed by the Iraqi Revolutionary Council the following day, and I was very much afraid that this was when we would learn of the strings that were attached. However, Jude assured me that it would be all right.

By now, the whole of my firm was buzzing with excitement and people kept stopping to congratulate me. I was trying to prepare myself for just another disappointment, but it was difficult to keep my feet on the ground. I telephoned Sue and discovered that she had been so overcome when she heard the news that she had been physically sick. She was just coming out of the bathroom when I got through to her, and we had a good cry together over the phone. She asked me if I thought it would really happen, and I replied that I was not sure but that it was a more hopeful sign than anything we had previously been given.

The telephone wires were becoming red-hot in Worcester that afternoon and British Telecom must have been making a fortune. The local evening newspaper was continually ringing my office, and when I eventually returned the reporter's call, he persuaded me to invite Sue and Sheila round to my house that evening so he could interview us all together.

I then left a message at Craig's school asking him to ring Judy because it was more difficult for him to get through to me when I was at the office. When he rang her, Jude told him what had happened and he was over the moon, and his teachers and schoolfriends were delighted for him. Meanwhile, Stuart's headmistress, Miss Probert, had already heard on the radio of Derek's imminent return, and she telephoned Judy to ask if she could tell my younger son. Stuart was also excited to hear that his dad would soon be back, but unlike Craig and me, he had never thought that Derek might not come home at all. He started talking about it when I picked him up from school later that afternoon, and he did not stop all the way home.

Our cul-de-sac seemed quiet and normal when I turned into it and parked the car in my front drive. I got out, and as I put my key in the latch, a woman reporter suddenly appeared and spoke to me. As I turned to reply, a number of journalists from a variety of newspapers and broadcasting stations just appeared out of the woodwork. Within seconds, they were all in my front room with me, and a succession of others kept coming and going half the evening. It was absolute bedlam. I did not even have time to throw together some tea for me and the boys, and I had to telephone Sue and ask her to stop off at a fish-and-chip shop for us on her way to our house.

Stuart had been going down with a cold earlier in the day, and by this time it was obvious that he was in for a bout of flu. He became very drowsy and a BBC Television camera team, who had already been coming round to film him in connection with his school Nativity play, had to abandon what they had planned. By the time an ITN crew arrived to interview us, he was already dozing off, and they recorded some film of him asleep on my lap. I managed to get him to bed at about 8.30 p.m., and shortly afterwards most of the press people left us in peace.

Sue, Sheila and the reporter and a photographer from the local evening paper had by now arrived, and we all sat down to have a good long chat about our feelings and the events of a very hectic day. I was still sceptical about whether the hostages were coming home, but Sue and Sheila were convinced that this time it was for real. I do not think that either of them ever had my doubts, but then they had not met the Iraqis or seen them in operation. Unlike me, when Nigel and Mike were taken prisoner while working in the Middle East they had both been safe at home in England.

When the 10.00 p.m. news came on ITV, we watched the film of us that had been recorded by ITN earlier the same evening. To get a different slant on the story, the local paper's photographer took a picture of us watching the bulletin. They all left at about 11.30 p.m. and I tumbled into bed exhausted.

There were two final stories about which I could afford to smile when Derek was finally back with us. The first was that the same morning, the visa application forms had arrived from the Iraqi Embassy for the trip to Baghdad that Sue and I had believed might help us to rescue our husbands. I hoped so badly that we would not now be needing them.

The second incident involved Stuart and his classmates at school. They had made a Christmas card for Derek and had all signed it, and Miss Probert had been intending to post it to him earlier that afternoon. When she heard of Derek's possible release, she asked if she should still send it, and I told her to carry on in case this was just another Iraqi false alarm. The card reached Baghdad after Derek had returned home and was sent all the way back to Britain by our former 'hosts'. It was eventually delivered to our house less than three miles from where it had been posted.

Friday 7 December

At last I could relax and join in the heady celebration that had been ringing from one end of Britain to the other for the past twenty-four hours. At last I could let go of my grim, self-contained sense of reality and taste the elation in which everyone else seemed to have been bathing. The Iraqi Revolutionary Council voted in favour of freeing the hostages. There would be no more vain hoping, no more lying to myself about Derek's long-term safety – this time he was really coming home.

I heard the Council's decision on the television news, and my heart skipped a beat and I burst into tears. I did think at first that I might not go to work, but then I decided I would be better off in the office. I would be too busy to worry about last-minute hitches and I would also be able to hide from the press. In any case, some of the Doubting Thomases in the media were now saying that it could be days, or even weeks, before the men got back, and this was the last thing I wanted to hear. In the absence of any further hard information, there was a good deal of confusion, which was something else I wanted to avoid.

The hostages at Derek's installation were celebrating their forthcoming repatriation in style. Jamal, the maintenance manager at the factory, had earlier promised to buy them all a drink the day before they were freed, and he was as good as his word. He turned up with two crates of beer which were quickly shared out among the jubilant detainees. The announcement of the Revolutionary Council's decision came round about midday, and this set the perfect seal on everybody's delight.

The guards, who had gradually become more relaxed over the past few days, now really started chatting with the hostages and opening up to them. They revealed how they were frightened of the danger that lay ahead for them in the approaching war and spoke of their sorrow at being parted from their own families, and, quite suddenly, the two groups of men reached an understanding as they discovered how much they had in common. Derek talked to one guard called Mohammed who had been guarding hostages for three and a half months and had seen very little of his five-month-old son, and Derek told him, 'You can imagine how I feel.'

Derek had already begun to feel a little better even before the repatriation was announced because the food supplies had been steadily improving during the past two weeks. The hostages were by now being given such things as honey, cornflakes, fresh milk, tinned vegetables, feta cheese, oranges, dates and even decent instant coffee. They also had enough sugar, cocoa and butter to try making their own sweets and toffee – although most of their efforts ended up like glue.

The ordinary Iraqi people remained grindingly poor, and every so often the hostages would give them small bits of their supplies. There was one old cleaning woman who regularly tried to cadge things from Derek, and, because she claimed to smoke and was always running out of tobacco, he would often give her a packet of cigarettes. Now, at the very end of his detention, he discovered that every other hostage had been doing the same, and she had almost certainly been selling her acquisitions on the black market.

More 'comfort packs' had arrived recently from the British Embassy, though the Iraqis had obviously pilfered things from them. The hostages knew what should have been in them because the earlier packs had included checklists, but these were missing from the latest parcels and so were a number of the items our men expected to find in them. There were still, however, a number of things to help make life more bearable – playing cards, notepaper and envelopes, tracksuits, trainers, woollen socks, warm jackets, novels, more whisky, simple medicines, orange juice, toothpaste and toiletries including razors and aftershave.

That evening, none of the hostages could get to sleep because they were so excited at the prospect of returning home, and they kept pestering the captain of the guard for news of when they might be taken to the Mansour Melia Hotel prior to leaving. This pleasant man had played a large part in keeping the guards relaxed and friendly, and had even ordered his men not to carry their guns when on duty in the installation. Even his patience started to wear a bit thin, however, and he could hardly wait to be rid of his charges so that he could get some peace and quiet. In the end, he assured them, 'Believe me – you will be the first to arrive at the hotel.'

Back in Worcester, the best day I had experienced for more then four months ended with a mishap which could have been serious. I had a car accident while running Stuart home from school. Another car pulled across the road in front of me and I drove straight into its left-hand back door and buckled my wing. Fortunately, neither Stuart nor I was injured, and I immediately called Phil and asked him to come and sort everything out for me. The driver of the other vehicle did not know who we were, but the police officer who arrived on the scene did – although for once, this did not have anything to do with our appearances in the media: the same constable had stopped me a couple of weeks earlier and warned me about speeding.

Saturday 8 December

What a miserable and anxious weekend this was for us because the last-minute hitch that I had so feared fell on us literally out of the sky. It had snowed overnight and now a real blizzard closed in on the whole of Hereford and Worcester and several other parts of Britain. Power lines were brought down, whole villages were cut off, thousands of houses were left without electricity for several days and nearly every major road and motorway became impassable.

Living on the edge of Worcester, we suffered less than most because we were more sheltered and our gas-fired central heating was unaffected, yet our electric power was off from 8.30 a.m. to 5.00 p.m. Stuart spent a fairly boring day because the howling wind and driving snow made it impossible for him to go out to play, and he had no television to help him while away the hours.

Most important, however, was the fact that nearly every airport throughout the country became snowbound and had to close down. How could Derek possibly fly home from Iraq when there was nowhere to land? How could this be happening to us, I asked myself. I just could not believe that Fate had once again shown us a glimpse of freedom and then snatched it away.

Derek's spirits were also lower this morning because the Americans were the first to leave the installations and the British were the last group to be freed. Only two Americans – Al and Keith – were now remaining at the complex where Derek had most recently been being held, and everyone got up early to see them off at 6.00 a.m. All the men had found friendship in adversity, and they warmly said goodbye to each other and promised to stay in touch.

By now, the atmosphere at the installation was almost like that at a boarding school on the last day of term, and the guards even allowed curious local people up to the perimeter fence to talk to these hostages who were so happy to be leaving their country. Our men decided to give their dates and oranges away to the children, and many of the adults started begging them for other luxuries they had never seen in their lives before and very probably never would again. Derek gave some junior aspirin to a woman who had two little children with her, and soon all the hostages were handing out things they no longer needed.

Medicines, soap, towels, toothpaste, tracksuits and even blankets – everything that had been given to them by Iraqi officials, the Britons now gave away to the ever-growing, excited crowd of ordinary Iraqi citizens who had to exist in such poverty while their illustrious leader built himself a luxurious palace and assembled the world's fourth-largest army with which to defend it. Many of the hostages had been equipped with little AM radio sets to listen to the various announcements of the Iraqi Government, and these, too, found their way into the eager hands stretching out to grab them.

Some of the guards and other officials at the factory asked

sheepishly if there was anything they could have, and their requests were granted. For despite their uniforms and their better pay, they were also very poor. The economy had been devastated by Saddam Hussein's wars: for example, the price of powdered milk for children had increased ten times. There were a rich élite who could afford the new prices, but the guards were not among them. Derek gave some paracetamol syrup to one of the interpreters and, in return, this man gave Derek his only pen and shyly told him, 'I don't want you to forget me.'

The hostages spent the rest of the day making a nuisance of themselves by asking the captain when they could go, and he just repeated his promise that they would be first at the hotel. They packed up their meagre belongings, and at 6.00 p.m. they climbed into the minibus and cars being used to evacuate them, and sat waiting for the telephone call from higher authority that would sanction their departure. When it came shortly after, the small convoy drove into Baghdad and deposited the men on the doorstep of the hotel, and when they walked inside, they found the place was practically deserted. The captain obviously had a friend somewhat further up the ladder of command and had kept his word.

The hostages booked in with the British Embassy staff, and one of the officials on duty greeted Derek with 'I've seen your name a lot because you have received so much mail. At least our postal system can improve and get back to normal once you've gone.'

The men then walked down the corridor to the interior of the hotel, where they ran straight into the arms of the press who had flown out from England to 'welcome' them. Derek wanted nothing to do with the journalists or their glaring, flashing cameras and, to get away from them, he hid in the bedroom allocated to him. Like us, he had been completely overwhelmed by the media interest.

When he eventually ventured down to the dining room, a surprise party and some old friends were waiting to greet him. Some of the wives from our estate in Kuwait – Gilly, Sue, Maggie, Laura, Ann and Augusta – had travelled out from England to meet their husbands and, unlike Derek and his colleagues, they had money with them. The hotel had by now ceased to be a prison and, while there were still plenty of guards about, it was definitely a hotel again . . . although the bar prices had increased sevenfold. Nevertheless, the women bought crates of beer, and soon everyone was having a drink together and chatting over old times. Derek also learned from them the latest snippets of news about me and the boys, as well as hearing a blow-by-blow account of 'Yellow Ribbon' day the week before. More and more hostages arrived at the hotel throughout the evening, and Derek kept bumping into people he had not seen since the days in Kuwait.

For once, he was enjoying a much better lifestyle than I was. I spent the whole weekend sitting snowed in at home while I waited for news of when he would be returning, and worrying in case the snow made it impossible for his plane to land. Time after time I grabbed the telephone as soon as it started ringing, only to find it was yet another journalist wanting to know if I had heard anything.

The people I felt most sorry for were Phil and Judy who faithfully stayed in constant touch with me by phone. They gave up their two-day break to be on stand-by in case I needed them to run me to the airport to pick Derek up.

Sunday 9 December

The telephone started ringing as soon as we opened our eyes this morning with one newspaper after another calling to see if we had heard when Derek was coming home. We held our breath every time it rang, hoping that this would be the call to say that he was on his way, but each time we were disappointed. This was hardly the start we wanted to the day, but at least one good thing had happened: we were relieved to see that the weather had improved and the snow was thawing, so the airports would probably be clear for the hostages' plane to land.

As soon as we had woken up properly, we switched on the television and kept watch for the slightest snippet of information about the returning men. We caught one or two news bulletins in which some of the hostages were actually being interviewed in the Mansour Melia, and they were all overjoyed that the end of their nightmare was in sight and that they were returning home to their loved ones. We were relieved to see that, although everyone looked a little the worse for wear and had lost quite a bit of weight, they were all in good spirits and appeared to be fairly well.

Craig and I were in a perpetual state of edginess, and we spent every minute either diving for the telephone whenever it rang or keeping an eye on the news broadcasts. Our excitement mounted as we kept recognizing familiar faces, but at the same time we became anxious because we could see no sign of Derek no matter how carefully we scanned our television screen.

Derek was busily engaged in keeping his head down and avoiding the press, but eventually a representative of the *Today* newspaper managed to run him to earth in his room. The reporter said that his news-desk wanted to fix up a telephone link between Derek and me, and he claimed that one of his colleagues had already approached me in England. That was strange, because at almost the same moment, a reporter from *Today* telephoned me and said that one of his colleagues had already approached Derek in Baghdad with the same proposition.

As it turned out, we did not need the help of any news-desk because, just forty-five minutes later, Derek managed to get through to me himself. The line was as clear as crystal and for the first time I believed that there were no Iraqi snoopers eavesdropping and we could speak freely to each other. Derek told me about the party the night before and how he had met Gilly and the other wives who were just then leaving with their husbands to catch an early flight home. He also spoke of the way he was being chased by the media, and jokingly asked what I had let him in for. I asked him when he would be returning, and my eyes filled with tears of happiness when he replied, *'Boukra inshalaa.'* Tomorrow, God willing.

As soon as he had rung off, I quickly gave Craig a summary of everything that had been said, then started telephoning round our two families to let them know the latest. Dear old Phil was still sitting patiently at the end of the phone waiting for the message that it was time to move, and he told me just to let him know the details of Derek's flight when I received them, point him in the right direction and he would take me wherever I wanted. It was such a comfort knowing that I did not have to worry about driving or finding my own way to whichever airport was chosen for the hostages' arrival.

One thing that did upset me was the fact that Judy was rather low-spirited because she would not be able to come with us. Because Mum was ill again and the children needed looking after, she had no choice but to stay behind. She had done such a magnificent job of supporting me throughout the months of anguish, and now she was going to miss the fun part for which we had all been waiting.

The rest of the day passed with mind-blowing slowness as we sat waiting in vain for the official call to tell us that Derek was on his way. By the evening, I could stand the strain no longer, and I telephoned the emergency unit at the Foreign Office. The officials on duty were as much in the dark as us, but they promised to ring back if Derek's name cropped up on any of the lists they were trying to compile. I impatiently telephoned the FO on a number of occasions during the evening, but each time I got the reply, 'He's still not on any lists we have.'

After what seemed like a century, the phone did eventually ring, but when I snatched up the receiver, I found that it was only Sue calling to see if we had heard anything. She was becoming quite unhappy at the lack of information, though she did report that Sheila had been told by the Foreign Office that Mike would definitely be on the flight arriving the next day. One thing we did manage to establish was that the plane was probably going to fly in to Gatwick.

Just before I went to bed, I telephoned Phil again and he agreed with me that we should go and meet this flight in case Derek was on it. I rang Sue straight back to tell her what we had decided to do. She said that she was of the same opinion, and she asked if she could follow us because Mark, the friend who was going to drive her down there, was not sure of the way to the airport.

Our long day of anticipation had affected my two sons in totally different ways. Stuart had taken little part in it because he was still under the weather, yet even he had felt something of the sense of excitement which flooded into every corner of our home. Craig was completely elated at the prospect of seeing his dad again, but he was still level-headed enough to see that I needed support as much as ever, and he kept telling me, 'Don't worry, Mum. If Dad's not on this flight, he'll be on the next.'

My mind was in a turmoil of happy expectation at my family's approaching reunion and the dread that I would have to face up to one last, awful disappointment. I went to bed that night hoping and praying that by tomorrow more than four months of heartbreak would be over, and Derek would be returned to us.

Monday 10 December

Our lounge was bombarded with telephone calls again from first light, but none of them was the one we wanted. Nearly all were from the ever-anxious media and we were very tempted to unplug the phone, but this was impossible because we would have risked missing the all-important message from the Foreign Office that Derek was homeward-bound. We had to answer every single call and we also had to keep going to the front door to speak to other journalists who started gathering in the street from 9.30 a.m.

My first job of the day was to telephone the Foreign Office's emergency unit, but although its list of returning hostages had been growing throughout the night, Derek's name was still not on it. My mind was in absolute turmoil and I rang Sue to see if she had heard anything, and she said she would ring back after she had contacted the emergency unit. When she returned my call a few minutes later, she was quite upset because Nigel's name was also missing from the list. We were still agreed, however, that we must meet the flight in case our two men were on it, and we arranged that she and Mark would drive round to our house at about 11.30 a.m.

I told Phil of our plans when he dropped round shortly after and he promised to be there on time. He had to run the gauntlet of waiting photographers to get to our front door, and he made us laugh when he repeated the old joke, 'If you'd let me know they were here, I'd have brought my firm's van for a bit of free advertising.'

Sue and Mark pulled up outside almost on the dot of 11.30 a.m., and Phil was only a minute or two behind them. The telephone was still going mad, and Phil answered all the calls for me while Stuart, Craig and I got ready. Stuart was still full of cold and I was a bit worried about taking him because he was so quiet and out of sorts, so it was something of a godsend when ITN telephoned to ask if we were going and to offer us the use of a room at the Gatwick Hilton while we were waiting. I was not certain whether to accept, but the news assistant assured me I would be under no obligation to them and said she would book the room for us anyhow in case we needed it. When I discussed it afterwards with Craig and Phil, we all agreed that the room could well be useful if Stuart become worse and it would be as well to keep our options open.

We rang the emergency unit again but there was still no news, and we decided to get on the road otherwise we would be dithering at home all day. The cameras started clicking at us as soon as we opened the front door, and we were very edgy as we climbed into our cars. A crew from Sky Television and two other reporters asked if they could follow us to Gatwick, and I replied shortly that it was entirely up to them, so we set off with a small convoy of four cars following us.

We had not travelled many miles before we had to make our first stop. Stuart was sick and I had to clean him up and put him into the change of clothes I had fortunately had the foresight to bring with us. The poor thing looked really rough, and he went to sleep as soon as I settled him down.

When we got to the large motorists' service area at Oxford, we stopped so we could try telephoning the emergency unit for the latest news, and the four shadowing media cars dutifully pulled in behind us. The Foreign Office still had nothing to tell us, however, and we decided to have a rest over a cup of coffee before continuing our journey. As we were about to start off again, the Sky crew offered us the use of their mobile telephone and the reporter said his news-room would be able to talk to us as we travelled along.

Craig was really taken with this idea, and we had barely pulled out of the car-park before he was telephoning Judy to see if she had heard anything new. She had not, but she was tickled pink by the idea that he could talk to her as he bowled along the motorway towards Gatwick. Unfortunately, when he had finished talking to her, Craig turned the phone off completely and the Sky news-room could not get through to us. It must have been very frustrating for them, but we were not really worried because we had far more important things on our minds. We felt a growing unease that we had still not heard anything and that Derek's name was still missing from the list of those about to be repatriated.

Derek's name was missing for one very simple reason. Unknown to us, he had been barred from the flight because of bureaucratic bungling by the Iraqis and the British Embassy in Baghdad.

It all started after breakfast when the hostages were called to the lobby of the Mansour Melia Hotel to be given their passports. About thirty of the men, who had been among the earliest to be taken to Baghdad when the emergency started, did not have any documents and Derek was one of them. The Embassy staff now realized belatedly that they would need temporary passports immediately if they were to get away, and the men were furious that nothing had been done about it during the two days they had just spent cooling their heels in the hotel.

There was such a need for haste that the men were photographed three at a time with a polaroid camera, and then their faces were cut out from the snaps and stuck on to the official documents. Even this did not get them their passports, however, because the application forms for exit visas had to carry some wording in Arabic as well as English, and the Iraqis insisted that they must also be marked with the official Embassy stamp. By the time this had been done, the Iraqi official who could issue the visas had gone off duty, and the Embassy staff had to chase round trying to find someone else with enough authority to process the documents.

Derek and his friends had to travel to Baghdad Airport without passports, not knowing whether they would be allowed on to the aircraft when they got there. When they arrived at the terminal, television crews walked up and down the queues of jubilant men who stood singing and chanting as they waited for their turn to be passed through the checking-in system. There was no such euphoria for the group without passports, however, because they were kept by themselves and were not allowed through the barriers. All they could do was watch the fast-dwindling queues with seething frustration and hope that their visas and passports arrived in time.

Eventually, the Ambassador himself arrived and explained what had gone wrong, and the men's bitterness spilled over as they surrounded him and complained loudly about the way they had been treated. It was more than they could stand to be so close to freedom after four months and then see it snatched away from them just because some faceless Iraqi official had not signed a few pieces of paper.

As a member of the Embassy staff continued to scour the city for someone who would authorize their departure, the men paced up and down and continually gazed out of the terminal window as they watched for his arrival. The Embassy sent out for food for them, but this was small consolation as the other hostages disappeared completely into the departure lounge and could still be heard singing together in the distance.

At one stage, British officials admitted that Derek's group would probably not be travelling on the flight and would have to be found overnight accommodation, and the men became really frantic. Purely by chance, they were bought a little more time when the plane's departure was delayed by the fact that it could not get airspace clearance in one of the countries it would have to fly over on the way home. It seemed, however, that even this would not be enough to get them on the flight, and they were told that if the visas did not arrive by 8.00 p.m. local time, they would have to abandon their dreams of returning home that day.

The whole group was close to tears as the minutes ticked away relentlessly, and the men had just resigned themselves to another night in captivity when, five minutes before the deadline, the Embassy official arrived with the documents. In a second, the last thirty hostages soared from the depths of despair to a perch on cloud nine, and they charged through the barriers whooping with delight. But Fate had still not quite finished with them. By now, the baggage-handlers had gone off duty, and it was several agonizing minutes before they could be found. Finally, when their hand baggage was checked, one of the men was found to have a map of Kuwait in his bag and was marched off to be grilled by the secret police. Luckily, the Ambassador spotted what had happened, dived into the room where he was taken and managed to free him.

Because everybody wanted to leave so badly, the airport clock now appeared to stand still, and it seemed ages before the plane was ready to leave and the men were strapped into their seats. The whole fuselage was filled with a deafening cheer as the aircraft lifted off the tarmac, but even now everybody was tense because there were no longer any Embassy staff with them and they were travelling in an Iraqi jet with an all-Iraqi crew. A half-rumour started circulating to the effect that the whole thing was a charade and they were just being taken to another installation, but this was dispelled with another mighty cheer when the captain announced over the tannoy that they were now entering European airspace. A man called Ted, who was sitting next to Derek, turned to him and said, 'We can crash now. I don't mind dying here.'

Many of the hostages, not believing that they were really going home, had smuggled some of their old rations on to the plane, and these were now passed along the rows as a party got under way. Tins of pilchards, cartons of cheese spread, cans of beer and bottles of whisky were passed from hand to hand as the men celebrated their homecoming. In the middle of it all, one of the detainees sat wearing an Iraqi steel helmet which he was taking back as a souvenir. Yet another cheer went up as the plane landed at Gatwick and the men looked out of the window and saw the comforting sight of the British Airways sign on the terminal building. There were jokes about what a nice installation it was, and when they climbed on to the buses waiting for them on the tarmac, one man said to Derek, 'The last time I got on a coach like this, I ended up at a generating plant.'

The rest of the Lockwood family heard that Derek was on the flight just after they had driven through the gates of the airport at 5.45 p.m. When Craig rang Judy on the mobile phone, she was bursting with the news which had just reached her from the Foreign Office. The relief was tremendous and I felt as if a ten-ton weight had been lifted off my shoulders, but we were very sorry for Sue and Mark because there was no further information about Nigel.

Because Stuart was still unwell, we thought it was a good idea to make use of the hotel room, so we parked the cars and walked into the Hilton. The ITN representative made us very welcome, and I quickly settled Stuart down for a sleep while the others ordered some drinks for us all. Sue then rang the Foreign Office and, to everyone's delight, discovered that Nigel was also on the flight. Before she rang off, I asked her to confirm once more that Derek was with him – I could not help myself because it all seemed too good to be true.

At 10.00 p.m., we were advised to walk over to the terminal ready to welcome the men home, but when we got there, we found an enormous queue of people waiting to get in. Hostages' families, friends and well-wishers were waiting to go through and, because the airport officials had already let in too many people earlier on, they now tried to stop anyone who was not an immediate relation – even Mark who had driven Sue down to Gatwick. In contrast to the wonderful reception we had been given at Heathrow, the whole thing was chaotic and Stuart's condition deteriorated as we had to queue in the bitterly cold night air for more than one and a half hours. The flight landed at about 11.30 p.m. and by the time we got through the barriers, Derek was already in the arrival lounge. Normally, he is the last to get off a plane, but for once he was first – and I felt distressed and guilty that I had missed his homecoming.

Just as on the occasion of my arrival at Heathrow, there was pandemonium as hundreds of people burst into tears and flung themselves into the arms of loved ones they had thought they would never see again. At that moment, I still could not see Derek in the crowd and he could not see me, and I walked around in a trance panicking about how I was going to find him among all these people.

It was Craig who spotted him first. I suddenly heard my

elder son shouting 'Dad, Dad' and saw him virtually climbing over people's heads to leap into Derek's arms. I do not know how he managed to get through the crush so quickly, and, with Stuart in my arms, I hurriedly pushed my way through with my heart pounding and tears streaming down my face. We hurled ourselves against Derek's body, and four months of pent-up terror and tension drained from me in an instant as I nestled against his chest and wept. There would be no more loneliness, no more fear, no more bitter helplessness – he was home and, in my heart, I vowed that we would never be parted again.

In all the confusion, I seemed to have lost Stuart. I now saw that he was just clinging to his daddy's neck, and that was where he stayed as Derek tried to cuddle all three of us at once. Phil joined us and he, too, was blinking back tears as he became lost for words for only the second time in his life.

I had waited for this moment for so long and had so dreaded that it would never happen, and now it had arrived it was completely different to how I had imagined it. Even now, I feared that the whole thing might be a dream and that I would wake up any second to the grim, twilight world that had so blighted our lives.

After all the hugs and kisses, I managed to calm down enough to look at Derek properly for the first time, and I saw how ill he really looked. I silently promised that I would devote myself to caring for him and nursing him back to full health.

We picked up his bits of luggage and, as we moved towards the exit, I started preparing him for the pressure we would have to face from the media. He replied that he had already had a sample of it in Baghdad and I was relieved that he apparently knew what to expect. I was therefore shocked to see the effect on him when we walked through the door to be confronted by a horde of photographers and reporters who stood just behind a barrier. Derek, still holding Stuart in his arms, stood rigid, with shock written all over his face as this crowd shouted his name and thrust microphones and cameras at him.

At Heathrow, the boys and I had been protected from the press, but now we were just thrown to them by the shambles that was Gatwick. As we stepped clear of the barriers, they flooded round us, blinded us with the flashes from their cameras and bombarded us with stupid questions. Were we glad to be back together? Was it good to be back in England? Would we be celebrating? . . . Did they really expect us to say 'No'?

Derek was obviously knocked for six by the cameras, and I became very distressed as they crowded about us and would not let us go. I was close to tears again because I was worried they would do him irreparable emotional damage after everything he had been through. Derek told them that we wanted to be left alone because we had so much time to make up, but they just ignored him and pressed even closer round us. They were trying to bully us into holding a press conference and there were so many of them.

I think we might have been there for hours if it had not been for a passing police patrol. Five officers saw what was happening and waded in to rescue us. They physically pulled some of the journalists away, threatened to arrest them if they did not leave us alone and then escorted us to the car-park.

With that mature thoughtfulness that he had found through all our trials and tribulations, Craig climbed straight into the front passenger seat. He insisted that Derek and I would want to be together in the back, and we sat hand in hand as Phil drove us to Worcester. We arrived at about 3.15 a.m. . . . and there was a local radio reporter waiting for us as we got out of the car. We brushed past her, stepped into our hall and, with a huge sigh of relief, shut the door on the free world that had given Derek such a terrifying welcome home.

Tuesday 11 December

The boys went to bed very soon after we got in, but Derek and I sat talking for another nearly two hours before we followed their example. I dropped off to sleep almost straight away, feeling secure and contented for the first time in my new home. Yet even now I had a stupid, illogical fear at the back of my mind that my new-found happiness was too good to be true and that when I woke up I would discover I was alone again.

Derek spent the first of the many sleepless nights he experienced during his early days of freedom, and at about

6.00 a.m. he got up to go to the bathroom. He was just returning to bed when he heard a clanking noise and the sound of voices outside the front of the house, and looking out he saw about a dozen men standing there. Immediately, the fear that had become so ingrained in him during his captivity came flooding back into his tired, bruised mind and reminded him of the many times during the preceding months that he had been brutally roused from sleep in the early hours to be moved to a new installation. He came anxiously tearing into our bedroom to ask what was going on and, being an old hand at dealing with such emergencies now, I was able to tell him, 'It's only the press.'

The clanking noise had actually been caused by a photographer taking from his car boot a small set of stepladders, which he intended to use later to get a better view of us over the heads of his colleagues who would inevitably crowd round us the moment we stepped outside our front door. Derek could not believe this was happening to us, and he peered out of the house at them round the edge of our curtain, just as the other women and I had had to do all those months ago when we had been imprisoned in our houses just after the invasion back in Kuwait. Armed Iraqi guards he could have coped with, but this was something outside his experience.

The telephone started ringing again at about 7.30 a.m. with calls from reporters whipped on by their news-desks to get an interview with us, and in the end we were forced to unplug it. This brought even more journalists flooding into our little cul-de-sac and eventually there were over forty of them. At 10.00 a.m., they knocked on the door and asked for a photograph and an interview, though I later discovered that some of them had wanted to disturb us an hour earlier and were talked out of it by their colleagues.

As the morning wore on, our close took on the look of a car-park as their vehicles clogged up the roadway. They stood about in small groups chatting, and every so often they looked at our house for signs of movement and then glanced at their watches. They got into conversation with our neighbours who were emerging from their houses to go about their daily routines. One lady in the next street even provided them with hot drinks, and suddenly a coffee pot and plastic picnic cups were being passed around among them.

We had planned to go out later because there was so much we needed to do. Derek had to sort out his bank account and then go shopping – he had little more than the clothes he stood up in – and, with my old Ford now being repaired following last week's accident, we also needed to hire a car. There was no way, however, that we were going to get past the waiting crowd without either giving them an interview or fighting them. As I had feared might happen, Derek was really upset by the media attention, and he wanted nothing to do with them.

About mid-morning, Sue came round to see us and she was followed shortly afterwards by Phil. Sue thought I should go and speak to the reporters, and I reluctantly agreed because I could see that it was the only thing that would enable us to escape from our home that had so suddenly become a prison. Phil went out to tell them what we proposed to do, and a few minutes later I appeared on our front lawn with Stuart as the group gathered round us and, once again, fired dozens of cameras and questions at us.

It was at this point that Stuart left me reeling with surprise because the reporters asked him what he wanted for Christmas. They doubtless hoped that he would say his daddy, but he actually said a train set. This was news to me because he had previously asked for a bicycle, and a gleaming new machine had already been bought for him and was now being hidden at my cousin's house.

As a result of Stuart's announcement being reported in every newspaper in the country, we were deluged with offers of train sets for the next week. Many were genuine and came from people who had an unwanted train set left over from their days of bringing up young children, but just as many came from companies who could see the commercial potential of our endorsing their product and wanted us to pose for photographs with the fruits of their generosity.

The short interview seemed to satisfy the journalists since they could see they were going to get nothing else from us, and they left us in peace afterwards. Derek could now get down to the serious business of enjoying his freedom properly. He took delight in such simple things as drinking a can of lager, strolling down to the corner shop for a newspaper and eating his meals with a proper knife and fork.

Later on, Phil took him to a car-hire place, and now we were equipped with our own transport, we went on the family shopping expedition we had so much looked forward to. We bought a copy of the local evening paper with the pictures of our homecoming taken at Gatwick, and wherever we went, strangers stopped us to congratulate us and say how glad they were that we were now back together. It was a pattern that was to be repeated time and again throughout the next couple of weeks as we went Christmas shopping. During one trip to Birmingham, a lady was so overcome that she ran up to Derek and threw her arms round him.

There was only one slight mishap during this first, hesitant expedition. When we returned to our hired car, we discovered that a parking ticket had been slapped on the windscreen. It was at that point that Derek really knew he was home.

Wednesday 12 December

Derek began catching up on Stuart's brief school career today. The two of us went to the school as a couple for the first time to see our younger son taking part in his Nativity play.

The headmistress, Miss Probert, marked the big occasion with a little extra special treatment for us. She invited us into the privacy of her office, welcomed Derek back and gave him a progress report on Stuart to make up for his missing the parents' evening. Derek's heart swelled with pride as she told him, 'Your family has done very well while you have been away. They have fared marvellously considering the situation they have been in, and Stuart is doing well in class.'

We attracted quite a bit of attention as we walked round the school. Teachers and parents whom we hardly knew often stopped us to say how glad they were to see us reunited, and Stuart's friends kept nudging one another and whispering, 'There's Stuart's dad – over there.' It really brought home to me how lucky we were to be a complete, proper family again, and I felt enveloped by a radiant happiness.

I had always described the school production as a Nativity play, but it was actually something entirely different. It was a little review of all the months of the year ending with a look at the Christmas season, and Stuart appeared in the section dealing with July and August. He stepped on to the stage wearing swimming trunks and took part in picnics and strawberry teas. The other thing he wore throughout his appearance was an enormous beam all over his face, and the whole audience could see how delighted he was to have his daddy back home. His delight was matched by Derek's: less than a week earlier he had still been a hostage and had never dreamed that he would be home in time to share this magical moment with his family.

It might have been thought that we had seen enough of the Middle East and its problems to last a lifetime, yet strangely the opposite was true. When we got home after the play, we could not resist tuning in to the television tea-time news to see what was happening in the Gulf. People we knew had still not been repatriated and we were worried about them, and once they were safely back we started worrying about the troops who had gone out there to fight. We were also anxious about Kuwait itself because it had given us four very happy years in our lives, and as a result we have remained keenly interested in events there.

We felt like a proper celebration after seeing Stuart in his school production, and so I cooked a full roast meal that evening. The joint I had chosen was pork and I think I may have bought it subconsciously as a symbol of the fact that we were safely home together. We all love the meat, but we had barely eaten it since first going out to the Middle East. In the eyes of Islam it is unclean and was therefore just about the only thing that could not be bought, even in the well-stocked Kuwaiti supermarkets before the invasion. Now, as the four of us tucked into it and sampled the delicious crunch of the crackling in our mouths, it was as if we were physically tasting the freedom we had in England.

Later on, after we had cleared away, Stuart was playing

about with his little Walkman and an odd cassette he had found. Suddenly, his beautiful eyes widened in surprise and he turned to Derek.

'It's me on this tape,' he cried. 'Here, Dad – have a listen.'

Derek took the Walkman from him and put on the headphones, and after a few seconds he gave a start and his eyes also widened. It was the recording of Stuart's interview on local radio which I had nearly included in the Christmas parcel I had planned to send out to Baghdad. Derek listened for a short while to the sound of children singing carols and Stuart saying that he wanted his daddy back for Christmas, and he fought back his tears.

Tuesday 18 December

I shall never forget these next two days. They were the proudest and happiest of my life, and were in stark contrast to the countless days of misery I had spent during the previous four and a half months. The four of us travelled down to London where Stuart was to be presented with a *Woman's Own* Children of Courage Award by the Duchess of York. Yet my motives for agreeing to become involved in the ceremony had been entirely different when the idea had first been mentioned.

I was approached by the magazine back in the dark days of November, and I was extremely doubtful about the whole thing. Although I was very pleased at the way Stuart had behaved when confronted by Saddam Hussein, I felt that he had been caught up in such a historic event only by accident, and had been exposed to enough publicity already. In the end, I was persuaded to let him take part, but only on condition that he accepted the award on behalf of all the brave children involved in the Gulf crisis. I also hoped the extra publicity might help the hostages who at the time seemed to be further away from freedom than ever.

One of the nice things about the *Woman's Own* staff was that they were among the few media people who acknowledged Craig's existence and tried to involve him, and they invited him to do one of the readings during the presentation service in Westminster Abbey. At first he refused, but after thinking about it, he changed his mind because he knew how proud his father would be and how much it would help his morale. Now his dad would unexpectedly be there to see him do it and would be even prouder.

We were due to meet up in London, stay overnight and then take part in the ceremony the following day. We caught the mid-morning train to Paddington and took a taxi to St Ermin's Hotel, behind New Scotland Yard, where reservations had been made for all the award-winners. Stuart caused a stir as soon as we arrived and introduced ourselves to the magazine staff, who were charming to us. The porter, who carried our bags up to our room, was an Egyptian, and he recognized Stuart and asked for his autograph.

We mingled with the other award-winners and their families over tea in the hotel lounge, and then at 6.00 p.m. it was time for Craig to go to Westminster Abbey for a rehearsal for the service. The other reader was to be the actress Dawn Acton, who plays Tracy Barlow in *Coronation Street*. Craig was extremely quiet and subdued. We waited for him at the hotel feeling tense and nervous for him, but when he returned he was far more confident. He had met the Bishop of Westminster and liked him, and the magazine representatives said he had done so well that there would be no need for a second rehearsal the next morning.

Later, we went down to the official dinner that had been laid on for the Children of Courage, and as we entered the dining room, there was a buzz of conversation among the waiters. The Egyptian porter had been telling all his colleagues about Stuart, and they now made a fuss of him.

The atmosphere of excitement affected Stuart because he was unusually full of mischief that evening. He managed to persuade one of the waitresses to give him extra Christmas crackers from nearby empty tables which had already been laid for dinner, and he was soon playing with the little toys that he found in them. He also took one of the mock Christmas presents from under the Christmas tree in the hotel foyer, and was later found hiding under a table while he opened it. He was very disappointed to discover that it contained only paper.

His cheekiest venture, however, involved a group of nearly a dozen hotel guests who were complete strangers and had nothing to do with the Children of Courage. These poor people were sitting on a chesterfield minding their own business, when Stuart spotted them. He crept up behind them, tapped one lady on the shoulder, and ducked down behind the sofa's raised back so that she could not see him when she turned round. He then went along the whole row doing the same to her companions.

Fortunately, when the group realized what was happening, they recognized the grinning face of their little tormentor and saw the funny side of it. The incident did nothing, however, for my and Derek's peace of mind. We were naturally anxious that he should be on his best behaviour in Westminster Abbey the next day, and we now had visions of him climbing all over the choir and organ, and pushing the organ stops in the middle of the service.

Wednesday 19 December

Our official duties began straight after breakfast with the first photo-call of the day. Reporters, photographers and television cameras assembled at the hotel to record the occasion, and Stuart was in great demand throughout the hour-long session. He was bombarded with requests for interviews and photographs, but all the attention made him switch off and his questioners did not find him very chatty. Some photographers pictured him standing in front of the hotel's Christmas tree with one of the mock presents, and one television reporter managed to coax from him the famous interview that was carried on the network news later the same day.

'Are you getting any toys for Christmas?' the reporter asked.

'Yes,' Stuart replied shyly after a short delay.

'Why? Have you been a good boy?'

'Yes.'

'How do you know you've been good?'

Stuart's eyes opened wide in amazement that anybody could ask such a question when the answer was so obvious, and for the first time he replied almost immediately. 'Because my brain FINKED it!'

Perhaps the most touching photograph was the one of Stuart and a tremendously brave little girl called Michelle Pratt who was on crutches and who had endured a number of operations to help her walk. This seemed to sum up what the award ceremony was about. The children there were from every walk of life, but the thing they had in common was that they had shown the most amazing courage, acting on impulse in often dangerous situations without a thought for their own safety. It made us feel humble to think that here was the next generation of Britons growing up, and they would be as great as any previous generation had been.

It was now time for us to go to the service, but the coach due to take us there failed to turn up, and we were driven across London in a hastily-assembled fleet of taxis. When we arrived, we found that some of the photographers who had been at the hotel had managed to get there before us and were waiting to greet us. As we got out of our taxi, they called out Stuart's name and snapped away at him as he waved to them.

It was a chilly winter's morning, yet as soon as we stepped through the mighty doors of Westminster Abbey and trod in the footsteps of the great figures of British history, we were hit by an atmosphere that was so electric that it actually seemed to warm us. The place was crowded with school parties and underprivileged children, and a large number of celebrities were also there to give the event their support. I remember seeing the children's television artist Tony Hart walking among the congregation doing little sketches and handing them out to some of the children. The old abbey seemed to be alive with optimism and a mighty, overwhelming presence of kindness, and Derek and I suddenly felt that it had been waiting for us and that we were meant to be there.

The dozen or so award-winners were shown to a row of seats right at the front on the left, and their parents were seated as close as possible behind them. Because he was taking part in the service, Craig was given a seat in the second row on the opposite side of the aisle. Now that his big moment was fast approaching, he was quiet and thoughtful again, and I could see how nervous he was, but he looked very grown-up and smart in the new suit we had bought him specially for the occasion.

A few minutes later, the choir and servers processed into the chancel, and the Duchess of York, accompanied by her bodyguards, walked into the abbey. She was met by the Bishop and by the actor Anthony Andrews, who gives up some of his time each year at the Children of Courage service to read the citations as the awards are presented. The Duchess was shown to her seat as the voice of a lone choirboy floated throughout the ancient building, and then the Bishop began the service with a short address.

He told everyone that today was an extra-special day for one family, and my heart pounded with a strange mixture of pleasure and embarrassment as I realized he was going to talk about us. Sure enough, he mentioned the names of all four of us, spoke of our ordeal and said how good it was that we had now been reunited. I could feel a lump in my throat and tears welling up in my eyes, and glancing sideways at Derek I could see that he was having the same problem.

As any mother would be in the circumstances, I was on tenterhooks over how both my sons would acquit themselves when taking part in such a grand occasion, and the time now arrived for me to find out. My heart started pounding for a second time as Craig walked out to the front to deliver a reading about the Nativity, but my apprehension turned to joy as his voice lifted clearly and confidently into the air and echoed among the rafters. He was really good, and I had to choke back a second lot of tears.

Stuart had spent much of the service turning round to us to ask which lady was the Duchess and was-she-the-one-in-the-red-coat-look-over-there? When the awards ceremony arrived, he was one of the last to be called out, and he kept turning round to me again to ask if he was next. After what seemed like an age, his name was read out and he strolled nonchalantly up to the Duchess with his hands in his pockets. I could have died at his casual behaviour, but I suppose it was hardly surprising because he knew she was important and he was shy. The Duchess, however, was wonderfully natural with him, gave one of her wonderful smiles and put him at his ease in seconds.

After the service, there was an official reception in the abbey's vestry where we met a number of celebrities and dignitaries, including the Lady Mayoress of London who asked for Stuart's autograph. A number of people commented on how well Craig had read the lesson, and Derek and I were so proud that we felt as if we were walking on air. For the hundredth time since the invasion of Kuwait had turned our world on its head, I was caught up in the middle of momentous events which I could not believe were happening to me – only on this occasion the experience was entirely pleasurable.

We met the Duchess, and she had a lengthy talk with us about some of the things that had happened to us and asked how we and the boys were adjusting now that we were finally back together. Stuart was completely captivated by her natural charm and would not leave her alone, and he followed her as she drifted away to talk to other award-winners and their families. One problem was that he could not pronounce her official title, and Anthony Andrews suggested that he should call her 'Ma'am'. Stuart innocently replied that he could not do that because she was not his mum, and in the end the Duchess solved the difficulty herself by telling him that he could call her 'Sarah'.

As the reception ended, we were taken back into the abbey for another photo-call, and Stuart disappeared in the crush of people. I started flapping, but the *Woman's Own* staff assured that he was being well looked after and had been taken outside for yet more pictures. He was actually in very reliable company for, unknown to us, he stepped out of the abbey hand-in-hand with the Duchess and was photographed with her for a final time.

When he reappeared, he was holding a little posy he said was for me. As he had earlier been admiring the flowers on the Tomb of the Unknown Warrior, I started worrying about where he had found it. A little later, I discovered that as the Duchess was leaving she had handed him one of her posies and told him to give it to me.

This, I feel, is the most fitting point at which to end my diary. There was so much more that happened to us during the weeks ahead as we hurriedly got ready for Christmas, met up with relatives and old friends whom Derek had once believed he would never see again, and set about the sometimes painful task of putting our nightmares behind us and readjusting to normal life once more. That, however, is the beginning of the story of the rest of my life, and it has nothing to do with our four and a half months of despair during which we plumbed the depths of misery, managed to hold on to our sanity and, by the grace of some higher, unseen power, emerged intact as a complete family.

For me, the nightmare that started with the sound of a jet screaming low over our house in Kuwait early one morning ended with the gentle song of a single chorister in Westminster Abbey. It ended with the words of congratulation from the Bishop, the winning smile of the Duchess of York and the sight of my two sons playing a leading part in such a fine ceremony. My mind flew back fleetingly over all the things that had happened to me and all the people I had met.

I looked briefly at the man by my side whom I once thought I had lost, but who was now very much with me and was singing carols lustily. I looked at Craig who had been my protector and strength for so long and who was now reading the story of the Nativity, and lastly I looked at Stuart who was receiving his just reward for refusing to be the puppet of a dictator. It was then I really believed that this was no dream and that, against all the odds, we were a real family again in time for Christmas. At that moment, the blight that Saddam Hussein had put on our four lives was finally exorcised.

AFTER

We – and particularly Stuart – have had messages of support from all over the world since we have been back home. Most well-wishers did not know where we live and some letters from as far afield as Australia and the United States have been addressed as vaguely as 'To the Little Boy with Saddam Hussein, England'. Every message has reached us because the Post Office has shown the most amazing imagination in interpreting the directions on the envelopes.

Perhaps the grandest communication arrived for Stuart last November about six weeks before Derek returned. It was a parcel containing the most magnificent ceremonial French fireman's helmet which was a gift to him from France's Minister of the Interior, Monsieur Pierre Joxe. It had been forwarded through the Foreign Secretary, Douglas Hurd, who enclosed a personally-signed letter explaining where the helmet had come from and congratulating Stuart once more on his courage.

Stuart has also received two bravery awards – the *Woman's Own* Children of Courage Award and, more recently, the *Daily Star* Gold Award. The latter was presented to him during a wonderful lunchtime ceremony at the Inn on the Park in London by Margaret Thatcher. Celebrities like Ernie Wise, Rodney Bewes and Derek Jameson had their photographs taken with him, and he also met Lady Bridget de la Billiere and Brenda Schwarzkopf, the wives of the British and American military commanders who had just led the Allied forces to such a resounding victory in the Gulf War.

Stuart's picture has again appeared on television and in newspapers all over the world and he was even offered a lucrative child modelling contract. This could well have opened new fields to him and set him up financially for life, but after considering everything carefully, we decided to turn it down.

*

For the time has come to say 'enough is enough'. The way Stuart and the whole family have been feted and applauded has been as much fun as the events that led to it were terrifying, but we are under no illusions about our place in the scheme of things. We have done nothing particularly clever. We were merely caught up – accidentally and reluctantly – in shattering events and we tried to behave with dignity in the most appropriate way. Derek and I do not want Stuart to be a miniature mannequin with an over-inflated ego; we want him to be a normal, healthy boy who grows up into a normal, healthy adult. Our thanks go out to the many people who have been so kind and generous to us, but now it is time for us to pick up the pieces and get on with our lives.

We do have pieces to pick up because nobody could go through such an experience and not be affected by it, although some of the changes have been for the good. One thing is certain: we shall never again be the same as we last were on 1 August 1990 – the day before the invasion of Kuwait.

Stuart had a number of difficulties in his first term at school. He retreated at times into a safe, fantasy world and had problems in his relationships with other children which could well have been caused by the media attention he was still receiving. Thankfully, these problems seem to be over now that Derek is back with us, though remnants of the old insecurities remain because he will rarely leave his dad's side for fear that they might be parted again. He is also anxious about going on long car journeys in case we get lost, and I am convinced that this anxiety is a result of that horrendous journey to Baghdad in the convoy.

The most serious long-term effect on Craig has been the considerable deterioration of his schoolwork. I firmly believe that this is not his fault and is due to the fact that since our detention he has found it difficult to concentrate on any one thing for very long. Again it is a problem that we can only hope will rectify itself with time. He also loathes being involved in publicity and this dislike has probably arisen from the way so many media people have ignored his existence.

Derek really went through the mill and was in a very poor

state of health when he came home. He suffered badly with a skin allergy called urticaria which may have been caused by stress, had an eye complaint and had lost a considerable amount of weight. These problems are gradually improving with treatment, but the long-term effects on Derek will be great. He could barely sleep at all when he first returned and even now he is a very light sleeper. At first he was continually looking over his shoulder and did not trust anyone, and, because he once thought that he would not survive to see his sons growing up, he thinks a lot about the meaning of life and death.

Finally, there is myself, though I am not certain what the future holds for me. I am a lot more confident and independent than I used to be, because I had to stand on my own two feet for nearly four months during Derek's absence. Yet I was nearly bled dry emotionally and there were times when I was not too far away from a complete breakdown. I think three factors helped me to get through the ordeal: the support I received from Craig; the help I got from my family and friends; and the fact that, for a month after our return, my mother was ill and I was too busy dashing about to wallow in self-pity. The longest-lasting effect on me appears to be that, like Craig, I find it difficult to concentrate and settle, and I always have to be on the go and doing something.

Ironically, the benefits to us all have been enormous. We now realize how lucky we have been to emerge from such danger as a complete family. We are much closer than we used to be, and although we have lost the wonderful and elegant lifestyle we enjoyed in Kuwait, it does not matter because material things now come bottom of the list of what we want out of life. In addition, because we have experienced such extremes of happiness and despair ourselves, we think far more about other people's feelings.

Since putting pen to paper to record the details of our involvement in one of the most dramatic events of the twentieth century, I have many times questioned my motives for wanting to do so. Having tried to think about it long and honestly, I believe that this diary has been written for four main reasons.

I felt that the way the British community in Kuwait was put in danger because of the sheer inefficiency of the British Embassy – and, in some respects, of the British Government – should not be allowed to pass without comment. I do not suggest for a minute that British officialdom acted as it did through irresponsibility or recklessness. These were a unique set of circumstances and no British Embassy in the world had received the right training to deal with the taking of hostages on a grand scale or the movement of large numbers of civilian people over vast distances. This is something that must now be put right so that, in the unhappy event of a similar situation arising elsewhere, there is a proper system that can be put into operation to protect British nationals.

Also I wanted to make it absolutely clear that at no time did the British hostages allow themselves to be used as willing tools of the Saddam Hussein propaganda machine. The world would have known this if it could have seen everything that happened during our meeting with the Iraqi President, but the recording was heavily edited.

Thirdly, I felt everyone should be reminded that I do have another son besides Stuart and I am every bit as proud of him. Craig – and indeed every British teenager I came across in captivity – became a man overnight and took on responsibilities that should not be expected of any fourteen-year-old boy. He could easily have cracked under the strain, but he did not and has emerged a better person for it. He has been a wonderful elder brother and, without malice or jealousy, has stood in the background while Stuart has attracted all the limelight.

Finally, I have written this diary for the benefit of Stuart himself. I have already spoken of my fears for his future and we really have no idea how our experiences will affect him in the years ahead. He is far too young to comprehend the political situation that so endangered us and it was no fault of his that he was forced into a moment of history. This is intended to be what I regard as a true record of what happened, so that if ever he needs to, he can read it and, I hope, understand.

Glenda Lockwood
31 March 1991